She's the Boss

# She's the Boss

The Rise of Women's Entrepreneurship since World War II

DEBRA MICHALS

Rutgers University Press
New Brunswick, Camden, and Newark, New Jersey
London and Oxford

Rutgers University Press is a department of Rutgers, The State University of New Jersey, one of the leading public research universities in the nation. By publishing worldwide, it furthers the University's mission of dedication to excellence in teaching, scholarship, research, and clinical care.

Library of Congress Cataloging-in-Publication Data

Names: Michals, Debra, author.
Title: She's the boss : the rise of women's entrepreneurship since World War II / Debra Michals.
Description: New Brunswick, New Jersey : Rutgers University Press, [2025] | Includes bibliographical references and index.
Identifiers: LCCN 2024040376 | ISBN 9781978818163 (paperback) | ISBN 9781978818170 (hardcover) | ISBN 9781978818187 (epub) | ISBN 9781978818200 (pdf)
Subjects: LCSH: Women-owned business enterprises—United States—History. | Businesswomen—United States—History. | Entrepreneurship—United States—History.
Classification: LCC HD2358.72.U6 M53 2025 | DDC 338/.04082—dc23/eng/20241004
LC record available at https://lccn.loc.gov/2024040376

A British Cataloging-in-Publication record for this book is available from the British Library.

Copyright © 2025 by Debra Michals
All rights reserved
No part of this book may be reproduced or utilized in any form or by any means, electronic or mechanical, or by any information storage and retrieval system, without written permission from the publisher. Please contact Rutgers University Press, 106 Somerset Street, New Brunswick, NJ 08901. The only exception to this prohibition is "fair use" as defined by U.S. copyright law.

References to internet websites (URLs) were accurate at the time of writing. Neither the author nor Rutgers University Press is responsible for URLs that may have expired or changed since the manuscript was prepared.

♾ The paper used in this publication meets the requirements of the American National Standard for Information Sciences—Permanence of Paper for Printed Library Materials, ANSI Z39.48-1992.

rutgersuniversitypress.org

For my sister Camie—a promise kept

Contents

	Introduction	1
1	From War Worker to Business Owner: Women, Enterprise, and Postwar Reconversion, 1945–1950	11
2	Motherhood and Its Discontents: 1950s Domesticity, the Cold War, and Women's Business Ownership	43
3	"Doin' It for Themselves": Gender, Race, and Women's Entrepreneurship in the Socially Conscious 1960s	74
4	Sisterhood Is (Economically) Powerful: Civil Rights, Feminism, and Women's Business Ownership in the 1960s and 1970s	103
5	Becoming "Entrepreneurs": Women's Businesses in the 1970s Recession and "Go-Go '80s"	140
	Epilogue: Women's Entrepreneurship in the 1990s and Beyond	171
	Acknowledgments	179
	Notes	183
	Index	227

She's the Boss

Introduction

In December 2020, as the world experienced the COVID-19 pandemic shutdown, Debra Ball was putting the finishing touches on Olive's, the coffeehouse and bakeshop she planned to open in Newburyport, Massachusetts, later that month. It seemed counterintuitive: starting a coffee shop in the middle of the lockdown when people were wearing masks, fearing for their safety, and cutting way back on restaurants and similar outings. But Ball was undeterred. She opened just after Christmas, and in the years since she has built a popular neighborhood spot.[1] What she could not know at the time was that she was in the vanguard of an important trend: since the pandemic, women have opened businesses at rates that far surpass those of their male counterparts, with women of color outpacing everyone. While many businesses closed permanently during the pandemic, women opened more ventures than they closed: from 2022 to 2023, the growth rate for women-owned businesses was 4.5 times that of men's.[2] In fact, one study shows that U.S. women open 1,817 new ventures every day.[3]

Ball's venture and many others are part of the long march of women into business ownership that began with increasing intensity after World War II. That was when women, some of them former suffragists, gained high-level government positions and advocated for women's economic equality through business ownership. Jane Todd paved the way; when she became the first woman deputy commerce commissioner in New York State in 1945, she used her post to help thousands of women nationwide start businesses. Todd recognized early on what has been true of women's business ownership ever since: that entrepreneurship can do for women what the labor market has not—provide autonomy, flexibility, and limitless economic potential for their own financial security and success. For Todd, this was about helping women pushed from wartime jobs for returning soldiers survive and thrive while also rebuilding the number of small businesses lost during the war. She launched forums designed to teach women how to turn their talents into thriving enterprises.[4] Todd's vision served as a unique form of activism, an attempt to fuse postwar reconversion capitalism and women's economic needs/rights with prevailing gender norms. By 1949, the number of women-owned businesses in the United States reportedly jumped from five hundred thousand to nearly a million.[5] It was the first of many moments when times of crisis led politicians, activists, and business leaders to consider and promote entrepreneurship for women.

This book project began with these questions: What is it about business ownership that has proven so attractive to women in the decades since World War II? What changed historically in the second half of the twentieth century to facilitate women's shifting perceptions about their relationship to small business and the economy? In attempting to answer these questions, *She's the Boss* chronicles women's increasing and evolving relationship with business ownership in the decades since World War II. It demonstrates that this early postwar moment proved transformative in the history of women's business ownership, setting the stage for the growing appeal of private enterprise in the decades that followed so that today women own more than 43 percent of all businesses nationwide.[6]

The study of women's business ownership is a study of women's history from the mid-twentieth century to the present. It offers insight into women's changing social, economic, and political status—the independent steps they took when they had few rights as well as the movements they launched to gain the rights that would enable them to not only initiate but excel in the ventures they took on. Women entrepreneurs did not exist in a vacuum; they experienced the obstacles, gender and racial norms and biases, that women throughout U.S. society experienced. But as business owners, they used their ventures to bypass roadblocks and stake a claim for themselves within the U.S. economy. They essentially opted out of a restricted and often biased labor market and into private enterprise as a vehicle to get back into the economy—ideally on terms they helped define. If the structure of the job market was not set up for women of any and all races, gender identities, sexualities, ages, and abilities—for those who may have had children or who needed or desired a more flexible scenario and/or who daily experienced discrimination—then women hoped entrepreneurship could be a far better, more egalitarian alternative. And when career women hit the glass ceiling in the 1970s and 1980s, many too looked to businesses of their own with their limitless potential for upward mobility.

The thread that runs through the history of women's entrepreneurship is simply this: the economy (the system) was not set up for women, but since World War II, women have nonetheless increasingly needed and wanted to work. Entrepreneurship made that possible in ways the job market may not have. At the same time, the changing social landscape—the rise of civil, women's, and LGBTQ+ rights movements—helped to create a new activist language of economic rights: the right to make a living regardless of gender, race, or sexuality; the right to be self-supporting; the right to survive and thrive.

While women have turned to business ownership throughout U.S. history to stave off exigency or after the loss of a spouse, since the postwar era, women's business ownership moved far beyond that to become a way that women could combine multiple roles and responsibilities—the need for an income or a sense of personal fulfillment—with the pressure to conform to norms about motherhood and femininity. The 1940s represents the first time the state actively sanctioned business ownership for women and promoted it as a legitimate option. That would happen again in the 1970s with the federal MBE and WBE (Minority Business Enterprise and Women's Business Enterprise) programs and in the late 1970s and 1980s with Jimmy Carter's and Ronald Reagan's outreach to women entrepreneurs and the 1988 Women's Business Ownership Act. In the interim years, women of all races and classes pushed forward, tapping into racialized gender norms and ideologies—as well as political challenges to them via the civil rights and women's movements—to justify and expand their growing relationship with capitalism as business owners.

In addition, the postwar era established the hallmarks of women's business ownership that prevail up to the present: that business ownership could solve multiple problems and needs for women and the state and that it could do so in very gendered ways that did not necessarily pose a challenge to women's traditional roles or to labor market and societal biases. By starting businesses, women of all races and classes could exit an often discriminatory labor market while remaining "in" the economy (or at least on the sidelines)—albeit in what, at least initially, was a privatized, often home-based, separate subsection of the economy.

That, of course, would change if the women's businesses grew beyond the home, as many did. Throughout the latter twentieth century, business ownership would prove flexible enough to enable women to redefine its role, place, and function in their lives in ways that would simultaneously thwart those who challenged their economic efforts and mesh with the changing socioeconomic context. That is, business ownership's inherent flexibility meant its role, place, and function in women's lives could be molded (actually and discursively) to change with the times by individual women and those who advocated for their entry into business ownership. The flexibility built into women's relationship to small business was both its appeal and its assurance of continued growth and reinvention throughout the changing social landscape of 1950s redomestication; 1960s and 1970s escalating divorce rates and the growth of feminism and civil rights activism; 1970s and 1980s economic fluctuations, growing government interest in and programs for small business owners, and mainstreaming of feminist egalitarian ideals in an economic context; and as a workaround when the glass ceiling stymied their professional progress.

Women business owners simultaneously used the language of capitalism, gender norms, and gender politics in a given historical moment to explain and rationalize their ventures. For example, women business owners in the 1950s adopted the language of domesticity and anticommunist, free enterprise social discourse to justify their moves from the home into business. Catalog maven Lillian Vernon, whose business started at home and grew within a few years to a multimillion-dollar venture with a warehouse of its own, would say repeatedly that she started the business to give her children a better life than they would otherwise have had on a single-breadwinner salary. By the 1960s, such justifications would extend to the rising divorce rates, the welfare/antipoverty debates, and for civil rights activists, as a means to help fund the movement. In the 1970s, feminists too—even socialist feminists—hoped capitalism would prove flexible enough so that their ventures could not only actualize their visions of gender equality but also promote a new, more humanitarian model of capitalism itself. While they may not have ultimately revolutionized corporate America, over time, these women business owners did indeed engage in what has continued to be a push-pull relationship with the very system they sought to change: the U.S. economy.

As *She's the Boss* demonstrates, in the decades since World War II, women have made vital and increasing strides into entrepreneurship, at times outpacing their male counterparts and even upholding the mythic American image of the risk-taking entrepreneur during more economically conservative times. In the process, women's increasing presence as business owners has reshaped the meaning of entrepreneurship itself from a term that once exclusively applied to self-made men to, by the late 1970s, one that included women who launched businesses and whose relationship to the profit motive inherent in capitalism and entrepreneurship may have been different from that of their male counterparts. By the late 1970s too, women not only began to claim the gendered word "entrepreneur" for themselves; they expanded its meaning beyond profit maximization and growth as the only measures of success. While women's ventures were built on filling market niches, they also often sought to control growth, provide a means to combine home/work responsibilities and ambitions, and serve community goals (such as aiding other women or advancing equality, as feminist and civil rights–based businesses wanted to do). Today, millennial / Gen Z entrepreneurs and LGBTQ+ business owners and advocates often expect their enterprises to function on two levels: the traditional, profit-driven model and a newer, socially responsible one that either gives back to society (social entrepreneurship) or provides jobs for those who face systemic discrimination and helps advance the larger goal of equality writ large.

A Note about Sources

Telling women's stories and giving voice to their contributions to modern history required the use of a wide range of primary and secondary sources, including magazine and newspaper articles, biographies and autobiographies, government documents, oral histories, and archival materials on individual women and women's organizations. It would be impossible to include every woman who ever started a business in the United States in a single book. Instead, the mission here was to make visible the many women long hidden from history and balance their stories with those who founded what became huge enterprises that garnered lots of media attention.

Tracking the number of women business owners across time proved tricky and required interpretation, since figures varied as did the government agency collecting the data until the early 1970s. The first government tabulations seeking to specifically track self-employed women did not occur until 1972, when the Census Bureau established an official category for women's businesses and self-employment to be studied every five years. Before that, agencies used ever-changing formulas that often lumped women's enterprises with professional and managerial jobs, making it impossible to tell just which women owned a business and which ones were employed as managers. Similarly, prior to the early 1970s, government data at times considered sex and other times did not, and when race was included, gender was not always an additional category for analysis.[7] Moreover, there was undoubtedly a gross underrepresentation of women's businesses in national statistics, in part because many women running businesses from their homes were more likely to list their occupation as "housewife" rather than "proprietor." These home-based ventures were also less likely to pay taxes, therefore not showing up on Internal Revenue Service rolls—which was the data used by the Commerce Department in its early studies. Not until the Women's Business Ownership Act of 1988 would there be a consistent definition of what constituted a woman-owned business and a mechanism for counting them. In addition, while most small businesses statistically fail in the first few years, there are no tracking mechanisms showing precisely whose ventures survived and whose did not.

A Brief History of Women's Business Ownership before World War II

Prior to the turn of the twentieth century, small business dominated the commercial landscape of America and, in fact, was its foundation. Rooted in the mystique of the small businessman was both the ideal of independence—political and moral—and the notion that like the yeoman farmer, the nation's economy was built on the backs of independent merchants, wholesalers, and artisans who found success through the ethic of hard work and determination. A mid-1970s Senate study of the place of small business in American life described the "spirit of private enterprise" as emblematic of national character and referred to Thomas Jefferson as understanding the value of the "economically self-reliant farmer-businessman" to the larger democratic society.[8]

A staple of American identity, the archetype of the self-made man may apply equally well to women, particularly women entrepreneurs. History is replete with stories of self-made women who turned necessity and hardship into self-supporting and sometimes lucrative ventures from the earliest days of European settlement through the present. That ingenuity, so often ascribed to pioneering men, has been at times more typical of enterprising women from all ethnic, racial, and class backgrounds. For much of American history prior to the World War II era, women's participation in small business ownership remained fairly consistent, albeit with cultural and individual variations by decade and business owner. Women traditionally owned businesses as a function of necessity, after becoming widows, or in the case of farm wives, starting a small market to trade vegetables or other items as an extension of work roles within the family. Women everywhere made handicrafts and food products, and urban women similarly took in boarders, laundry, and sewing. Often too, women's ventures were characterized as merely for "pin money." Historically, "pin money" has meant anything from money given by husbands to wives for pins and needles, as in the fourteenth-century usage, to money women secreted away to buy little trinkets without making a dent in the family budget. It has also referred to money women literally pinned to brassieres as a means of hiding it from the prying eyes of spouses, as in twentieth-century references. Engaging in business prior to the twentieth century was often marked by exigency, downward mobility, and declining class status, and starting a business was an attempt to stave off all three.

Women then, as has often been the case since, commercialized their domestic skills or worked in service of others, concentrating in traditionally feminine categories: food preparation, housekeeping, apparel, small retail, and beauty, to name a few. From the start, small business ownership for women enabled them to exist simultaneously within and outside the larger economy. For widows, women abandoned by spouses, or the unmarried, business ownership was often an acceptable way to provide for themselves and their families without stepping outside what were perceived as acceptable gender roles. Women typically launched ventures in ways that marketed their domestic skills, thereby staying within their gender role, even while moving beyond it. For single women such as Mary Catherine Goddard, who owned the printing press that produced an early version of the Declaration of Independence, it could be a mark of unusual status. For widows and those left on their own, it was a means of survival. Many owned taverns or hotels, again in keeping with their gender roles. Rebecca Lukens, who was a widow, staved off bankruptcy at her late husband's Brandywine Iron Works in the 1830s. Pregnant with her sixth child at age thirty-one when she inherited the business, she not only turned a profit for the renamed Lukens Iron Works but left an estate of $100,000 at her death in 1854, considered a small fortune at the time. By 1974, the company Rebecca Lukens saved was worth $283 million in sales. White women became pioneering entrepreneurs in the late nineteenth and early twentieth centuries as milliners, as noted in

Wendy Gamber's pathbreaking work.[9] Newly freed as well as enslaved women in early America such as the seamstress Elizabeth Hobbs Keckly also found enterprising ways to support themselves and generate needed cash by marketing their talents and skills. Keckly, who purchased her freedom in 1855, became First Lady Mary Todd Lincoln's dressmaker in 1861 and had nearly two dozen women working for her.[10]

In truth, while the postwar era represents an important rupture in the continuous history of women's business ownership, there had been another moment of unreached potential in the early twentieth century, in the era described by women's historians as that of the "New Woman." Charlotte Perkins Gilman's 1898 *Women and Economics* was the first polemic about the centrality of money for women's true equality, and though not its intent, it provided a powerful legitimation for New Woman entrepreneurs.[11] During the 1910s, for example, women traded on new images of their autonomy and founded businesses that would provide a comfortable living, at times free of the requirements of marriage. Elizabeth Arden, for example, was driven to build a major corporation from her burgeoning cosmetics business, regarding it as a way to remain free of marriage. She even distinctly stated that men were in fact "the problem" in women's personal development.[12] Her arch rival, Helena Rubenstein, shared Arden's determination to build a major corporation. Other women likewise launched ventures with a goal of profit maximization as well as making a name for themselves, among them Ida Rosenthal, founder of Maidenform, and Madam C. J. Walker, the nation's first African American woman millionaire, who made her fortune on hair care products for Black women.

In an age when women increasingly took chances and revised standards of femininity to include rebelliousness and independence, the dawn of the twentieth century served as the first laboratory for both entrepreneurship itself and an economic justification for women's business ownership. In 1903, Maggie Lena Walker became the first woman of color to open a bank when she launched St. Luke's Penny Savings and Loan in Richmond, Virginia, to provide other African Americans with an institution of their own.[13] In 1922, just two years after women gained the right to vote, sisters Clara and Lillian Westropp opened the Women's Savings and Loan in Cleveland, Ohio, the first savings and loan association founded and operated by and for women. The pair took pride in their all-woman board, and the bank grew to assets of more than $576 million in 1983, when it was renamed Women's Federal Savings. It merged in 1992 with Charter One Financial.[14] Future First Lady Eleanor Roosevelt partnered with friends Nancy Cook, Marion Dickerman, and Caroline O'Day to open Val-kill Industries in 1926 as a crafts cooperative in Upstate New York. The vision was to create reproductions of early American traditional furniture and find a way to pair artisan work (and vocational training) with agriculture as farms increasingly declined.[15] Other women too sought to create ventures in the suffrage and post-suffrage eras that celebrated and promoted women's capabilities.

The 1929 stock market crash and coming depression curbed this spirited drive for women into business ownership and progressive ideologies about gender roles. The Great Depression with its reactionary climate imposed a silence about women's initiatives. Women did not stop seeking creative, entrepreneurial solutions to their growing fiscal crises; rather, they were forced to dissemble about them in the interests of maintaining the male breadwinner myth and, in so doing, keeping their families intact. As male unemployment rates soared, women took in laundry, boarders, and sold homemade products to maintain the family's survival. The mythic norm that women only entered the world of business when there were no other available options (read: a male breadwinner) was underscored in the 1934 film *Imitation of Life*. Raising daughters on their own, the two female protagonists—a white woman and her Black housekeeper—market the Black woman's pancake recipe as a last chance at economic survival. Their success, much greater for the white woman who spearheaded the venture, was driven by the singular purpose only a woman driven to desperation without a male breadwinner could achieve.[16] Despite such public norms, some women—like Estee Lauder, Margaret Rudkin of Pepperidge Farm, and Olive Beech of Beech Aircraft—nonetheless continued in the progressive footsteps of the New Woman era, launching in the late 1930s what would quickly become large-scale corporations focused on staking a claim in the economy.[17] Others, such as Hattie Gray, a woman of color who moved from Chicago to Saratoga Springs, New York, made a living serving the racetrack and Jazz Age nightclubbers at Hattie's Chicken Shack. "I didn't have but $33," she recalled years later, noting that the twenty-four-hour restaurant served only her fried chicken recipe: "I bought a stove, an icebox, table, and chairs. It was very shoestring."[18]

In the crisis years of the 1930s, small, often home-based ventures were seen more as a solution to joblessness than as an end unto themselves. Many women in the Depression era looked to small business as a way to stave off poverty and stretch the family's resources, particularly when male breadwinners were out of work.[19] Starting home-based ventures could prove more desirable than facing the rising public acrimony leveled at women workers, who were often accused of taking jobs that men needed, despite the fact that the gender segregation of work made women's jobs undesirable to men.[20] In a 1936 Gallup Poll, for example, 82 percent of the respondents said married women should not work if their husbands were employed.[21] This cultural disdain for married women's employment, combined with pressing financial needs, often accounted at least in part for women's preference for home-based business ownership.

Born in part of necessity and in part of changing social mores, women's businesses have flourished precisely because of the odds against them—namely, their lack of access to institutional capital and their invisibility in mainstream capitalism prior to, and in the decades following, the post–World War II period. That is, denied equal access to capital, women's businesses were started with little or no money and often at home, a fact that ironically facilitated a propensity for risk-taking. In effect then, the history of women's business ownership is a tale of both triumph—for the individual women business owners and the march of women into entrepreneurship—and continuity. As women left the workforce, they also left in place the discriminatory practices that blocked all women's advancement.

Scholarship

In 1999, historian Mary Yeager published an article asking if there would ever be a feminist business history. Since then, and especially in the past decade, women's/feminist and business historians have begun to answer the call, merging social and cultural history and intersectional gender analyses with business history and capitalism studies. These scholars have published new work that highlights not only the long and steady march of women into business in the last century but also the at-times political underpinnings of their initiatives. Tiffany Gill was an early trailblazer in seeing the social and activist connections in women's enterprises in her work on African American beauty salons. More recently, Kristen Hogan demonstrated similar intersections in her 2016 book *The Feminist Bookstore Movement: Lesbian Antiracism and Feminist Accountability*, as did Alex Ketchum in her thoroughly researched 2022 *Ingredients for Revolution: A History of American Feminist Restaurants, Cafes, and Coffeehouses*.[22] In his brilliant 2017 book *From Head Shops to Whole Foods*, Joshua Clark Davis looked at both gender and race for links between activism and entrepreneurship, studying Black-owned bookshops, countercultural head shops, and feminist businesses.[23] Scholars have also produced studies on women entrepreneurs in a particular location and time period, such as Edith Sparks's *Boss Lady: How Three Women Entrepreneurs Built Successful Big Businesses in the Mid-twentieth Century*. Sparks's book concentrates on Margaret Rudkin, founder of Pepperidge Farm; Olive Ann Beech, who was the cofounder (with her husband) of aerospace giant Beech Aircraft; and Tillie Lewis, who inherited an Italian tomato canning business that was drowning in debt and made it one of the largest and most successful companies of its kind.

Other works that have offered useful insights into the relationship between women and the economy include studies about the entrepreneurial nature of direct sales work for women in the postwar world, such as Katina Manko's 2021 history of Avon, *Ding Dong! Avon Calling! The Women and Men of Avon Products, Incorporated*, and Jessica Burch's 2015 dissertation "Soap and Hope: Direct Sales and the Culture of Work and Capitalism in Postwar America." Additionally, there has been exciting new scholarship on workplace issues and their intersection with both gender and race, among them Kirsten Swinth's *Feminism's Forgotten Fight: The Unfinished Struggle for Work and Family* (2018), Agatha Beins's *Liberation in Print: Feminist Periodicals and Social Movement Identity*

(2019), and Allison Elias's *The Rise of Corporate Feminism: Women in the American Office, 1960–1990* (2022), to name a few.

She's the Boss is the latest entry into this field, providing an overview of the forces that pushed and pulled women into business ownership as well as the place and meaning of those ventures in women's lives. The book sits at the apex of women's/feminist history and capitalism studies and contributes to a lively and growing scholarship in both areas. Organized chronologically and thematically, each chapter highlights the key trends of a given period along with narrative accounts from women business owners themselves. The opening chapter on the 1940s shows the ways in which business ownership fused women's needs and desires to continue their wartime relationship to the economy with government interest in ensuring a burgeoning postwar economy. The section on the 1950s demonstrates that despite public efforts to limit women's roles to home and family, women not only continued to launch small businesses but did so within the prevailing language of motherhood, family, and consumerism.

Chapters 3 and 4 focus on the 1960s and early 1970s. Chapter 3 looks at the impact of both changing family structures—rising divorce rates and a rapid expansion in the number of single mothers—and national trends, such as growing immigration or government initiatives via the Small Business Administration or the War on Poverty, on women's business ownership. It further discusses how new federal programs to alleviate long-standing economic and political inequities were not truly inclusive of women, especially women of color, and often imposed gender and racial biases. Chapter 4 focuses on the links between activism and entrepreneurship in the 1960s and 1970s, exploring the complicated relationship between civil rights, gay liberation, and feminism with entrepreneurial capitalism. The problem of the 1970s recession and the so-called Reagan Revolution of the 1980s that purported to solve it are the themes of the fifth chapter. The economic downturn took its heaviest toll on women workers, particularly women of color, and pushed many of them to create their own income via private enterprise. This chapter also notes the significance of women business owners claiming the label "entrepreneur" for the first time and, in so doing, altering the public understanding of the word in subtle but important and enduring ways. The final chapter explores the rise of the modern woman entrepreneur from the 1990s to the present and discusses whether the advent of internet technology with its potentially low start-up costs and crowd-funding truly matched expectations that it would level the playing field for would-be women entrepreneurs. It also addresses the ongoing question of whether entrepreneurship and feminism are compatible or antithetical.

1

From War Worker
to Business Owner

Women, Enterprise, and
Postwar Reconversion,
1945–1950

On October 2, 1946, two hundred African American women gathered at the 135th Street Branch Library in Harlem, New York City. They were there for the first of two opportunities to listen to Jane Todd, New York State's first woman deputy commerce commissioner, discuss the potential that awaited them from starting businesses of their own. Sponsored by the local chapter of the Negro Business and Professional Women's Clubs, the evening's program was Todd's brainchild, a forum she dubbed a "small business clinic" and made available to women's groups of all races through the Woman's Program she established in the Commerce Department. Todd, a longtime Republican politico and former suffragist, saw her new role as an opportunity to keep the economy going and empower women through business ownership. The clinics she created blended exhibits of homemade products that could be mass produced, success stories of women who made a tidy living running ventures, and personal, one-on-one advice from government and business experts—among them, cosmetics mogul Elizabeth Arden—about the risks and rewards (mostly rewards) of running their own enterprises.

While explaining to the Harlem professional women in the auditorium that they too could turn hobbies or hidden talents into businesses, Todd was quick to point out that this wasn't just about extra pocket or "pin" money by selling to family or neighbors. This was *real business* with potentially long-term and lucrative outcomes for both the women and the nation's recovering economy in the postwar era. As such, she "urged that housewives merchandise through large outlets, 'rather than through friends.'" New York State, Todd informed the audience, lost one hundred thousand small businesses during World War II, and by commercializing foodstuffs and other homemade goods—some of which had been in short supply during the war—would-be women business owners could help rebuild the state's economy. What's more, Todd made a bold claim about women's propensity for risk and their value to the larger postwar economic goals. "If women—who are more daring than men—go into commercial activities, the loss to our economy will be partially recovered," Todd declared.[1] This was not the first time she made such optimistic predictions; a year earlier, just after her appointment, Todd said that she expected "25,000 women to open small shops in the next decade."[2]

Individual women were similarly recognizing the potential of small business ownership in the postwar era. Faced with an ill husband and unpaid medical bills, Dorothy Chase, a white woman in New York, launched a home-based business as a way to provide for her struggling family. Chase borrowed a friend's herring recipe and sold containers of prepared fish door-to-door before landing accounts with specialty retailers who agreed to carry it on consignment. By 1948, Chase's business, Betty Lee Foods, had annual sales of $250,000 (adjusted for inflation, that would be roughly $3.2 million in 2024). Such growth required her to relocate the business from her kitchen to its own facility with forty employees. In upstate New York, Agnes Hose's smoked turkey products business was outgrowing her kitchen, and she too moved and expanded to a staff of sixteen women and ten men to meet supermarket and specialty store demand. Not all women's ventures were food related, but they were typically businesses that could be started at home, often by commercializing domestic or other feminine skills, and were likely to appeal to the changing social climate and marketplace in the postwar era. In Cincinnati, Ohio, for example, Desiree Steiner launched a babysitting service for local mothers, who eagerly responded to the convenience it provided.[3] The beauty business—hairdressing in particular—was also a big draw, albeit with white and Black women opening businesses for racially distinct clientele.

While women throughout American history have turned to money-making ventures as a way to extend family financial resources, their enterprises were historically met with resistance or were represented as either supplemental or as a way to stave off hardship, often after the death or abandonment of a breadwinning spouse. There were exceptional women, notably in the late nineteenth and early twentieth centuries, who started ventures much as men did—because they saw a market opportunity or had ambition—and built them into sizable companies. Many more, however, justified their ventures based on gender norms or familial needs, with few, if any, institutional resources or support systems. But the post–World War II reconversion period changed that, marking the moment when the state first sanctioned and promoted business ownership as a legitimate economic role and identity for women. Contrary to popular conceptions of the postwar period, public ideology and government initiatives did not simply encourage women to leave the workforce and return to hearth and home at war's end. Rather, fears of another world war, desires to continue the economic prosperity triggered by the nation's entry into World War II, and utopian ideas about reconfigured gender relations in the postwar era converged to facilitate and encourage women's movement into small business ownership. State and national governments, as well as women's organizations, picked up Todd's model and not only ran programs to entice women to launch ventures but similarly promoted these businesses as vital contributors to rebuilding the country's economy.

Government initiatives coupled with women's private endeavors signaled the new importance of women's business ownership in the postwar United States. For business and government leaders, small business served multiple goals. First, it provided a handy way to help stimulate economic development and boost women's spending ability in the conversion from wartime production to consumer goods. But it also aided efforts to push women from wartime jobs to make room for returning soldiers while ensuring that women continued to see themselves as economic agents and workers to be tapped again in the advent of another war. For women themselves, small business made it possible to combine domestic roles with the need to provide for their families, especially when soldier-husbands did not return from war or returned too injured to work. Business ownership also enabled women who had enjoyed the earning potential of, and sense of fulfillment from, wartime jobs to bypass the gendered, often lower-paid and discriminatory labor market options available to them in the postwar era, such as work as waitresses or secretaries.

For leaders such as Todd, women's business ownership took on the zeal of an activist mission, an attempt to fuse postwar reconversion capitalism with social norms about gender roles and with women's economic needs/rights and their potential for independence. In some ways, this was a feminist agenda, although not explicitly labeled as such; in other ways, simple economics drove Todd's work. As Todd saw it, if women could indeed start and run businesses, it would mark both a micro and macro victory—a win for the individual (ideally, thousands and thousands of them) and for the broader economy's need to replace small businesses lost before and during the war. What's more, leaders and individuals who embraced the small business solution seemed to regard capitalism as a flexible tool—one that could conform to prevailing gender norms about women's household roles while also tacitly challenging them. Women who started businesses could be every bit the feminine domestic, even as they transcended that realm. To Todd and other male and female leaders who embraced the small business promise, there was no incompatibility between women as business owners and their roles within the home and family; in fact, these roles were portrayed as mutually beneficial. Women could start a business from home that would enable them to balance the need to make a living with domestic tasks.

Capitalism was so flexible, it seemed, that its proponents thought it was also inherently gender- and race-blind; that is, they regarded the economy as neutral and nondiscriminatory except in terms of what made money—even as capitalists used business ownership as a vehicle to promote the values of the white establishment. The color of one's skin or one's gender mattered far less to those touting small business than the potential marketability of an idea, its ability to become a successful business, and its role in boosting economic growth. This made the small business solution a useful and nonpolitical tool in the era of "Double V" (victory abroad and against racism at home) wartime and postwar civil rights activism—hence Todd's and others' occasional outreach to African American women with their small business programs. Still, leaders such as Todd who advocated business ownership for women did so in terms that reflected the place of white women in society with little if any focus on the particular circumstances or needs of women of color. In this way, business ownership was as much about whiteness as it was about gender for those promoting its potential to women. But Black women would attend available workshops like those offered in Harlem and interpret for themselves the value of entrepreneurship as a means to bypass ongoing discrimination. One woman at the Harlem clinic proposed a "volunteer shop" where women could collectively sell their products to their Harlem neighbors, for example.[4] The ventures they launched would become an increasing source of racial pride and interconnected with the growing civil rights movement in the decades to come.[5]

Even if many business and political leaders promoted the links between women's ventures and their familial roles, they also expected their businesses to move far beyond the home, as did many women owners themselves. As such, the period from 1945 through the completion of reconversion by 1950 marks an important shift in political and social ideology that shaped not only the nature and scope of women's enterprises for generations to come but also their legitimacy as an economic option for women across race and class lines, most notably married women with children. Women too were eager to take their place as equal partners in the nation's future and responded in large numbers to every reconversion opportunity available to them. By 1951, Todd happily reported that there were eleven thousand new women-owned businesses in New York State.[6] The predominantly white National Federation of Business and Professional Women's Clubs (BPW), the nation's largest professional women's organization, was rapidly spreading the gospel of small business and Todd's Woman's Program and clinic model to its membership via its magazine, *Independent*

Woman. BPW chapters began offering similar programs and encouraging their state governments—many of which consented—to launch commerce department initiatives for would-be women business owners. The national media too promoted and praised such efforts. The result was that by 1949, the number of women-owned businesses nationwide reportedly jumped from five hundred thousand to nearly a million.[7]

Rethinking Gender Roles in the Postwar World

In the two years before the war ended, business, government, and academic leaders were beginning to debate what U.S. society might look like after the war. At the center of these discussions was an awareness that wartime jobs for women and parallel changes within American households might reconfigure gender roles. Many saw a moment of revolutionary possibilities for the future, and they urged the nation to embrace social change in postwar planning, including an end to gender and racial biases, at least in the economic sector. "No longer are there to be artificial barriers against useful employment and opportunity on account of sex any more than there are to be bars on account of race, color, creed or national origin," said New York governor Thomas Dewey.[8] Texas defense contractor and director of the Federal Smaller War Plants Corporation Maury Maverick agreed, arguing that "women had learned too much to go back" and would find great opportunities if the country "roll[ed] into full production after the war." In a nod to altered social roles, Maverick further said that home life had been so dramatically changed by the war that "no stigma would be attached to a man if his wife happened to be the moneymaker."[9] A YWCA pamphlet similarly spotlighted the flexibility of family roles in the postwar era: "We must accept the fact that in modern living women and men may play interchangeable roles. . . . No place remains today for the tradition that the man who is 'the provider' does not 'allow' his wife to work. Reality tells us that many of us who are wives must work either for economic or personal reasons."[10]

Utopian visions of reconfigured gender roles also featured altered household roles—including increased duties for men—in ways that would prove compatible with women's business ownership. In 1944, labor leader and business owner Elizabeth Hawes told attendees at the *Newsweek* symposium on "American Women in the Postwar World" that she conceived of a future where "everyone works a 30-hour week (and) both males and females will have time for home chores and pleasant recreational activities."[11] Economist Hazel Kyrk and magazine writer Edith Stern took a more extreme position, arguing that individual housework performed in private households would prove inefficient in the near future. "Home is the only part of the whole American economy where one person has to do everything," argued Stern. "Ten million women making ten million baked potatoes is absurd. Hot meals should be delivered like they are to airplanes every night."[12]

Similarly, as World War II ended and the Cold War intensified, fear of another world war produced a discourse of preparedness that included maximum use of womanpower. In 1949, *Woman's Home Companion* conducted a survey of its readership about whether they expected another global war in five years: "We asked them: In the four years since the end of the war do you feel the likelihood of continued world peace has improved, lessened or remains the same? Almost five out of ten think the likelihood of permanent peace has lessened."[13] Drawing on the lessons of World War II, the ideology of preparedness stressed that America must never be caught off guard again.

Antiquated ideas about gender roles meant lost time in training and recruiting women during the war for previously male jobs in defense and industry. Instead, advocates of preparedness argued that if women were kept economically viable in the postwar years, they could easily be called upon again to assist with manpower shortages at home if men were again called to serve in a war overseas. "Our planning for the effective use of womanpower can start at a much more advanced stage today than it did in 1942, for we can build upon the progress and learn from the mistakes made during World War II," affirmed Dorothy C. Stratton, former director of the Coast Guard World War II SPARS project, in 1950.[14] But if women's wartime jobs after World War II were to be returned to soldiers, how, then, to keep women seeing themselves as connected to the economy?

What to Do with All Those Working Women?

By war's end, the nation's vision of its future had yet to crystallize. Haunted by the failed economic legacy of the Great Depression and desperate to secure wartime prosperity for the long term, policymakers grappled with immense uncertainty, stressing the need for full employment to stave off another major depression. As historian William O'Neill has noted, "The war had brought prosperity and excitement to many Americans, tragedy to a few, but a sense of the future's possibilities to almost no one. Psychologically, most people were still living in the 1930s."[15] The recessions of 1946 and 1948–1949 only underscored the fears of economic naysayers. U.S. commerce secretary Henry A. Wallace's book *Sixty Million Jobs* posited that *only* if the nation acted in time and took definitive steps could it create new jobs in the postwar era and avoid another depression.[16]

The Depression, however, laid the groundwork for women's increasing understanding of economic contributions as part of their household obligations.[17] Many of the women who would become business owners in the 1940s and 1950s came of age during the Depression and learned then the centrality of women's economic efforts in family survival. "In hundreds of thousands of families, it takes the wage of both husband and wife to pay the bills," argued Mildred Adams in a debate over women's roles that appeared in a 1939 issue of *The Forum* magazine.[18] Women who would later turn to business ownership subsequently recalled the lessons of the Depression as formative in spurring these impulses.

"Grandmother told me, 'Every tub must stand on its own bottom,'" noted Mary Crowley, who in 1957 founded Home Interiors and Gifts, Inc., a multimillion-dollar home demonstration company in Dallas. "This was important advice that I would need to remember through the hard times of the Depression years. Married and a mother right after high school, I quickly learned that I would have to be the provider for my children—my husband was not ready for family responsibilities."[19] She took in sewing and sold homemade bread to buy food for her family.

During the war years too, women were rethinking their relationship to business. The *Boston Globe*, for example, ran a column by Polly Webster entitled "War Time Wife," which offered tips on everything from coping with scarce supplies during the conflict to generating an income. In the early 1940s, a group of primarily Jewish women in Cambridge, Massachusetts, started a consignment/gift shop and café, the Window Shop, to generate money to aid Jewish and other refugees from Nazi Germany. Proceeds from the business funded their transport to the United States as well as job training and employment assistance once they arrived. Partially, the venture stemmed from a long legacy of Jewish women as economic contributors to family life, but in large measure it derived from the direct necessity of wartime humanitarian crises. The nature of the Window Shop's business would change many times in its history of more than thirty years, with a restaurant and gift shop showcasing women's crafts as its primary focus.[20]

With full employment taking center stage in postwar efforts to avoid a return to the Great Depression, policymakers feared that prosperity would be difficult to maintain if women flooded the workforce and competed with men for jobs. They worried, for example, that women's ongoing presence in the workforce would drive unemployment statistics endlessly upward as war plants were shut down or retooled for commercial production. Government leaders also recognized that leaving women out would alienate a growing and viable political constituency of women's organizations and female voters, many of whom were becoming increasingly visible during the war years and believed that wartime labor force participation entitled women to be included in the full-employment economy. "The adaptability of women during the emergency points to a future trend for women in industry and the economic life of the postwar world," Jane Todd said during a 1945 press conference announcing her goals for the newly formed New York Woman's Program.[21] *Independent Woman* ran several articles in the mid-1940s strongly urging women's inclusion in the full-employment economy.[22] Even *Ladies Home Journal* and *Atlantic Monthly* took up the cause, arguing, "Only if there is employment for women as for men, and only if wages are based on occupations and not on sex, shall we achieve a sound economy."[23] Republican representative Clare Booth Luce told a meeting of the Women's Military Service Club in 1943, "It's absurd to think that women by the millions will vacate good jobs voluntarily."[24]

Women who entered the postwar era with faith in wartime promises expected policymakers to ultimately make good. Research on the era reveals that 37 percent of all adult women worked in 1944, and nearly half of all women were actually employed at some time during that year.[25] "During the war period we proved our capacity in this country, and women should insist on keeping their skills or getting re-training, if necessary, so that they can continue to be useful in the industrial field to which they contributed so much," said Margaret Culkin Banning, BPW coordinating committee chair, at a 1946 conference titled "Living and Working in the Peace-Building Years."[26]

As early as 1944, however, some female leaders feared that women had been misled by false promises of postwar careers to lure them to wartime employment in skilled positions as welders and riveters that were traditionally held by men exclusively. In 1944, Democratic representative Mary Norton of New Jersey accurately predicted, "Women are going to be pushed in a corner, and very soon at that."[27] In truth, by the end of World War II, many women lost wartime positions. Once factories were reconverted, sexual and racial discrimination kept women from resuming lucrative manufacturing jobs, with 60 to 80 percent—and in some cases as much as 90 percent—of these positions reserved for men only.[28]

Nonetheless, women's employment remained a critical, if completely unresolved, concern through the early phases of postwar reconversion. World War II casualties numbered over 400,000, with an additional 671,000 returning home wounded.[29] Although most were young, single men, the figure was high enough to alarm politicians.[30] Many women, they feared, needed postwar jobs to help them weather the hardship of single motherhood or the difficulties of providing for children and an injured spouse. Leaders also debated whether there would be a shortage of men available for marriage. As a result, many noted that women would have to plan for the potentiality of perpetual singlehood (translation: self-support). "Looking beyond the war, with its casualty totals," said economist Colston Warne in 1945, "it becomes evident that some women will not be able to marry because of the smaller masculine population. Others will have to assume the sole support of families either because they are widows or because their husbands are physically or mentally unable to carry the burden."[31] Such concerns fueled a legitimation of women's economic roles, even if they did not offer a singular or clear solution.

The Small Business Solution

Enter the notion of women as business owners, commercializing domestic skills, selling products that were scarce during the war, and functioning as economic citizens. As early as 1944, political pundits posited the benefits of small business ownership for women, particularly war workers whose jobs would be necessary for returning soldiers.[32] Newspapers extensively covered the many postwar economic planning conferences and symposiums and interviewed leaders such as

Federal Smaller War Plants Corporation director Maverick, who outspokenly advocated for women's move into business ownership as an easy transition from wartime jobs to a postwar economy. Maverick repeatedly pointed out that the home was the basis of small business, and as such, small business would provide a natural economic role for women in the postwar world. While commercializing domestic talents was one option for women, Maverick saw no limits to the kinds of businesses they might open, even arguing that women had and would make excellent small defense contractors.[33]

Because women's enterprises were often either home based or centered on domestic skills, business ownership—while transformative—seemed to pose less of a threat to traditional notions of gender roles than the idea of mothers continuing to work in war plants, factories, or offices after the war. Instead, women's business ownership in the postwar era occupied a liminal—and therefore far less controversial—space both within and outside broader market capitalism and standard definitions of entrepreneurship. Business and government leaders labeled women's enterprises as "home-based businesses," "small businesses," or "sideline or pin money" ventures—words women business owners themselves embraced—thereby also reinforcing their separate status.[34] Until well into the 1970s, the term *entrepreneur* was reserved exclusively for men who participated in the broader corporate world, chasing a profit motive and blazing fresh trails with new business ideas that could grow from start-up to conglomerate.[35]

At the same time, however, wartime changes to family life also served as a legitimation—at times even a feminist one—for pushing women into business ownership. Economists, academics, politicians, journalists, and labor leaders repeatedly noted the growing number of single mothers and sole heads of households in the mid-1940s.[36] Economist A. G. Mezerik estimated a total of fifteen million women would want or need to generate an income—among them women who held wartime jobs and "the newly created army of breadwinners for war-crippled husbands, brothers, and fatherless children."[37] Some writers such as Harrison Smith in 1947 even agitated for a renewed feminist movement to solidify the gains women made during the war and their continued need and desire to work: "I have now become one of several men and women who are attempting to turn back this tide [against taking women's jobs and all they earned during the war] even if it is necessary to start a new feminist crusade."[38] Three years earlier in 1944, Mary Anderson, director of the Women's Bureau of the Department of Labor, called traditional ideas about women not working "cultural hangovers (that are) no longer appropriate and even dangerous."[39]

That said, leaders and individuals alike walked a line between the progressive ideology of new opportunities for reshaping gender roles and the goal of restoring so-called normalcy with traditional (read: prewar) idealized notions of family life that included a male breadwinner and stay-at-home mother. This balancing act between a new gender order and an old-guard value system contributed at times to a public relations focus by political and business leaders on the separate and distinct nature of male and female economic contributions and roles in the postwar era. And in turn, by linking women's businesses partially to the home and to the economic transformations in home life posed by war, these leaders helped shape the categories women would pursue—most specifically marketing domestic skills—in ways that continue to define women's enterprises to the present day. Women who found themselves alone, did indeed turn to business as a way out of financial crisis. In 1959, Louise Williamson received an award from the U.S. Chamber of Commerce as one of the "Great Living Americans," honoring her for turning tragedy into triumph when in 1948 she found herself alone with no means of support. She opened a candy shop next to her home and eventually grew her Lou's Candy Kitchen in Edwards, Mississippi, to national acclaim. In the process, as *National Business Woman* magazine noted, "she set about in the good old American way to make a place for herself in this nation's business life."[40]

Such ventures in the 1940s had government backing at the federal and state levels. In a tacit nod to women interested in marketing homemade products, federal agencies such as the Commerce Department published pamphlets encouraging new ventures. Notable titles included *Establishing and Operating Your Own Business, Gift and Art Shop, Make It for Profit*, and *Salad Dressings, Mayonnaise and Related Products*—the latter referring to products that had been scarce during the war years.[41] While not specifically targeting women, many of these brochures nonetheless focused on products or services traditionally considered feminine and therefore likely to attract a female audience. Others offered guidance for traditionally female categories such as beauty salons, including a 135-page guide from the U.S. Department of Commerce entitled *Establishing and Operating a Beauty Shop*. Handbook chapters provided detailed instructions on everything from choosing location, financial needs, laws, taxes, advertising, personnel, and even civic obligations.[42] In her 1948 book *A Job for Every Woman*, author Louise Neuschutz not only encouraged women to act on their desire to start a home-based business but also provided a lengthy list of government booklets to help them do so.[43]

Saving America? Women and the Free Enterprise System

The emphasis on small business opportunities for women was also part of a broader political and economic conversation about the future of small business within the American economy. During the war years, the federal government effectively subsidized the formation of megacorporations by placing the bulk of its defense contracts in the hands of a relatively few large companies. The justification at the time was that these firms were better positioned than smaller manufacturers to fill the huge orders placed by the Department of Defense. While the formation of the Smaller War Plants Corporation in 1942—itself a precursor to the Small Business Administration that was established in 1953—was designed to allay fears about government interference in, and control over, private enterprise, it did little to shake these concerns.[44] Instead, business leaders and organizations took it as their personal mission to preserve the future of small business and the free enterprise system. Such concerns even found their way into the 1944 G.I. Bill of Rights, which included among its benefits for veterans loan guarantees for small business ventures.[45]

With an eye to stimulating and protecting small business, the U.S. Chamber of Commerce (COC) held a series of talks and produced literature from 1944 through the end of reconversion advocating the free enterprise system. "Economic freedom and political freedom are inseparable," noted one booklet, which further averred that the only safeguard to free enterprise would be the removal of government price controls and other regulations of business practices.[46] For the COC, the solution lay in the establishment of small business as the core of the U.S. economy.

Like the COC, the National Association of Manufacturers (NAM) expressed concern about the future of small business and developed economic education programs on the importance and centrality of small business to a free enterprise system. A big part of this effort included outreach to women via its "Home and Industry" series of lectures and symposiums conducted in conjunction with women's groups across the country from 1944 through 1949. "Women must know more about the economics of our country and of these economic interests which produce our food, our clothing, our shelter," noted a speaker at the Home and Industry "consultation between women leaders and business managers" in Pittsburgh in 1945.[47] Lecturers used the analogy of home management not only to educate women on the world of business but also to urge their support for political candidates and positions sympathetic to NAM's pro-business agenda.

In their literature and outreach efforts, NAM also appealed to women, albeit primarily white women, as capitalists—investors, workers, and mothers who would provide a legacy of opportunity to the next generation—and sought to enlighten women on the benefits of a profit system. The association likewise used white women as examples in educational materials, some of whom in fact did own independent ventures. In one case, NAM cited a woman who owned a baking business to demonstrate how profitability not only enabled her business to expand but also had economic benefits for the entire community.[48]

The U.S. COC and NAM, in their bid to preserve the free enterprise system, frequently articulated the potential of postwar consumer economy in their public appeals, including those made to women.[49] In essence, they saw women's role in consumption as crucial to facilitating ongoing economic growth generally as well as the well-being of local small businesses. Nonetheless, it was not a far leap for women to go from consumers of goods and services within their communities to producers of needed products and services themselves.

Championing Women in Business: The New York Model Goes National

New York State took what would become the most dramatic and transformative step in the history of women's small business ownership. In 1945, governor Thomas Dewey appointed Jane Todd as deputy commerce commissioner, the first woman in the state to hold the post, and launched the Woman's Council—an advisory board of thirty-two leading business and political women who could be called upon to provide advice or assistance. Todd almost immediately established the Woman's Program, a department-level initiative that was designed to assist both women—many of whom were being pushed from wartime jobs they wanted to keep—and the state's economy. Todd's staff made a serious study of women's needs and contributions. There were 5,382,267 U.S. families in 1940 where women provided the sole means of support, Todd and her team frequently averred in speeches and interviews. Moreover, women controlled 70 percent of the wealth and 65 percent of the savings accounts, and they owned 44 percent of public utilities and 40 percent of real estate—making them a powerful economic force that could be easily tapped in reconversion.[50]

Early on, Todd saw greater opportunities for women via business ownership than jobs. That worked just fine for policymakers such as Dewey, who regarded business ownership as a way of skirting the more complicated question of women's inclusion in the full-employment postwar economy. Consequently, while the Woman's Program had taken as its original mission the goal of helping women establish careers *and* small businesses, within a few short months of its inception, the program focused almost entirely on the latter.[51] The career portion was abandoned in favor of an emphasis on small business ownership, which served this middle category neatly and at the same time enabled leaders like Todd to promote a more progressive agenda.[52] New York's Woman's Program was the first of its kind nationally, though it would later inspire similar initiatives in other states.[53]

The centerpiece of Todd's program was training for would-be women business owners. Toward this end, the Woman's Program ran a series of small business clinics across the state throughout the latter 1940s and 1950s. Participants could bring proposals or product samples to be reviewed for marketability by business experts—many of whom themselves were female. Women, such as Elizabeth Arden or the Ogilvie sisters, who had launched what became large-scale companies in the era of the 1910s and 1920s New Woman, were active and visible counselors.[54] The typical women's business clinic combined the structure of a state fair with an educational seminar, thereby bridging the domestic and professional realms. There were tables with free books and brochures. Similarly, there was a farm component to the nature of these meetings, which in many ways, particularly in rural areas, built on the 4-H tradition of product demonstrations and prizes for the best farm or homemade items.[55]

The women's clinics covered a broad range of categories where women might have existing skills or resources, including roadside farmers' markets and canned produce for rural women and eclectic boutiques or typing services for more cosmopolitan types. They reached out across color lines and not only held clinics for Black women in Harlem but used these women to illustrate how clinic advisers could help a woman expand her business. In a 1948 radio promotion of an upcoming clinic, the New York Woman's Program told the story of Grace Bell, a Harlem housewife who turned her penchant for southern cooking into a thriving specialty business with the advice she received at a small business clinic. Equally important to Bell's story, however, was the fact that she returned to the Woman's Council for more advice when demand for her services soared.

The clinic highlights, for attendees and potential publicity, were the speeches and displays under the banner "Success Stories." During these sessions, women who succeeded in business beyond the home-based level would exhibit their wares, tell their stories, or meet with individual women. Strategically, these women served a public relations function for the New York Woman's Program, which not only kept hundreds of minibiographies of successful women on file but also used them to drum up media interest. Women such as the Mauger sisters, who sold gourmet fruitcakes, or Thelma Manter and Ann Wood with their odd-job service were frequently featured in national publications touting the small business clinics, including the *New York Times*, *Woman's Day*, and *Reader's Digest*. The Woman's Program frequently spotlighted Helen Morgan's prepared spaghetti sauce, Evelyn Costello's baby formula delivery service, Ellen Grey's Madison Avenue gourmet shop selling devilled crab, and of course, its lucrative favorite: Dorothy Chase's pickled herring. The Woman's Program even made a film about its efforts for national distribution in 1953.[56]

The Woman's Program also produced pamphlets on how to start a business, counseled women by phone or mail on finding suppliers or developing marketing strategies, and used the media to showcase women who achieved success as business owners with the help of the clinics.[57] Women were so eager for information on starting a money-making venture of any size that in 1948 the New York Woman's Program reported more than 750 requests per day from as far away as Alaska and Hawaii for its booklet "A Business of Her Own."[58] California alone sought nine hundred copies in 1949.[59] Women from around the country—and even, in some cases, Europe—also wrote to the council for advice on handling specific concerns, such as federal health regulations for making and storing cheese products, securing product labels, or researching demand for a party planning service. Mrs. Donald Ross came to the program from Brooklyn to ask whether her French salad dressing had market potential and how to go about selling it. Consultants not only suggested apothecary jars to "make a quite ordinary product appear out of the ordinary" but they also suggested suppliers for her ingredients, shipping containers, and a list of retailers who might be interested in the product. As a result, her business grew "well out of the pin money class"—the label given to either early stage, home-based ventures or those started simply for extra cash.[60] Such an important leap forward underscored not only the potential of small business but an understanding on the part of clinic organizers that women's businesses fit into a variety of categories—from the serious small business competitor to the hobbyist or part-time sideline venture that might last only as long as the founder's need and interest. The clinic programs sought the former, but since the goal or end of the enterprise was often unspoken, they equally served the latter as well.

The first and by far the most ambitious program, New York's small business clinics did not stand alone in linking reconversion, at least in part, to women's enterprises, however. From 1945 through the mid-1950s, the National Federation of Business and Professional Women's Clubs (BPW) spearheaded efforts to bring the clinic format to women in more than a dozen locations, relying on its own state chapters to sponsor clinics and urge government leaders to establish a women's division within their home states.[61] The BPW became one of the biggest boosters, not only of the various Women's Programs that would be launched across the country, but also of women's business ownership more generally. In its member magazine, *Independent Woman*, the organization gave Jane Todd a forum to advocate for business ownership for women. In at least two issues, Todd outlined step-by-step instructions for setting up a Woman's Program within other states.[62]

National publicity and demand from women led as many as twenty other states to adopt variations on the New York women's small business clinic model. In some states, such as Maine, California and Ohio, officials sought to replicate the entire program right down to establishing a women's division within the appropriate government agency.[63] Other states, such as Texas and Massachusetts, adopted only the clinic portion and relied on Todd and her staff to aid in facilitating and inaugurating their initial endeavors.[64] Todd was invited to consult with officials in both states on how to run such a program and attended at least their first clinic in each case.[65]

To further champion the opportunities of small business ownership for women, the BPW used its magazine throughout the 1940s and 1950s to regularly spotlight club members who had found success through independent enterprise. It also awarded citations to clubs that had either secured state government participation in these ventures or actively conducted clinics on their own. By 1951, BPW members in Ohio, Arizona, Oklahoma, Kentucky, South Dakota, and Minnesota had made inroads into establishing women's divisions within their state commerce departments to help women start small businesses or had secured government and university support for a series of clinics—which sometimes meant a more gender-neutral program. Some states didn't always know quite where to place these women's programs: In Kentucky, the commission was part of the State's Agricultural and Industrial Development Board, while in South Dakota a similar commission was located within the State

Natural Resources Commission.[66] That year, California governor Earl Warren approved the appointment of a Small Business Commission. The clinics also began to have a male following. BPW records point out "a letter from a small businessman's association in Omaha (Nebraska), telling us about how one man was helped so greatly at that business clinic of the women."[67] In fact, during the 1950s, state governments and universities across the country began adopting the women's small business clinic format to include men.

In its annual meetings and conventions, BPW officials not only noted the high demand for small business clinics but also advocated, "We must be prepared for carrying on small businesses, analyze the types and kinds of enterprises women get into, and give examples and demonstrations, and so forth—whether the business fits the community."[68] The BPW produced its own how-to brochures, notably *Bread and Butter Sidelines* and *A Plan of Operation for the Small Business Clinic*, and wrote articles advising women on what market research is and how to conduct it.[69] BPW member Julietta K. Arthur even wrote a book advising women on starting a business which was published in 1949, entitled *How to Make a Home Business Pay*. Arthur encouraged her readers to consider the skills they had to sell (from kitchen products to handcrafts and services), including a chapter on "Turning Home into a Factory."[70]

Whether promoted by the various women's programs or the BPW, success stories that demonstrated the vast sums of money to be made by women in home businesses no doubt fueled the overwhelming success of the small business clinics, as well as the growth in women's private enterprise overall. Women could aspire to follow in the footsteps of clinic legend and oft-cited success story Llewewlyn Jones of Gansevoort, New York, who turned her needlework hobby into a business selling lingerie cases to major department stores nationwide; "Mrs. Robert Dehlendorf" of Scarsdale, New York, who created a national brand, Market Basket Farm Mayonnaise, from a favorite family recipe; or Eleanor West, who developed a $50,000 annual business from home-baked breads made from soy products.[71]

Such successes, widely touted in local and national media—including *Life*, *Woman's Day*, and *Reader's Digest*—produced large crowds at small business clinics around the country. In New York, where the Woman's Program held as many as seven clinics per year, attendance at each averaged five to six hundred but ran as high as fifteen hundred to three thousand. Even in remote outposts such as Iowa farm country, as many as two hundred women would turn out at the clinics, some traveling great distances. Over six hundred women attended the clinic held in rural Bangor, Maine, while three thousand showed up in Fort Worth, Texas.[72] The small business clinics remained one of the most popular programs in New York State through the mid-1960s, and among BPW members until the late 1950s.

There was also a feminist component to efforts to promote women's business ownership. The title of New York's Women's Program brochure, "A Business of

FIG. 1.1 Jane Todd, New York State Deputy Commerce Commissioner, proudly showcasing her twentieth small business clinic for women. NYSPIX-Commerce; Jane Hedges Todd Papers, #2763. Division of Rare and Manuscript Collections, Cornell University Library.

FIG. 1.2 A view of the displays at one of the many small business clinics run by the Woman's Program in the New York State Commerce Department. NYSPIX-Commerce; Jane Hedges Todd Papers, #2763. Division of Rare and Manuscript Collections, Cornell University Library.

FIG. 1.3 Women flocked to the small business clinics; shown here, a packed auditorium of women listen to advice on how to start a business. NYSPIX-Commerce; Jane Hedges Todd Papers, #2763. Division of Rare and Manuscript Collections, Cornell University Library.

Her Own," was a deliberate reference to a quintessential feminist text, Virginia Wolfe's *A Room of One's Own*. Program leaders, at least initially, made that connection clear to audiences. In a speech at a women's leadership conference at Keuka College in Upstate New York, consultant Helen Thompson noted, "Many of you have read Virginia Wolfe's 'A Room of One's Own'—this is the first step in the emancipation of the female (on the records) sex. We have found, in laying small business plans before the women of New York an intense interest in 'a shop of one's own.'"[73] She went on to speak about the potential small business offered women in terms of vast financial, creative, and personal opportunities.

Promoters of women's business used statistics as a strategic tool for showing just what women could and did accomplish. Beginning in the late 1940s, government leaders, and especially Todd, frequently touted the exciting new data that the number of women business owners nationwide nearly doubled to one million, assisted in large part by these vocal and active public campaigns.[74] In truth, the actual figure is complicated. The data from Census sources included business owners with those who ran firms, though did not necessarily own them, under the heading "managers, owners and proprietors." Even so, given the long-established tendency for women to underrepresent their efforts as businesses, the figure may in fact be accurate. More important than the question of accuracy, however, is the utility of such figures for leaders such as Todd. The Census

Rewarding Loyalty: Feminism, Women's Business Ownership, and the Legacy of Suffrage

In some ways, Todd's ambitious efforts on behalf of women were due in part to women's newfound political clout. Political leaders were conscious of the debt many of them owed not only to women war workers but to the female voters and activists who helped get them elected. Just twenty years after the passage of women's suffrage, the 1940s marked the arrival of women on the political scene, and with so many men sent off to war, politicians came to rely on and build solid relationships with female voters. At the annual BPW conference in Washington, D.C., in 1948—amid a close election contest with New York's Governor Dewey—President Harry Truman took time out to give a speech lauding women's achievements during the war and urging them to aid in the fight against spiraling prices and recessionary trends. Via the Women's Bureau of the Department of Labor, the president said that "there should be monuments" to women for their social contributions to the nation. Labor secretary Lewis B. Schwellenbach further averred on Truman's behalf, "The solution to economic problems today, to a great degree, falls on women."[75]

For other leaders, the payback was more direct. Jane Todd, for example, used her considerable political influence with women to get Dewey elected governor in 1942. Todd, a well-known and highly regarded politician, had been an active suffragist as a young woman in the 1920s and successfully fought to allow women to serve on juries in the 1930s.[76] Todd was the first woman elected to the state legislature from Westchester County, where she secured passage of the state's Equal Pay Law. She also helped organize both the Negro Republican Women's Club and the Republican Business and Professional Women's Club. In 1937, when she first met Dewey, she was vice chairman of the Republican State Committee, and her leadership in garnering women's votes for the would-be governor was well-documented. An article in the widely read *Look* noted, "As district attorney, he talked with her about contacting women who could help him win the governorship. Jane Todd has been one of his best salesmen ever since."[77]

The *Look* article not only demonstrated Dewey's awareness of the importance of women voters; it also noted the way he continued to position himself as "the woman's candidate" during his 1948 presidential bid. The subhead to the article pointed out, "The Republican candidate (Dewey) has counted on women to fill key administrative jobs in New York. Their common quality: loyalty to Dewey. As friends and advisers, some will work for him in Washington."[78]

The article went on to profile all "Dewey's Women," beginning with his mother and moving through his wife and female staff members.

No doubt, Dewey implemented the Woman's Program in New York in 1945 as much to include women in the state's economic recovery as he did to create a political position for Todd and maintain his relationship with female voters. During Dewey's presidential bid, Todd told the press, "A great many of them (women) told me they had been following the record of Mr. Dewey as Governor since he was elected to that office in 1942. They like especially his recognition of women."[79]

Dewey was not the only political leader to recognize an obligation to women. No doubt Marion Martin, who was appointed Maine's first woman Commissioner of Labor in 1947, earned her position because of longtime service to the Republican Party and the state's leadership. Like Todd, Martin was a former state representative, elected in 1931 as the youngest woman ever to serve in the legislature. In 1937, she was appointed director of the Women's Division of the Republican party and, as one article pointed out, spent the next several years traveling from state to state "organizing clubs and exhorting the women of the nation to spend five minutes a day studying political issues." Also, like Todd, Martin understood her role not only as an advocate for women but also as proof that women *belonged* in public life: "In accepting this post, I realize that I am assuming a responsibility to the women of the whole country as well as to the women of Maine. If I make good, people will be more inclined to look with favor on the appointment of women to public office."[80] Perhaps it is little coincidence, then, that under Martin's direction, Maine became the second state to implement a Woman's Program designed to encourage and aid women in forming small businesses.

For these women, there may well have been a connection between coming of age in the era of women's suffrage and the economic programs they developed once in office. Historians have written extensively about the high hopes for equality many suffragists placed on the vote only to be disappointed later when the vote itself did little to change women's social status.[81] By the 1940s, many suffrage activists had either abandoned politics or transformed their agendas, but in either case, they were the generation coming to power in the war years. Where Todd was a suffragist, Martin was in her teen years as women gained the vote in 1920. Women like Todd and Martin who knew that the vote alone was not enough began to see in the economy the real potential for equality. In speech after speech, Todd linked the celebration of women's power through the vote with the opportunities for achievement in business and industry.[82]

Personal experience had some influence on the public speeches by female leaders urging women to consider small business. Todd herself had owned a kitchen business in her late teens and early twenties after her mother had died and she was left to help raise her siblings. She learned to cook just as World War I broke out, opening a canteen to supply a local hospital with cakes and pies for patients and staff.[83] This personal experience as well as the need to package herself as a "true, feminine woman" to succeed in politics undoubtedly inspired her tenure as Woman's Program director. In article after article, Todd carefully noted her cooking skills and the importance of homemaking aptitude for every woman, and she even let photographers photograph her "stirring up something" in the kitchen.[84] As one writer so aptly pointed out, "Laws and lamb chops, constitutions and cakes are irretrievably bound together in the life of a woman politico."[85] Martin too knew how to play the game as a woman in politics; her public persona balanced her cooking skills and femininity with her no-nonsense approach to solving the state's labor problems. She worked in the state legislature to improve Maine's labor laws while simultaneously promoting business ownership as a way out of economic problems for women.[86] BPW leaders who likewise brought these programs to women in Iowa in 1946 and Texas in 1948 similarly stressed that financial independence, however slight or grand that income may be, would lead to broader political equality for women.[87] Consequently, in addition to small business programs, the BPW held workshops on money management and investing.[88]

The Media Weighs In

Acceptance of women as business owners was becoming so popular at war's end that in 1945 when *Reader's Digest* held a contest offering $25,000 in prizes for the best new business ideas, women were visibly and unquestioningly present. Female entrants garnered more than 22 percent of the $250 first prizes and 28 percent of the $100 second prizes. In a book published a year later about the contest, these women were celebrated for their ingenuity in turning family recipes or handicraft skills into money-making businesses. The book also revisited Depression-era female business owners, retelling their stories not as tales of exigency or short-term ventures, as it would have a decade earlier, but rather to inspire a new generation of women to see the promise of independent enterprise. Women such as Lane Bryant Malsin, whose thirty-nine-year-old women's apparel and mail-order business had sales of $49 million in 1950, were perennial favorites of women's groups, books, and the popular press. Malsin's story made great copy: in 1900, a year after her son was born, Malsin's husband died leaving nothing but a pair of diamond earrings to his widow. Malsin pawned the earrings and bought a sewing machine in an effort to combine full-time motherhood with a paid income. From her home, she sewed nightgowns for garment manufacturers and private customers, eventually moving into her own business of stylish clothes for pregnant women that ultimately launched her empire.[89]

Similarly, the *Reader's Digest* book included a chapter devoted entirely to women's businesses, many of them started on as little as five dollars—an issue that was a constant subtext of women's ventures in an era when they had almost no access to traditional sources of start-up capital. Women were often told that they could start a business with just a few dollars as a way of reinforcing the home's centrality as a site of their ventures and a means to leave unaddressed biases in lending practices. But start-up funds aside, what mattered most, according to *Reader's Digest*, was having a good idea and the determination to make a go of it. One notable example is Ann Honeycutt, who was likely a pioneer in prepared takeout meals. The genesis for Honeycutt's business was an acute awareness in 1944 of a shortage in domestic help. She rented a storefront for her Casserole Kitchen in New York City, where she prepared a daily menu of meals priced from $1.10 to $1.65 to be delivered by boys on bicycles between 5:30 and 8:00 p.m. The final section included a list of books and pamphlets offering advice to the would-be business owner.[90] Other books published prior to the end of the war and in the years that followed similarly encouraged women to consider small business ownership as a valid and rewarding endeavor.[91]

Barely a month after V-J Day, the film *Mildred Pierce* further underscored the nation's growing acceptance of business as a legitimate means of women's self-support. Debuting in October 1945 to rave reviews, this murder mystery starred Joan Crawford in the title role as an enterprising California housewife with a knack for turning her cooking skills into cash. The film chronicled Pierce's rise from a suburbanite who extended the family budget by selling cakes and pies from her kitchen to her success as an independent female restaurateur. Faced with the end of her marriage—amid insinuations that her professionally unsuccessful husband was having an affair—Pierce set out to prove that she could not only make it on her own but also support her two children in high style. After a brief stint as a waitress, Pierce combined what she learned from the job with her intuitive business acumen and culinary flair to build a chain of lavish supper clubs bearing her name. Although the film was highly critical of her indulgent child-rearing and of the materialistic excesses of suburbia, it took for granted the acceptability of her venture or its success. The *New York Times* review was typical, hailing Pierce for building "a fabulously successful chain of restaurants on practically nothing" while also lambasting her for being "dominated by a selfish" daughter.[92]

That Pierce's story of business success could both serve as backdrop for a popular mainstream film and go virtually unchallenged by critics says much about gender roles, especially women's relationship to business enterprise, in the immediate postwar era.[93] In many ways, Pierce represented what women had proven during the war; that in times of crisis they could shoulder the economic burdens of their families and the nation.[94] Certainly, the image of women filling in as providers due to financial hardship or the absence of a man was familiar to Americans in the context of the Depression and war years.[95] But when she launched her own business, she did so by commercializing her homemaking skills, thereby challenging and also not challenging notions of women's proper roles. As such, Pierce foreshadowed the ways in which small business ownership would prove an increasingly viable and socially acceptable option for women seeking a place in the postwar economy.

Similarly, a spate of business books from 1945 into the early 1950s reconceptualized women's ventures in the 1920s and 1930s as serious commercial activities—rather than desperate measures to help families survive the crisis—and held them as role models for women starting a business in the postwar era.[96] Many of them recounted the story of Margaret Rudkin, the wife of a Connecticut businessman, who in 1937 used her bread recipe to establish Pepperidge Farm Bread, a company that by the early 1940s had forty-five employees and an annual payroll topping $50,000. The company in fact was built from necessity: Rudkin developed her famous whole wheat bread initially as part of a nutritional diet for one of her three sons who suffered a serious case of asthma and allergies. As the child's condition improved, his doctor asked Rudkin to supply the bread to other patients. Within six months of starting her business, she was baking one thousand loaves a week; by 1939, production hit thirty thousand loaves, and two years after World War II ended, she bought her first modern factory, supplying five hundred thousand accounts by the end of the 1940s. At her death in 1967, her company generated $50 million in sales, producing seventy million loaves of bread each year.[97]

These articles, books, and other materials about women and small business buttressed the efforts of the women's clinics and validated individual women who may have had doubts about the legitimacy or potential success of a business idea. In the postwar era, *Boston Globe* writer Polly Webster renamed her column "Careers at Home" and published two books for women considering a business start-up—*How to Make Money at Home* (1949) and *Start Your Own Business on Less Than $1000* (1950).[98] The popularity of these books and columns likely points to the advice and inspiration they offered readers about women finding fulfillment and making money as independent business owners. Louise Neuschutz's book also included a list of autobiographies and how-to books by successful women business owners from the mid-1930s to the late 1940s such as Alice Bradley's *Cooking for Profit* (which had three editions by 1936) and Madeline Gray and Vass De Lo Padua's *How to Cook for Profit* (1947).[99] The growing number of books and articles kept the idea of business ownership for women in public view as policymakers, the media, and families across the country wondered about economic prosperity and the changing social landscape.

Commercializing the Feminine: Home/Business

The Woman's Program exemplified prevailing ambiguity about the nation's future as well as women's place in the postwar economic order. On the one hand, leaders like Governor Dewey, Todd, Maverick, and Martin expected women to create legitimate, competitive small businesses that would rebuild the postwar economy. At the same time, however, women were enticed to commercialize domestic skills as their entrée to private enterprise. In fact, Governor Dewey and his staff frequently urged women to see the home as an untapped reservoir of potential business ideas.[100] Decorating services, catering, apparel manufacturing, and other functions women normally provided to their families free of charge were suggested at war's end as products or services others would be willing to buy. There was also a recognition of pent-up demand during the war years for even the most basic products, such as mayonnaise, which had been in scarce supply, and which women could manufacture for a profit in the postwar economy.[101]

In either case, homemaking abilities did indeed have increasing commercial potential. Within this argument, there was a tacit recognition of the emerging category of working mothers, who would now purchase products or services such as homemade sauces or desserts that they would be too time-pressed to prepare themselves. "The laundering of clothes and the cleaning of houses and apartments could be done much more quickly and efficiently by trained experts with proper equipment," noted one article. "The gradual transfer of domestic labor from the home to the world of business enterprise will cause more and more women to seek remunerative employment outside the home, if, for no other reason than to earn the money to pay for the new and attractive services available to them."[102] Todd pointed out in 1950, "The sandwich and the take-home dinner are here to stay, in peace or war."[103]

For women with children, small business ownership could enable them to combine familial and breadwinner roles in ways labor force participation never could. This proved a universal truth across ethnic backgrounds. Women with young children saw in small business a way to earn a living and raise their children at the same time. This was especially true when the business was located in the home, as in the case of Mrs. Sidney Phelps, who opened a Christmas shop in her home. To leave plenty of time for her family, Phelps only received customers from 1:00 to 5:00 p.m. each day.[104] Asian American women in a study of Hawaii's women entrepreneurs also noted that business ownership let them earn money to provide a better life and education for their children in the future while enabling them to be good mothers in the present. One woman, who could barely read or write herself, described long days running her restaurant business with her children playing at her feet.[105]

By linking women's business enterprises to their domestic skills, the Woman's Program could keep women both in the economy and in the home at the same time. As a study by the New York Woman's Program would point out in 1946, not only were women's businesses traditionally concentrated in beauty shops, small retail, and food production, but future female business owners indicated a strong interest in these and other feminine categories, including restaurants, laundries, and gift shops.[106] In essence, then, women's businesses became part of the broader economy by virtue of their ability to generate an income, employ workers, and fill a market niche—all vital components of any successful and legitimate commercial venture—even while they remained within a separate and feminized realm.

The other advantage was this: commercializing domestic talents was, frankly, cheap and required little of the kinds of start-up capital that traditional (i.e., white male) ventures required and could get but women typically had no access to. Woman's Program efforts to channel women into small businesses based on homemaking skills at least in part seemed to be influenced by concerns about start-up capital. Embedded in the New York State Woman's Program literature was a tacit understanding that gender bias would continue to make credit and other institutional sources of financing unavailable to women. Consequently, women would need to consider ventures that could be started on a shoestring or with family money. Home-based business, of course, was ideally suited to such undercapitalized ventures, since so much could be accomplished without additional rent, utilities, or other overhead costs.

Even the government programs designed to spur women's business ownership were funded on shoestring budgets. The Woman's Program and its counterparts elsewhere were often praised for how little they cost the state governments—the average small business clinic could be held for under $100, and New York's entire program, including salaries, had an annual budget of just $75,000.[107] There was virtually no discussion of bank loans or external sources of seed money at the women's clinics, and only rarely did the Woman's Council note assisting someone with financing questions.[108] Instead, clinic advisers around the country often pointed out the advantages of commercializing domestic skills because of the minimal costs involved.

The proliferation of business books for women in the late 1940s and early 1950s likewise focused heavily on domestic skills, again emphasizing their low initial costs, and steered away from discussions of start-up capital or financing expansions that were typical of advice manuals for a male audience. *Reader's Digest's* 1946 guidebook for men and women praised women's ventures for how little they cost to launch—in one case, just five dollars. Some women's books even built the money problem into the title, such as *Start Your Own Business on Less Than $1000* or *Making Money in Your Kitchen: Over 1600 Products Women Can Make*. These books finessed the topic of money, suggesting women rely on friends or husbands well-versed in accounting to keep their books or hire an accountant as the business grew.

In this way too, women moved into small business without upsetting the status quo of the financial services segment of the business world, still largely a male bastion, and they made no challenges to discrimination in lending. Banks were resistant to give money to women, despite the occasional article or study noting that women owned the titles to 74 percent of the nation's homes and controlled more than 65 percent of savings accounts. Research by the Federal Reserve Board that noted women were better credit risks than men received scant mention in a single paragraph buried at the bottom of a page in the *New York Times* in 1948. The study pointed out, "Men's clothing stores wrote off as a 'bad debt' 56 cents out of each $100 worth of sales last year. . . . But women's apparel stores showed only a 34-cent loss."[109] Legally, there was no prohibition on gender discrimination in lending until 1974; before that, married women seeking credit required a husband to cosign, and single women were often asked for a father or brother's signature. Whatever success women achieved as business owners was typically built on ingenuity rather than access to capital. This lack of financial resources, in part at least, may explain why women's businesses often remained small in size, since they would have to use their own profits or personal income if they wanted to open additional locations, add new products, or otherwise expand.

The Case for Small Business Ownership: Sidestepping Bias

For women of all racial and class backgrounds, small business was a way to sidestep discrimination and increasingly limited wartime and postwar workplace opportunities. Black women, shut out from not only war production jobs but also the clerical positions open to their white counterparts, often saw in small business ownership a way to avoid being channeled almost exclusively into domestic service. In 1945, Rose Morgan, for example, partnered with her friend Olivia Clarke to open the Rose Meta House of Beauty in Harlem, New York, which *Ebony* magazine hailed a year later as "the biggest Negro beauty parlor in the world." Morgan had come a long way in the seven years since she moved to New York from Chicago, initially renting a chair for ten dollars a week in other salons—a fairly common practice—and gradually building an increasingly prestigious clientele, including famed blues singer Ethel Waters. In early 1945, Morgan bought an abandoned house and spent three months converting it into her beauty emporium. Clarke, who had degrees in biology from both Virginia State College and New York University, was a skin care expert, and with their combined talents, the salon served as a site of pampering for women of color, with three floors of treatments and thirty employees providing facials, massage, manicures and pedicures, and of course, hair care. Morgan and Clarke each had their own separate apartments on upper floors. Congressman Rev. Adam Clayton Powell Jr. cut the ribbon for the salon's grand opening.[110]

Morgan's business grew rapidly, earning $3 million in its first few years and establishing Morgan as an icon of the potential of women's business ownership for women of color, increasingly hailed in the Black press for her role in advancing the race. Morgan too, increasingly understood her business's significance for both herself and other Black women beauticians and prospective business owners. In 1947, she was the only Black woman invited to serve on the newly established New York State Minimum Wage Board for the beauty service industry, an appointment she accepted as an opportunity to ensure Black beauticians' viewpoints were represented.[111] Morgan would own several businesses in the years ahead, including an even larger beauty business a decade later. With them all, her consciousness continually grew about the ability of business ownership to provide opportunities for women of color that the job market—which typically relegated them to work as maids and domestics—did not. Morgan saw her

FIG. 1.4 Advertisement for the grand opening of Rose Morgan's beauty emporium that ran in the Black press nationwide. This ad was featured in the *Detroit Tribune* in May 1948. *Credit: The Detroit Tribune* (Detroit, Mich.), May 29, 1948. *Chronicling America: Historic American Newspapers*. Library of Congress. Image provided by Central Michigan University, Clarke Historical Library.

FIG. 1.5 Salon owner Rose Morgan styling the hair of renowned soprano Margaret Tynes (1960). *Credit:* George Morris. Photographs and Prints Division, Schomburg Center for Research in Black Culture, New York Public Library.

role as not only providing jobs for other women of color (up to eighty women as her salon grew) but also validating Black women's beauty—especially their hair. An *Ebony* article quoted her as saying that notions of Black women's hair as inferior were "a reflection of the extent to which white America [had] warped the values of certain Negroes who [felt] that the more Negroid a Negro the less attractive."[112] She also expanded into her own cosmetics line, which the *Pittsburgh Courier* considered as "a potential threat to Elizabeth Arden, Dorothy Gray, and Helena Rubenstein."[113]

Similarly, women who had experienced independence through military service in the Women's Army Corps (WAC) and Women Accepted for Volunteer Emergency Service (WAVES) looked to replicate those experiences in the postwar world through business ownership. Margaret Mischke, a twenty-nine-year-old ex-WAC, joined forces with a friend in 1946 to establish their own beauty parlor in Meriden, Connecticut, called "Marg-Ru." Mischke's military service led her to the strong belief that "things were going to be different when she returned to civilian life." Pooling their savings and each borrowing $625 from relatives, these women invested $2,368 to start their beauty shop.[114] Whatever the venture, business ownership afforded a wider range of options to women than employment.

Wartime and postwar anti-Asian bias would have a profound impact on Japanese American women. Aside from a long tradition of family businesses, Japanese American women felt an urgent need to help reestablish the income and property taken from their families during wartime internment. Roughly one hundred thousand Japanese Americans fell victim to racism after the attack on Pearl Harbor and were rounded up and detained in camps throughout the west. Some, like one Japanese American widow who lived with her family in rooms behind their California dry-cleaning business, had time to sell homes and property before being carted off by U.S. military officials. Even then, however, their desperate bid to sell undermined any attempt at receiving full market value for their belongings.[115] In total, Japanese families had income and property losses estimated at $350 million, including business and farm ventures.[116] By 1947, only a fraction of the evacuated businesses had been reestablished: for example, in Los Angeles, prior to internment, there were roughly 240 Japanese-owned restaurants; in 1947, about forty restaurants were reestablished.[117] Women recognized within and after internment that they would have to take on greater economic roles to rebuild family finances, including starting businesses, as Precious Vida Yamaguchi has noted in her ethnographic study of women postinternment.[118] After internment, many women initially had few job options, mostly in domestic service and some factory jobs. Others transformed the enterprises they started in the internment camps into postwar ventures. One pregnant mother who gave birth to her second child in the camps, for example, did hairdressing while interned; afterward, she ran her own salon in Cleveland, Ohio. Another woman opened a sewing school and a hotel; yet another launched what would become a popular nightclub and restaurant in Los Angeles.[119] With pressure to prove themselves "worthy Americans" in the postwar era, many Japanese American women sought to provide educations for themselves and especially their children; business ownership made that possible.[120] One woman who owned apartments and a tavern in Hawaii noted that she started the business in the postwar years out of "necessity . . . to make added salary." She continued, "I had seven children. Everyone wanted to go college (and that) took a lot of money."[121]

Other forces such as age discrimination, prevalent in the 1940s and 1950s, proved a powerful draw for both women and those who promoted the potential of small business. Employers were not only reluctant to hire women over age thirty but also within their rights to bar such women from applying for job openings in their advertising. Nonetheless, statistically speaking, women between the ages of thirty-five and fifty-four accounted for nearly two-thirds of the labor force as a result of World War II.[122] When age discrimination led the corporate world to shun them, women who wanted or needed to work simply turned to independent enterprise. In 1948, Ann Taylor—a gray-haired, Washington, D.C., economist—expressed frustration with the limited opportunities available to her in the job market, especially the increasing number of service sector, "pink collar ghetto" jobs that were designated for women. As a result, she abandoned a ten-year career to set up a catering business called Ann's Kitchen, she said, because "she valued independence over a guaranteed salary."[123] Upon reaching "retirement age," Kate O'Neill and Beulah Hall, for example, weren't ready to stop working, and they instead decided to open a laundering service for delicate fabrics in Washington, D.C.[124]

Moving beyond the Home: The Potential of Women's Businesses

Although the initial emphasis may have been on the home, the Woman's Program, the BPW, and the women business owners themselves often did not expect women's businesses to stay within the home for very long. In the pamphlet "A Business of Her Own" and its follow-up, "102 Ideas for a Business of Her Own," the New York Woman's Program advised women on how to conduct business in a professional manner that would make their ventures competitive in the broader capitalist marketplace. As Jane Todd told Texas women at their small business clinic in 1948, "Even if she starts on a shoestring, as many women do, the woman in business today must have a professional stance."[125] The pamphlets stressed the importance of product quality and appearance as well as the need to do initial research before starting up. Similarly, the pamphlets developed by the BPW for national distribution at clinics, such as "Bread and Butter Sidelines," saw the home as having untapped commercial value in the wider economy. Across America, clinic leaders, like those in Iowa, stressed that no idea was too small to become the cornerstone of a large company.[126]

More important, the New York Woman's Program and its counterparts in other states made a clear distinction at the clinics between two classes of business ownership: the "pin money" class, which referred to either women at the starting stage or those who merely sought an additional source of part-time income, and the "professional" class, which described women whose businesses advanced beyond the home. While the clinic organizers saw it as their mission to counsel women in both categories of business ventures, their literature and speeches placed an emphasis on the ability of any idea to secure a lasting place within a given market or business category.

As such, clinic advisers not only evaluated whether there was a long-term need for a product or service a woman might seek to establish, but they would also counsel her on how to proceed regarding expansion. Dorothy Orefice had already rented a plant, installed machinery, and hired women to produce her French designed baby shoes when she approached the Woman's Program for assistance. Woman's Program case files stated, "Her problem was simple: How shall I sell?" According to its own notes, the program's consultant "discussed Mrs. Orefice's marketing problems, suggested buyers, and proper approach to them, told her how to go about advertising, and laid out a preliminary publicity campaign." The result was that "in six short months, (she) was selling in 24 states and had made plans to export to Japan." By 1950, her Glamourette baby shoe factory produced four hundred pairs per day, and they were sold in the ever-popular Sears-Roebuck catalog.[127]

For the women's clinic organizers, it was less important—in fact, it was virtually irrelevant—whether a business idea originated from homemaking skills. What mattered instead was its commercial potential, its professional quality, and the ability of the woman herself to produce the product to meet demand. While most women's businesses in the late 1940s remained in traditionally feminized professions, some women moved beyond the beauty parlors and catering concerns to open air cargo delivery services, filling stations, construction companies, and stock brokerages.[128]

"The Feminine Difference"

What ultimately made women's businesses consistent with popular ideology was that these enterprises and their owners were content to exist in a separate feminine economy. This was due, in part, to the fact that women in the 1940s saw no incompatibility between feminine difference and equality in the political, economic, and social realms. Where 1970s feminists stressed the ways in which they were equal to men, women in the postwar society embraced those qualities and attributes that set them apart from men. Women understood their contributions to the war effort as having been different but no less vital—they maintained the home front that the men would come back to, while the men fought the war. Definitions of equality, then, were intertwined with prevailing notions of femininity. At war's end, women participated in government policy and planning, sought postwar leadership roles and representation in federal agencies and committees, and urged that goals of full employment include jobs for women—all because they believed feminine integrity and nurturance could have public benefits.

Femininity had an equally important function in rebuilding local communities and the national economy, the argument went. Jane Todd, for example, noted on several occasions that women had "particular aptitudes" that would prove valuable to overall economic growth. In a commercialized version of turn-of-the-century public housekeeping, she pointed specifically to women's affinity for service jobs and enterprises that "make everyday living attractive and comfortable for all of us."[129] She added, "Women in business had an unusual opportunity for lifting the face of Main Street and making the community a better place to live."[130] Women in traditionally unfeminine businesses such as construction nonetheless relied on definitions of femininity to sell their wares. Tulsa resident Mrs. R. B. Butler, one of the few women builders in the U.S. in 1951, said being a woman gave her an advantage over her male competitors: "As a homemaker as well as a builder of homes, she believes she knows what women want, and she puts those wants into every house she builds," noted an article in *Independent Woman*. To further lure female customers, Butler called her company and the residences she built "Personality Homes."[131]

In countless cases, women on planning committees insisted that what made women suitable for leadership or employment were those very qualities that made them different from men. BPW member Kathryn Brummond argued in 1946, "In numbers alone, woman is superior to man. In union, she can change her world. She must first develop a clear understanding of her importance, her sanctity as the mother of the race, [and as such] she deserves a special reward."[132] Eleanor Roosevelt noted, "Women can help make a lasting peace [because] women will try to find ways to cooperate where men will think only of dominating."[133] This notion of equal citizenship through different attributes and contributions was also present in the ways the small business clinic programs positioned themselves to both women and the public at large.

Consequently, women could understand their ventures as both feminized and separate yet equal in professionalism and status within the economy. The Academie Moderne, a women's finishing school established in Boston in 1941, relied heavily on the feminine difference to build a booming business throughout the war years and well beyond the 1960s. Its stated mission was "to develop and dramatize feminine charm to the point where it brings the greatest possible returns, both financial and social."[134] In effect, this charm school merged feminine grace with professional achievement, deeming the two the apex of female potential.

Women's ability to merge social expectations with their personal needs and goals would prove useful to women seeking to open businesses in the 1950s heyday of domestic ideology. When the end of the Korean War in 1953 lessened fears that another World War was imminent and eliminated the urgency associated with keeping women economically viable in preparation, few state governments were as eager to implement or support programs encouraging women's business ownership as they had been in the 1940s. Those interested abandoned notions of women as economic citizens through business ownership and looked exclusively at business ownership as facilitating women's consumer roles.

42 • She's the Boss

Nonetheless, under the leadership of the BPW, Jane Todd, and the states with programs already established, small business clinics remained popular until the end of the 1950s. But as Americans became increasingly comfortable with their new positions as world leaders and with the stability of their economy, a debate over women's proper place in the socioeconomic realm emerged in full force. Tinged with the specter of communism and Cold War rhetoric, these debates did not dampen women's interest in economic enterprises. Rather, women would once again find a new way to position their independent ventures within their personal lives and in keeping with the prevailing social ideology about gender roles.

2

Motherhood and
Its Discontents

1950s Domesticity,
the Cold War, and Women's
Business Ownership

Lillian Hochberg had only one thing on her mind in 1951 when she placed the ad that would spark her mail-order business: supplementing her husband's income. Four months pregnant, she worried about the kind of life the pair would be able to provide for their first child. During the two years of their marriage, the couple had been getting by on Sam Hochberg's seventy-five-dollar weekly salary at his parents' haberdashery combined with Lillian's part-time income from odd jobs such as selling pots and pans by phone or dresses at the Lerner Shops.[1] She joked about the crooked ceiling in her Mount Vernon, New York, apartment and didn't give more than a passing thought to what their financial future might hold. But her impending motherhood forged a new economic reality that her newlywed status had not. Sure, she knew her husband would make a good father, but as a provider, she had her doubts. "I noticed, for instance, that he would go off every afternoon to play tennis, leaving his mother to watch the store," she would recall years later in her 1996 memoir. "To me, such behavior was inconceivable."[2]

If her child were to have the upper-middle-class life, complete with piano lessons and other luxuries Lillian Hochberg herself had known as a child—first in Leipzig, Germany, and later in New York—the twenty-two-year-old would have to make up for the ambition her husband lacked.[3] "We did not, in my evaluation, have enough to live on, to have an apartment, have a child, have a car," she noted.[4] Day after day, she sat at her yellow Formica kitchen table, struggling to find a way to combine being a good mother with making a living: "Hovering in the background was always the accepted idea that a working wife was an embarrassing commentary on her husband's earning power," she recalled in her autobiography. "Even so, I could read the numbers. It was a dilemma: I had to earn money, but I couldn't leave the house."[5]

In time, Hochberg devised a compromise: work from home, using her sales skills to begin a small mail-order enterprise. Such ventures were a burgeoning part of the postwar consumer economy, and business leaders had begun to highlight the growth potential of the direct mail industry. With $2,000 of wedding gift money, Hochberg placed an ad in *Seventeen* and other women's magazines for monogrammed handbags and belts—to be made at her father's leather factory—selling for $2.95 and $1.95, respectively, under the trade name Lillian Vernon.[6] She would ship them from her kitchen. What she expected was a few, small orders and a profit of no more than $1,000—just enough for the little extras she sought to provide; what she got was over $16,000 in orders in the first few weeks and $32,000 by the end of 1951.[7] In the years that followed, she would seek out other products that appealed to America's growing appetite for consumer goods, building what would become a mail-order empire with sales of $41,000 in 1954, $195,000 in 1956, $6 million at the time of her divorce in 1968, and $238 million at its peak in 1999.[8] In 2003, Hochberg, who was in her late seventies, sold the business for $60.5 million and remained on staff as "honorary chairwoman" for another three years.[9]

Around the same time and across the river in Newark, New Jersey, Rosemarie Simmons turned her dining room into a handbag shop. Married with a six-year-old daughter, Simmons saw the business as a way to supplement her husband's income, already stretched thin by his need to send money home to his mother.[10] Rose Totino made a similar decision a year before Hochberg, using her mother's pizza recipe to augment the family income by opening the pizza parlor in her hometown of Minneapolis, Minnesota, that would spawn a frozen foods empire (Totino's Pizza) by the 1970s.[11] In 1951, Norma Purvance joined the ranks of home-bound business women when this military wife launched her cake delivery service for students at Colorado A&M University. With her husband attending school full-time, Purvance knew that the couple and their children could not get by on his GI salary. Facing this economic challenge, she turned her "hobby" into an income-generating venture with a 50 percent return.[12] And Joyce Chen, a Chinese immigrant in Cambridge, Massachusetts, began her takeout Chinese food business in the mid-1950s as a way to earn money while raising her children, who as toddlers, sat by her feet as she worked. In the decades that followed, her business would become a major restaurant, prepared foods, and kitchenware company and land its founder her own television cooking show.

What united these women and thousands like them throughout the 1950s was a shared understanding of their roles as mothers, consumers, and providers of increased purchasing power for the family in the midst of a postwar consumer products explosion and growing Cold War. In fact, the decade stands as a vital moment in the history of twentieth-century women's business enterprise, one in which the changing socioeconomic landscape redefined the nature and context of women's ventures for decades to come. The brief window of progress via 1940s postwar policy supports for women's businesses faded in the 1950s. Gone were the early postwar days, when women's enterprises were seen as helping to rebuild the nation's economy and reestablish small business as its base. Political leaders such as New York's governor Thomas Dewey were no longer talking about women's economic roles as having "an increasingly important place in the whole economic structure."[13]

Instead, as the 1950s progressed, what emerged were multiple Americas when it came to women's business ownership. The dominant discourse, driven as much by white heterosexual gender norms as by Cold War anxieties, celebrated motherhood as women's primary (and oftentimes exclusive) gender role. The image most typically promoted by leaders and mainstream media was of white, suburban, stay-at-home motherhood with a breadwinning father. Certainly, not all women could afford to or wanted to acquiesce to these norms, though the message was powerful and linked closely to notions of containing communism through both free enterprise and women's containment in the home.[14]

Even as the language of women's economic citizenship through business enterprise waned after the 1940s, the need for additional income nonetheless increased in the face of new pressures on the household budget. Postwar reconversion and rising economic stability produced a vast assortment of new consumer goods. Many were beyond the purchasing power of GIs attending college or organization men joining the corporate ranks, as Hochberg experienced. Statistically too, from war's end well into the decade that followed, women—particularly married women—noted that they *wanted* to continue working.[15] Throughout the 1950s, the number of women in the workforce topped nineteen million—half of them married. As more women joined their ranks, public pressure intensified to discourage this rapidly growing trend. Instead of retreating into their household duties, women increasingly turned to business ownership, often configuring their ventures so that they reconciled with prevailing notions about gender roles—and they did so at a time when the very nature and meaning of small business in America was itself in flux. For many married women who started businesses, motherhood became the rationale for launching ventures of their own, much as Hochberg did when she started what would quickly become a mail-order empire. This could also have been a deliberate marketing strategy: company origin stories that downplayed women's ambitions and depicted their successes as accidental

46 • She's the Boss

might be more appealing to the gender expectations of a potentially conservative customer base.

But there was another America for women on the margins—people of color, immigrants, and lesbians—who faced legal and systemic discrimination against their right to earn or even exist. While small business became a means of economic freedom and sometimes survival for all women, for those on the margins it was much more—certainly a way to earn a living but also a tool to build community and possibly expand outreach for emerging social movements. In Los Angeles, Doña Natalia Barraza opened the Nayarit in 1951 with a mission to serve Mexican food and create community for the growing number of Mexican Americans there.[16] Black women understood their ventures as a form of racial pride and uplift, especially as the civil rights movement became increasingly and visibly activist in the middle and later parts of the decade. Even those women who did not participate in the movement nonetheless served as a model of what business ownership offered that the job market—with limited, low-paid, and often predominantly domestic work—did not. Similarly, lesbians in McCarthyist, anticommunist Cold War America were fired from jobs, expelled from the military, arrested, harassed, and even blacklisted from future employment. For some, business ownership provided a means of economic survival. At the same time, while Cold War anxieties may have prescribed containing women in their homes, the era also provided a rationale for small business ownership by promoting free enterprise as a way to defeat communism. Business organizations such as the U.S. Chamber of Commerce promoted a notion of patriotism for women that was fused to the ideal of free enterprise and women's roles as consumers in an age of postwar prosperity and mass consumption.

Together, these socioeconomic forces would ally with public gender norms about women's household roles to create a tacit rationale for private enterprise for women, particularly married women with children. That was true for women of color and immigrant women as well, who likewise felt the public pressure of the motherhood ideal, sometimes in combination with cultural or ethnic prescriptions for women. Ultimately, not only would these trends fuse women's household roles with their ability to generate an independent income, but in doing so, they would solidify the place of women's businesses in a separate economic substructure distinct from the world of their male counterparts. Heterosexual, white gender norms would also gain institutional support both in terms of ending some of the programs designed to channel women into small business ownership and in the way the newly formed Small Business Administration in 1953 defined what constituted a legitimate business in ways that largely excluded most women's businesses.

Would-be women business owners were not simply passive recipients of a changing public culture, however. They were active agents whose individual strategies collectively helped define and shape the position of small business both within the broader society and their own personal lives. Using the language of the day and cognizant of the rising sanctions against working mothers, female small business owners in the 1950s increasingly referred to their ventures as "sideline businesses," "pin money projects," or even "profitable hobbies" rather than legitimate and equal competitors in the commercial sector, as they might have done a decade earlier.[17] Women of color too framed their businesses at times to both conform to public norms about women's domestic roles and align with racial politics of inclusion and civil rights. In effect, then, while 1940s pro-business advocates—male and female—described enterprise as intrinsically female because it was home-based, women in the 1950s combined this legacy with the new language of women's primary role as mothers or exemplars of their race to position their economic enterprises in a publicly acceptable way, even if their businesses and ambitions would ultimately grow well beyond the home.

Motherhood as Justification for Business Ownership

Many 1950s women business owners came of age during, and took their initial inspiration from, the liberal climate of the postwar era when political and economic leaders championed women's contributions to all aspects of national life. But in the 1950s women and policymakers alike described women's businesses as tied to the home and a way for a wife and mother to better serve her family by combining child-rearing with generating presumably additional household income. Anna Owens, who ran a personalized plate business with a friend, noted that having her children around while she ran the business was "the fun of it."[18] By running a small business from her home—typing, catering, or even babysitting—a woman could earn money without the childcare needs presented by paid employment.[19]

Most women—even those who went out to work—described their business activities almost exclusively as "helping the family," either by providing essentials or by earning additional income for such extras as a new carpet or an air conditioner.[20] One article on "money making at home" in the *Woman's Home Companion* underscored the point by addressing readers with this knowing remark: "Most of us don't fool ourselves. We know we're not businesswomen and don't want to be.... Still it would be nice to make a little money, we think.... Not a lot of money, but, say thirty or forty dollars a month. Enough to pay for those extras."[21] Mrs. Watson, for example, told the *Woman's Home Companion* that she used the money she earned from her part-time curtain business to "buy a new carpet and pad for her living room and [was] saving for another for her dining room."[22] By justifying her venture in this way, Watson and countless women like her could avoid criticism from within their homes and from the larger community. To the women who ran them, their businesses were as much about financial contributions at home as they were an outlet for the woman's creativity, an opportunity for unexpressed ambition, and a means to, as subsequent generations would say, "have it all." Kay Bowe—wife, mother, and owner of a

New York–based hand-knit business in 1953—noted, "I believe a woman can stay at home and still have a career!"[23]

In effect then, employing domestic language as a rationale for starting a business shielded women's multiple motivations as well as the fact that many found running an enterprise more rewarding than the little extras it could yield. Women may have positioned their ventures within the ideology of home and family as their primary roles, but while owning a business, these women also uncovered a new sense of self, a pleasure derived from work, and perhaps even independent achievement outside the confines of family life. This might provide at least a partial explanation for why so many major women-owned corporations trace their roots to the 1950s. While it is true that many women-developed companies would last only as long as their economic need existed, the 1950s gave birth to a considerable number of ventures that would become large corporations in the decades that followed, including the Lillian Vernon Co., Mrs. Totino's Pizza, Liquid Paper Corp., and Home Interiors and Gifts, Inc.

This tendency to see small business as a solution to problems the corporate sector was unwilling or unable to address continued to solidify throughout the 1950s. It provides at least a partial explanation for why contemporary and subsequent generations left unaddressed the question of childcare for working women or their limited career mobility—labeled "the glass ceiling" decades later. If a woman did not fit the existing corporate paradigm, then she could simply opt out via small business. With the increasing prevalence of the small business solution, the corporate world could simply continue with business as usual rather than change with the times.

Articles and books for would-be women business owners made the case, continuously advising them that home-based ventures would let them earn a living *while* rearing their children. Bette Nesmith (later Graham), founder of Liquid Paper, was an oft-cited example. A divorcee with a young son, Graham developed the formula for Liquid Paper in the early 1950s while working as a secretary. She hated typing and with the introduction of the electric typewriter made too many mistakes with the sensitive keyboard. An amateur artist, she created a white paint-based product to camouflage typing errors, and by 1956, she was selling "Mistake Out" from her Dallas, Texas, kitchen and garage. Demand skyrocketed, and she changed the name to "Liquid Paper." While her son grew up to be 1960s Monkees band member Michael Nesmith, Graham went on to revolutionize secretarial work in over thirty-one countries, selling twenty-five million bottles a year by 1975. She sold the business to Gillette Corp. in 1979 for $47.5 million.[24] Her success aside, however, even as she developed her business, Graham was ever conscious of the bias against women in the business world. To obscure her sex, she signed company correspondence with the gender-neutral "B. Nesmith," and she typically received orders and letters addressed to "Mr. Nesmith." Still, as late as the 1970s, Graham often highlighted both her son's involvement in the business and her home as its base until he was grown.

Like many women business owners in the 1950s, Joyce Chen started a restaurant through her role as a mother and in turn used her work experience to influence her children's upbringing. A refugee from communist China in 1949, Chen made egg rolls for her child's 1955 school bake sale in Cambridge, Massachusetts, which sold out in minutes. She taught cooking classes in her home and at adult education centers before she heeded the advice of friends to open a restaurant. At that time, the nation's understanding of Chinese food was limited to Americanized versions of chop suey or chow mein. Chen's restaurant not only introduced the country to the Mandarin-style cuisine of her homeland, but it also aided the introduction of multicultural cuisine and created a business empire for her. Chen became the visible centerpiece of an enterprise that included a PBS series (*Joyce Chen Cooks*), several restaurants, retail food products, and cookbooks. From the start, the business was a family venture. After deciding to go into business, Chen took her young children to the abandoned Waltham Fruit Company storage house that would become her first restaurant. Throughout their formative years, the children helped, and her son and daughter took the helm of the company decades later.[25]

Other women similarly expanded the concepts of motherhood and business with distinctive racial and ethnic implications. A member of the White Mountain Apache tribe in Whitewater, Arizona, Mary Velasquez Riley became the first woman elected to the tribal council in 1958, where she spent two decades fighting for her tribe's right to control its own resources and promote economic development. Surveying the tribe's long-term needs and immediate problems, Riley made several bold moves. First, she established the Sunrise School to

FIG. 2.1 Joyce Chen on the WGBH *Joyce Chen Cooks* set. From *Joyce Chen Cooks* © WGBH Educational Foundation.

50 • She's the Boss

ensure quality education for future generations. Second, she applied her business acumen and lobbying skills to help develop two businesses that would provide income and jobs for her tribal family for decades: the Sunrise Ski Resort and the Fort Apache Timber Company. Both rapidly rose to become multimillion-dollar enterprises owned by the tribe and continue to provide income and jobs into the present.[26] Through her position on the tribal council, Riley extended women's traditional concerns with education and household management beyond the private realm and into the broader tribal family.

Business Ownership for the Woman Who Doesn't "Fit"

Increasingly, small business proved an option for married women as their children grew up and left home. Often the target audience was white, though the prescriptions about gender and age seemed to be universal. Discussions throughout the late 1940s and into the 1950s pointed out that by their middle to late thirties, most women were finished with their mothering responsibilities and yet had several decades left to live. That, combined with the fact that women long outlived their male counterparts, made their economic survival a paramount social concern.[27] Women's Bureau Director Alice K. Leopold launched "Earning Opportunities" forums for older women during the 1950s in cooperation with the National Federation of Business and Professional Women's Clubs across the country.[28] Noted one article, "Employers in business and industry still manifest a reluctance to employ older workers or to retain them on the pay roll—and this despite the large and constantly growing body of facts which prove that older workers not only bring to their jobs an amount of experience and soundness . . . but [also have a] better record for attendance." The term *older* here applied to women ages thirty-five and up. The solution to this corporate brick wall was, as Leopold advised, "Go into business for yourself."[29]

In the hands of magazine writers and other promoters of small business, a home-based venture also seemed a natural option for aging women who had been out of the job market while raising a family and perfected many of the household skills that could now be marketed commercially. Take in mending, repairing or remodeling of clothes, suggested some articles. "You may have to begin at home with only a sign over your door, but more than one flourishing business had its start in just this very way," writer Annie Greenwood advised readers of *Independent Woman* magazine.[30] Other articles directly advised or used anecdotal examples to urge readers to consider "the possibilities that small business holds for women who are looking toward their retirement years."[31]

Offered as models of success: seventy-two-year-old widow Fanny Lee Davis, who owned and supplied the Fanny Lee Apron Shop in her Cherryvale, Kansas, apartment. After raising a family and making aprons for local church bazaars, Davis decided it was "natural that she . . . turn those talents into cash," making and selling 1,200 aprons a year. An article on Davis in *Profitable Hobbies* noted,

"Making aprons is a good business for an older person, Mrs. Davis says, because one's output can be regulated to suit her convenience as she grows older."[32] Likewise, eighty-one-year-old Mrs. George McCollum of Illinois turned her hobby of making doll clothes into a lucrative home-based venture to supplement the shrinking value of her fixed retirement income. Among her customers were Chicago department store Marshall Field and Company and manufacturing mogul Henry Ford, who saw her work on display at the Women's Exchange in Detroit and scooped up her designs for children at the Ford Hospital.[33] Other articles highlighted the energy level of youthful retirees. Not long after Miriam Mason sold her chain of Southern California drapery stores, she was ready to take the plunge with a new venture—an ultramodern car wash she called the Boulevard Auto Laundry on Los Angeles Miracle Mile. "Sounds crazy," she said in 1955, "but business must just flow in my veins."[34]

Many women too became automatic, if unintended, business owners after the death of their enterprising spouses. Just three years after her husband died, Mrs. Hedwig Welander took over her husband's Chicago bakery business, noted *National Business Woman* magazine, and "began the first frozen food business on record when she froze her cakes and dared her customers to differentiate between her frozen products and the fresh."[35] As the magazine of the BPW, *Independent Woman* (later renamed *National Business Woman*) demonstrated a sense of responsibility to show women that age and achievement—especially in business ownership—were hardly incompatible.

As the 1950s progressed, it was not at all unusual to see books and articles on small business linking women and the disabled together as those who might benefit from such ventures. Women and men with physical "handicaps" (the term used at the time)—like Patricia Mae Anderson, who was paralyzed, or Bessie Sawyer, who was blind—further demonstrated the power of small business to fit neatly into individual circumstances the way paid employment did not. Anderson, who faced rheumatic fever as a teenager in 1948, refused to be stopped by her physical limitations, an article heralded, and instead opened a real estate brokerage business from her home in Lebanon, Indiana, six years later. "Walking and showing houses proved to be more than somewhat of a strain," the article pointed out, "but she found that she could wheel her chair to her desk in a pine-paneled annex next to her bedroom, operate a typewriter, commute by chair to her files and—most importantly of all—enlist the telephone as an important business ally."[36] In Sawyer's case, despite her blindness, she opened a telephone answering service from her home in Orange, California. The Braille-based switchboard was set up next to her bed so that "day or night, weekday, Sunday or holiday, Miss Bessie [could] serve any or all of her 42 subscribers," one article described.[37] In effect, then, by the 1950s, the language surrounding small business highlighted its potential as a solution to an array of personal, economic, and gender-defined needs.

While the media may have talked about business as a vehicle for those who did not "fit" the needs of the job market, some groups of women—lesbians, in particular—saw business as a form of survival. In the heyday of the Cold War "lavender scare," gays and lesbians were fired from government jobs and dishonorably discharged from the military on the flimsy and unproven claim that they might be a security risk in the hands of enemies of the United States. Homosexuality was illegal in the United States in this era, and gay men and women were forced to hide their sexual identity or risk arrest and the possible embarrassment of family and friends as well as their own blacklisting in the job market. This kind of high-stress, high-stakes economic situation led some to live closeted lives, but as historian Lillian Faderman has noted, some launched businesses including bars and clubs that served other lesbians and gay men and created a sense of community.[38] Initially bars were mixed spaces for gays and lesbians in cities such as New York, San Francisco, Houston, and Detroit, but in 1959, Charlotte Coleman opened one of the first lesbian-only bars, The Front, in San Francisco.

During World War II, Coleman had served as a member of SPARS, the women's auxiliary of the U.S. Coast Guard. Like many lesbians, she forged relationships and community with other women during her time in the military. Afterward, she took a job in San Francisco as an auditor for the Internal Revenue Service rather than return home to New England. When she applied for a promotion, however, she discovered that the government had been monitoring her and kept a file with "evidence" of her lesbianism. She resigned to escape any potential legal action by the IRS and used the last of her savings to buy the bar. "I had to do something and I heard about this bar for sale for practically nothing, some guy wanting to get out," Coleman recounted years later.[39] Her membership in the Daughters of Bilitis, one of the country's first lesbian movements, made Coleman's bar a hub for other lesbians. For its part, the Daughters of Bilitis produced a magazine that was a precursor to the publishing ventures that would become a vital component of lesbian feminist entrepreneurship in the 1970s.

Racial, Ethnic, and Cultural Supports for Women's Business Ownership

As 1940s public and policy supports waned in the 1950s for women's business ownership, some women's aspirations were validated, at least in part, by ethnic heritage or racial politics. Jewish women, like Hochberg and fashion designer Pauline Trigère, whose families both fled the Nazis during their childhoods, could maneuver within a mixed heritage of domesticity and upward mobility that made the white middle-class domestic ideal less rigidly oppressive. Both women, for example, learned their craft from their parents; Trigère acquired tailoring skills from her Russian émigré father, and Hochberg picked up business acumen from watching her father in his various ventures over the years.[40] As historian Susan Glenn points out, Jewish women have a long tradition of walking the line between homemaking and breadwinning, "sometimes assuming entire responsibility for the family's welfare."[41] In part, this came from a heritage that valued the intellectual and religious commitment of men and encouraged women to take on breadwinning responsibilities if they were blessed to marry a scholarly man. Knowledge or experience of the Holocaust also led some Jewish women business owners to prefer the free enterprise politics of the Republican Party. Bud Konheim explained about his businesswoman mother, "Being Jewish, and aware of the Holocaust, she knew what bigness in government had traditionally meant for Jews."[42]

Jewish immigration to America combined familial obligations with the desire for the upward mobility promised by their new homeland. After her family settled in New York, Hochberg's parents worked together in the family lingerie business, and as a girl she internalized the lesson that it was a wife's legitimate place to aid her husband, and in turn, promote the family's survival.[43] Hochberg simultaneously internalized another, more traditionally gendered, message: "Despite my evident interest, it was an unspoken assumption that I would not end up a full-fledged businesswoman. It was understood, though, that my brother would become a businessman and I, a wife and mother."[44] When she decided to launch her business two years into her marriage, her father supported the idea, perhaps partly because the son who was to have followed in his footsteps perished during World War II but also because he recognized his daughter's talents and women's roles in economically aiding the family. Though a working woman herself, Hochberg's mother steadfastly opposed her daughter's venture.[45] To her, Hochberg's duties were to her husband and children, not as breadwinner.

For African American women during the heyday of the civil rights movement, business ownership also had multiple meanings. Aside from providing a living for their families, Black women's businesses were hailed by civil rights leaders and the Black press as an example of the role entrepreneurship could play in racial advancement. This was part of a long tradition of racial uplift as a means to combat racism dating back to the turn of the century.[46] In 1955, as the civil rights movement was building momentum and the Montgomery bus boycotts were creating a stir in Alabama, Rose Morgan, a Black beautician in Harlem, was once again making news. Morgan unveiled her second and the nation's largest and most lavish beauty salon catering to Black women, particularly women from the emerging middle and upper classes.[47]

Morgan had been in the beauty business for more than ten years. Throughout her career, the press, especially the Black press, presented her life story as a rags-to-riches narrative.[48] The tale began with her early days, when she could barely make ends meet renting a booth from another beautician, and continued to the opening of her first shop with a partner in 1945.[49] That early salon—not to mention her marriage to boxing champion Joe Louis—helped Morgan create a public persona that throughout her life (and divorce) gave her celebrity status.[50] The gala opening of her $225,000, five-story salon captured the attention of neighborhood Blacks and elite whites, such as Mayor Robert Wagner's wife, with more than ten thousand people standing in line to witness Morgan's latest endeavor. She went on to create a chain of salons, with similar beauty palaces in Chicago and Detroit, and in doing so became a symbol for African Americans generally and women specifically about the power of business to convey status and legitimacy.

Morgan's business, while hardly typical of the small home-based shops run by Black women, existed within a larger political context of racial progress and civil rights, which would continue well into the 1960s and 1970s.[51] But even in the 1950s, Black leaders, ministers, and press encouraged African Americans to pursue business ventures as the avenue for achieving both racial solidarity and progress.[52] Black hairdressers, like other Black business women, found it impossible to separate their identity as beauticians/entrepreneurs from their gender, race, and class distinctions. These women shared and embraced the belief of other Black leaders that through their economic successes, they could potentially put an end to racial discrimination.[53] Hence they relied on business ownership to create an image of respectability that would silence white critics and be inspirational to other Black women. They also received messages from African American writers and leaders about the potential power of business ownership. A series of tracts beginning in 1949 and throughout the 1950s argued that Blacks had a long history of owning businesses and that there were fourteen million potential members of the "Negro public . . . becoming more race conscious and hence more eager and willing to support Negro businesses."[54] While most of the discussion was about business for men, leaders did point out that women owned more than one-third of all Black businesses, 96.7 percent of the Black-owned beauty shops, and 88.2 percent of related beauty schools.[55] There was an urgency and sense of racial responsibility in these discussions, since many noted that whites were beginning to encroach on these mainstay Black businesses.

Such arguments made the visibility of women such as Morgan all the more important. Other women of color similarly heeded the call to connect their individual goals as business owners with efforts for racial advancement and rights. "It meant you could be the boss of something," said Marjory Joyner, who represented Black beauty workers and educators as president and founder of the United Beauty School Owners and Teachers Association (UBSOTA), a Black trade group. With a strong commitment to helping other women of color, Joyner, who had a long legacy as a shop owner, said, "I know I felt I was setting an example that no one is superior to me and that I can be whatever I want to be. I wanted white society to know that you can't keep me from that . . . from the chance to be known as a business person."[56] Black beauticians combined their efforts to make these political statements through their work when, in 1954, 195 beautician members of UBSOTA broke the color barrier by going to Paris, France, to gain training reserved for whites in the United States. The wide press coverage they received afforded an opportunity to present a professional image and serve as symbols of progress in the struggle for racial equality.[57]

Fashion designer Ann Lowe also symbolized what was possible for people of color in business. Born in 1898 in Little Rock, Arkansas, the descendent of former slaves, and raised by a single mother, Lowe came from a long line of seamstresses and tailors. She moved to New York in 1928, where she made and sold dresses and started a millinery school in Harlem. Lowe designed the gown that actress Olivia de Havilland wore to receive her 1939 Oscar for *Gone with the Wind*. Her gowns

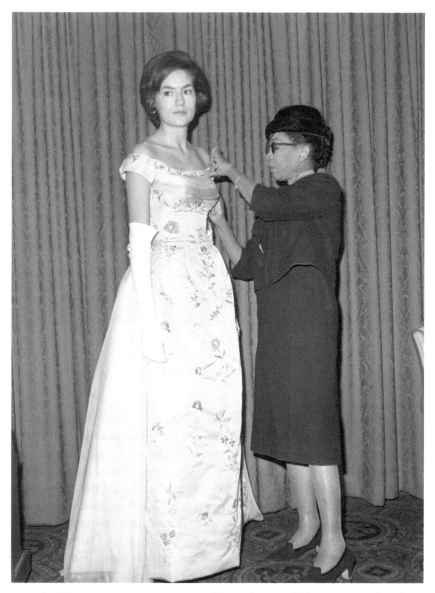

FIG. 2.2 Designer Ann Lowe working on one of her haute couture gowns in the 1950s. *Credit:* Bettman via Getty Images.

FIG. 2.3 Jacqueline Bouvier Kennedy with her new husband and future president John F. Kennedy on their wedding day. She is wearing a wedding gown created by African American designer Ann Lowe. *Credit:* Toni Frissell, Library of Congress / John F. Kennedy Presidential Library and Museum.

were carried in upscale boutiques catering to elite, often white women and high society. She opened her first shop, Ann Lowe's Gowns in 1950 and would own a few other salons, always commuting from her Harlem apartment to her business on the Upper West Side of Manhattan. A career coup, she was hired to design the wedding dress that Jacqueline Bouvier wore when she married then-senator John F. Kennedy in 1953. In her heyday, Lowe designed one thousand gowns a year, grossing more than $300,000 annually. But an incident over the Kennedy wedding dress revealed the depths of Lowe's dignity and racial pride. When hired to make the dress, she agreed to confidentiality as was the standard of the day; this way, society women could keep their favorite designers to themselves. Later, when *Ladies Home Journal* quoted Jacqueline Kennedy describing Lowe by name as "a colored woman dressmaker, not the haute couture," an insulted

Lowe fired off a letter to Kennedy. She wrote, "You know I have never sought publicity but I would prefer to be referred to as a 'noted Negro designer,' which in every sense I am."[58] In fact, acclaimed fashion designer Christian Dior and Hollywood costume designer Edith Head had both named Lowe among their favorite American designers. Lowe's pride was also linked to ambitions for her race. In a television interview with talk show host Mike Douglas, Lowe noted that a driving force in her life was "to prove that a Negro can become a major dress designer."[59]

Cold War Consumer: Women's New Patriotic Duty

The need to keep women economically prepared in the midst of the Cold War and fears about the potential for another world war fueled government and public acceptance of their workforce participation and shaped perceptions of their business ownership.[60] But when the Korean conflict (1951–1953) proved not to be World War III, the energy behind such womanpower discussions and programs faded dramatically, save for ambiguous new fears of a nuclear war by the end of the 1950s.[61] Shifts in emphasis were already evident by the mid-1950s, when leaders began to fuse women's economic roles with both their previous national contributions and their place at home as mothers. In 1957, for example, the National Manpower Council's conference on womanpower focused on easing concerns that working mothers would upset gender roles at home. Instead, the conference emphasized how these second incomes facilitated traditional roles by enabling greater numbers of families to purchase homes, automobiles, and appliances.[62] According to published proceedings, its follow-up conference a year later was almost wholly consumed by the question of "the impact of increased employment of women upon family life, the rearing of children, and the self-development of women."[63]

By 1959, when Women's Bureau director Alice Leopold delivered her speech "Womanpower in a Changing World" at a Purdue University conference, she seemed more to be pleading for the recognition and inclusion of women's capabilities in the public realms of politics and economics than demanding they get their due. "It is pertinent for this gathering to know what role women will play in America's future economic growth," she said tentatively. Although she noted that there were five million women in the workforce and that they comprised a "national resource," she maintained the position of humble petitioner rather than righteous claimant. She cited the ever-visible women business owners in her appeal, noting, "More women than in earlier years have become accountants, editors and reporters, lawyers and judges—and yes, such top executives as managers, officials and proprietors, as the census calls them. These women 'bosses' total more than a million—over twice their number in 1940 and about five times that in 1920." In a more desperate plea, she argued, "As a free nation, we must always remember another aim, that of encouraging the individual to realize his own personal goals."[64] Despite such determined appeals, by decade's end, leaders and policymakers had a diminished interest in women as an untapped reservoir of economic potential.

The Ebbing of the Small Business Clinic Model

In this context, organizing around women's business ownership would take a decidedly different tone and course in the 1950s compared to the previous decade. By 1952, fewer and fewer states engaged the idea of institutionalizing women's divisions, and while many continued to sponsor the small business clinics popular in the late 1940s, it was often at the nudging of the National Federation of Business and Professional Women's Clubs (BPW). For several years, virtually no other states added women's divisions to their government offices. Still, with the Korean War underway, the BPW argued for small business—and the clinics—as a preparatory measure. Advising their members in May 1951, the group wrote in its newsletter, "Give special emphasis to the establishment and maintenance of small businesses needed in the emergency, development of resources important to the state economy, and development of services needed because of emergency employment. Send for 'The Small Business Clinic 1951–1952' [brochure]."[65] While New York maintained its women's division until 1971, Massachusetts was the last state to implement one in 1957. In its early years, the Massachusetts Women's Division offered few programs despite its mission, as quoted by the BPW's magazine, to "promote business opportunities and economic projects for women in the Commonwealth and . . . provide an advisory and counseling service for the purpose of increasing opportunities for women in business."[66]

The abandonment of state programs came at a time of peak interest by women in owning enterprises and by the nation generally in the future of small business. The BPW national and local chapters consistently noted in their meeting minutes throughout the 1950s both the success of the programs and ongoing requests by members and nonmembers alike for more sessions. New York's Jane Todd responded to such enthusiasm among New York women through a variety of programs, including "Business-of-Your-Own Career Conferences." The Women's Program even produced a 16 mm movie in 1953 highlighting the how-to activities of its small business clinics, to be shown to women across the state. Along with the film, Todd continued to generate publicity through women's and national magazines and newspapers. The results were that the New York Woman's Program counseled 1,676 women on business issues, of which 597 sought advice on how to start a new enterprise and 489 had questions about expanding existing businesses.[67]

Such hands-on efforts by women's groups were so successful, in fact, that by 1952, many of the small business clinics that women developed were being adapted by private programs and universities to include training men. No doubt, the declining interest of men in small business and their rising complacency among the ranks of employed "organization men" in part contributed to this concern. It was further exacerbated by fears about the survival of small business amid increasing corporate agglomeration and the rise of what would come to be known as the military-industrial complex in the years after World War II and the Korean War. Iowa was among the first BPW state clubs to include men, with the *Iowa Business Woman* noting, "The clinics are for everyone—members and non-members of BPW, and include men as well as women."[68] State agencies that served the entire area populace, for example, might mandate that any programs it sponsored be open to the general public, regardless of gender. That meant the BPW had to slightly reconfigure the clinics. Moreover, in smaller communities with limited populations, the only way to garner the attendance necessary to make these events cost-effective as the 1950s progressed would be to include men.[69]

Despite public interest by women and men, however, policymakers' interest in institutionalizing the clinic model continued to diminish, leaving the business of training and advising would-be women business owners largely in the hands of the BPW. Well into the 1960s, this group's national and local chapters continued to note that interest in small business clinics ranked highest among club activities. *Independent Woman* magazine noted in 1954, "Since our Blue Print for the Small Business Clinic was published in 1949, no other project of the Education and Vocations committee has [had] so much active participation."[70] Iowans would travel great distances to attend clinics, and rarely was an event reported with fewer than one hundred to two hundred people in attendance, even in the most remote areas.[71] The groups continued to hold clinics and put out brochures explaining how to launch a business including "Plan a Bread and Butter Sideline," "Marketing a Home Product," "Small Business Clinics, 1951–1952," "The Voice of Experience on Small Business Clinics," and "A Woman's Way with a Shop."[72] Todd and BPW president Marguerite Rawalt publicized the success of the clinics and the women who launched business because of the advice they received there. But the tone of the articles shifted dramatically from gender-based arguments for equality to the use of women's distinct and private roles to squelch fears that these ventures were more than "pin money projects."

Although the BPW small business clinics continued to find support from women everywhere, as the decade progressed, the clinics were slowly folded into other categories. Initially, they found a home under the banner "Career Clinics" or "Career Advancement," which might attract job seekers as well as potential business owners. Over time, however, the serious focus on business was lost. Instead, in the years that followed, they were either renamed or collapsed into everything from "Hobby Clinics" to "Personality Workshops," and by 1959, "Self-Improvement Clinics."[73] This changing language signaled the beginning of the end for the small business clinics.

Gender and the Future of Free Enterprise

While the small business clinics struggled to survive, the state of small business in America faced a similar challenge. The Depression, World War II, and the Korean War initiated a downward spiral in the number of small businesses in the economy, due largely to consolidation during the war years and the rise of the industrial complex during the 1950s. From 1940 to 1947 alone, 2,500 firms disappeared due to mergers alone.[74] Groups such as the National Association of Manufacturers (NAM) and the Chamber of Commerce of the United States (COC) had expressed concerns about the future of free enterprise. In a 1953 report, for example, the COC noted that 58 percent of total assets of all corporations were held by just 1,179 firms each with total assets of $50 million or more.[75]

Corporate trends aside, American males were also becoming increasingly risk-aversive in the decade after World War II. Driven by an insatiable quest for security after the turmoil of the Depression and war years, most men opted for stable positions in corporations, giving birth to that 1950s icon, "the organization man."[76] This army of men in gray flannel suits abdicated the image of pioneer that had long been the emblem of American manhood, earning the reputation of being "even more conformist and prudent than its elders."[77] In 1945, novels celebrating the entrepreneurial success of fictional heroes were among the most popular sellers to male customers. Just ten years later, however, themes reflected heroes making choices between work and leisure, family and the public. Male protagonists in the 1950s were more likely to be heroic for choosing to accommodate themselves to the workforce and a secure place in the organizational hierarchy.[78]

Media watchers and academics were puzzled by the odd stability of this younger generation—soon labeled "the silent generation"—and noted that the men of the class of 1949 "[seemed] to a stranger from another generation curiously old before their time. Above everything else, security [had] become their goal." Not much had changed by 1955, when sociologist David Reisman "concluded that the typical class of '55 senior sought a place on the corporate ladder, planned which branch of the military he would enter (guided missiles was a favorite one) and knew what his wife would be like at 45 (the Grace Kelly, camel hair coat type who would do volunteer hospital work and bring culture into the home)."[79] To this generation, big business served as a private welfare state, which offered, as one historian later noted, "modest advancement, numerous fringe benefits and a reasonable security" over the risks, adventure and potential profits of entrepreneurship.[80] Concern about men's declining interest and success in small business during the twenty-five years after 1950 led the media to coin a new term: "The New Forgotten Man."[81]

Yet the image of the small businessman as the backbone of American society was not easily erased, and ironically it would be women who maintained this pioneer spirit, albeit in a covert way, throughout the 1950s. In a 1959 pamphlet on starting a business, the COC noted, "1,100 firms on average, go out of business every working day. Roughly 650 percent of them are retail, service, or wholesale firms. About 70 out of every 1000 retail businesses went out of operation in 1959." While no doubt the authors' main target audience was the COC's male membership, their emphasis on retail and service—two areas of strong female concentration in business ownership—indicated that they expected at least some readers to be women.[82]

Both the COC and NAM reached out to women's organizations during the Cold War to help maintain the American system of Free Enterprise. Throughout the 1950s, the COC tracked the number of chapters with female members or auxiliaries and urged local branches to welcome women.[83] By 1954, thirty-one COCs had a Women's Division, charged with promoting citizenship in the community.[84] In 1957, NAM held a special women's program at its annual convention entitled "Women Mean Business." Noting that statistics about women's central economic roles could no longer be ignored, NAM's data showed, "Women own fifty-three percent of all stockholdings, sixty-five percent of all accounts in mutual savings banks, hold title to forty percent of all homes, pay forty percent of all property taxes."[85] A year later, NAM encouraged its women's club members to follow in the footsteps of two Midwestern sisters who hitch a wagon to their car and "bring beauty to approximately 100 women every week." The sisters created a beauty shop on wheels during the summer, traveling to rural towns with populations of five hundred to seven hundred people that had no beauty parlors. Good businesswomen, the traveling beauticians averaged "a customer a mile in their weekly travels."[86] Through such outreach, NAM and the COC were, however ambiguously at times, providing a model of legitimation for women's economic roles.

While men abandoned independent enterprise for the corporate sector or shuttered their businesses due to competition from larger companies, women posted increases in the number of self-employed or independent proprietors. According to a report by the Women's Bureau, in April 1959, there were 335,000 women in the retail trade, up from just 242,000 in 1950.[87] Meanwhile, from 1955 to 1960, the number of self-employed women increased from 12.2 to nearly 13 percent of all women workers. While this may not seem significant, it deserves closer scrutiny. Nearly 13 percent of women who *defined themselves* as employed in 1955 were self-employed, compared to barely 10 percent of employed men. Measured as part of an ongoing trend, from 1955 to 1986, women increased their rate of self-employment by 113 percent.[88] Other categories showed similar increases.

Obtaining an accurate count in this era is difficult, however.[89] During this period, the Department of Health and Human Services reported self-employment figures, while the U.S. Census Bureau tracked business owners under the heading "managers, officials and proprietors." In the latter category, which lumped administrator-employees with business owners, women's figures held steady at about 4.8 percent of the total employed. But one might make

62 • She's the Boss

the case that the consistency accounts for declining numbers of women in high-ranking jobs, a tendency to underreport ownership, and a confusion about the meaning of the category itself.[90] Sex was only a sometimes category in data collection, and surveys of women business owners or self-employed were sporadic. In addition, women who ran small ventures from a kitchen or spare room were unlikely to consider or report themselves "proprietors" to government agencies. Consequently, one can easily assume that the total number of women who were self-employed in this era remains grossly underreported. It is doubtful too that many home-based businesses paid taxes on their ventures or in other ways reported their incomes.

Defined Out of Existence: Women's Businesses and the Small Business Administration

While women turned their enterprising ways toward the home, on the national front, fears about the impact of corporate agglomeration on small business fueled the establishment of the Small Business Administration—an organization that would ultimately reify gendered norms about business ownership. The new agency evolved from the World War II Smaller War Plants Corporation (Small Defense Plants Administration during the Korean War). According to the Act establishing the SBA in 1953, it was to "aid, counsel, assist, and protect, insofar as is possible, the interests of small-business concerns in order to preserve free competitive enterprise, to insure that a fair proportion of the total purchases and contracts for property and services for the Government be placed with small-business enterprises, and to maintain and strengthen the overall economy of the nation."[91] Introduced with strident language that the essence of the American economic system "of private enterprise is free competition," the Small Business Act of 1953 charged the new agency with making loans and guaranteeing capital for small independent enterprises. It was also to ensure that they received a fair portion of government business and serve as an advocate within the government for the interests of small business.[92]

Aside from debates over whether such an agency was necessary, the biggest problem facing the new Small Business Administration came in defining "small business." Definitions ranged from firms with fewer than 2,500 employees to those with earnings below $1 million.[93] Ultimately, the SBA opted for what it considered an industry-specific and flexible definition of a small business as "one which is independently owned and operated which is not dominant in its field of operations." Size would vary depending on the industry; for example, in manufacturing, this meant firms with no more than five hundred employees; in wholesaling it referred to companies with sales below $5 million, and in retailing, receipts could not top $1 million.[94]

Whatever the definition, what was instantly clear was that such terminology—and other SBA catch phrases—precluded all references to the kinds of enterprises women typically launched. Small business virtually always referred to companies that existed outside the home, with a base of employees that easily topped one hundred or more, and that in general fit a model of business as existing within the corporate sector. The occasional woman did indeed procure a small business bank loan, such as Mary Crowley, who founded Home Interiors and Gifts; however, not only is her case atypical, but it is difficult to know whether her loans were SBA-backed.[95] Moreover, Crowley herself pointed out that it was hard convincing the bank to lend money to a woman and even more difficult when she explained her business would depend on the efforts of a network of housewives.[96] To bank officials and SBA program officers, this feminized business strategy seemed alien and outside the realm of viable business investment.

In fact, SBA administrators intended to provide loans not to the mom-and-pop establishments many Americans regarded as the definition of 'small' business, but instead to medium range firms with the potential to keep the relative growth of big corporations in check.[97] While this would be in some measure corrected a year later, nonetheless, it established an enduring connection between small business and *man*. After all, for the most part, it was men who had the resources to own firms of this size in large numbers and men who fit the traditional definition of what constituted a business used by creditors in making lending decisions. It was the entrepreneur—virtually always defined in male terms—who took center stage in political discussions surrounding the SBA. Women's ventures fell out of these conversations, virtually disappearing into the home or into a separate economic subculture.

In effect then, although the Horatio Alger myth and the term *entrepreneur* had throughout much of American history referred to male-owned enterprises, there was a brief window of opportunity in the immediate postwar years to expand that term to incorporate women's businesses. But the abandonment of progressive postwar initiatives by Cold War policymakers, and more specifically the founding of the SBA, slammed shut any initiatives to see women's businesses as on a par with men's. Instead, the term *entrepreneur* was reinscribed in rigid male terms, defined as a person who "becomes aware of a need, be it for a product or service, and creates a business enterprise to fulfill that need. The entrepreneur seizes upon opportunities presented by our national economy and begins to do things that were generally not done in the traditional business routine."[98] Entrepreneurs placed their own personal capital at risk and labored to turn their business into a vast enterprise. Part manager, part inventor, part administrator or marketer, "the entrepreneur is a *man* who takes risks."[99] Men such as Henry Ford, Andrew Carnegie, or John D. Rockefeller were its prototypes.[100] Consequently, a line of demarcation—a kind of "separate spheres" of business—arose between public, professional businessmen entrepreneurs and home-bound, enterprising women. Where by definition, the entrepreneur was a person of high achievement concerned with uniting labor and capital to produce a profit for themselves and investors, the small businesswoman in this era was concerned more with earning a livable wage while doing work she enjoyed and possibly also rearing a family.[101] As historian Kathy Peiss has noted, what distinguished women's ventures from men's in public parlance was this: women commercialized the feminine while men—the real entrepreneurs—were engaged in "vital industries."[102]

Even women who reached millionaire status such as Mary Kay Ash, Lillian Vernon, Mary Crowley, or Bette Nesmith Graham would not see the term *entrepreneur* applied to their ventures until the late 1970s and 1980s.[103] Lillian Vernon lay claim to the term in the early 1990s, funding a chair in entrepreneurship at New York University and casting herself as the embodiment of the American entrepreneurial spirit in her 1996 autobiography. But in the 1950s and 1960s, as Vernon's business was blossoming, she did not use such language to describe what she was doing. She was running a business and raising a family, nurturing both carefully.[104]

A Boon for Women's Business: The Rise of the Consumer Economy

Despite the neglect of women's ventures in the founding of the SBA, other trends in the 1950s nonetheless kept women's interest in small business burning bright, most particularly the rise of the consumer economy. With the end of the Korean War in 1953, the nation swung into full postwar prosperity, and even the scant recessions of 1953–1954 and 1958–1959 did little to slow the new assortment of postwar consumer goods. Private housing topped the list, and studies show that 25 percent of all existing homes in 1960 had been built during the 1950s. Some historians have argued that the need for housing starts to bolster the economy at least in part explains the forcefulness of the domestic ideology of the era.[105] Levittown, New York, home buyers found units equipped with "a Bendix washer and Admiral TV at no extra cost; there were swimming pools and play areas that would ensure good recreation for the kids."[106] In the years after the war, spending on household furnishings and appliances rose 240 percent.[107] Such big-ticket items may have started the trend, but smaller consumer goods followed right behind.

About a sixth of the nation's income went for leisure products in the 1950s, and with seventy-six million babies born between the 1946–1964 baby boom years, spending for a host of consumer goods went way up. According to historian James Gilbert, "Money spent on diapers increased from $32 million in 1947 to $50 million by 1957; toys and children's clothes soon became boom industries." Over $300 million was spent on doll replicas of icons Hopalong Cassidy, Roy Rogers, Wyatt Earp, and the Cisco Kid. Davy Crocket raccoon caps brought in $100 million in sales. About $1.6 billion was spent on teenage entertainment—record albums and record players, cameras, and tickets to rock 'n' roll shows. Breck shampoo sales jumped by $1 million from 1956 to 1959.[108] Taken together, such purchases could put heavy new demands on the household budget.

Aside from the mere proliferation of products, however, Americans recognized the underlying message that without ongoing consumption, the nation's economic stability would again be in jeopardy and Depression-era conditions could return. "In times such as these, excessive saving can be as harmful as excessive spending," exhorted one politician.[109] Ad campaigns for everything from furniture to cars exhorted consumers, "Eisenhower Urges Consumer Buying!"[110] The *Wall Street Journal* responded to all this pressure with a sardonic column, arguing, "It seems that if we don't buy, the recession will become a depression and there will be a revolution or something and the Communists will take over."[111]

In reality, the person feeling the pressure to consume was the woman of the house. A 1957 article in the *Christian Science Monitor* cited NAM data that women controlled as much as 85 percent of household spending.[112] As economist Julie Matthaei points out, in the 1950s, "the homemaker was transformed from a home producer to a consumer of commodities. . . . It was her job to see that the family's needs were filled."[113] Homemakers at every end of the socio-economic spectrum, save the very richest, found themselves caught up in what Matthaei describes as "permanent, unending neediness."[114]

Suburban shopping centers that sprung up in the late 1950s likewise recognized shopping as the woman's domain. Historian Lizabeth Cohen notes, "As families strolled and shopped together at the mall, they engaged in what was becoming a form of leisure that was female directed and hence bore witness to a wife's or mother's control."[115] Women were spending an average of $15 billion per year—$250 per woman—for their wardrobes alone.[116] Men's salaries, however, could not often keep pace with wives' perceived household needs, thereby creating internal conflicts and a sense of deprivation, albeit relative. "It is not that they believe they are particularly disadvantaged compared to their neighbors," as sociologists wrote in 1959; "rather it is that they feel their incomes are just not large enough to cover the things they think they should buy, are entitled to have."[117]

It was not a far leap, then, for the home-bound consumer to look inward for a solution to the limited finances provided by her organization-man husband. In fact, throughout the 1950s, with its dual discussion of domesticity and consumption, women of all classes fused the ability to consume with their roles as wife and mother. Matthaei calls this "vocational homemaking." She and others argue that this quest for additional funds to better provide the finer things in life for their families beyond a husband's income allowed women to extend homemaking into income generation.[118] As one working-class homemaker explained, "My husband says I don't have to work, but if I don't we'll never get anywhere."[119]

If a mother's job was to keep her children healthy, well-dressed, and in league with their school chums, then it may fall to her to come up with the extra income to do so. According to the U.S. Department of Labor, married women in 1950 comprised 52 percent of women in the labor force, up from barely a third in 1940.[120] What's more, data from the Women's Bureau indicated that in 1950, 68 percent of women "managers, owners, and proprietors" were married with husbands present.[121] When Bud Konheim's mother, Shirley—born as he describes her with "a silver spoon in her mouth"—saw that life with her musician husband would mean downward mobility for herself and her children, she decided it was up to her to engage in an economic endeavor that would assure this never happened.[122] She turned to the business that had made her grandfather wealthy: apparel manufacturing. Borrowing $500,000 over the years from her wealthy friends, in the early 1950s she set up a teen clothing company with the label Connie Sage. Eventually, Konheim's ventures would lead to the P. J. Walsh Company of moderate women's apparel in the mid-1970s, where her son Bud joined his mother and met his future business partner, Nicole Miller.[123] Konheim, like many married women of her era, provided a powerful example of this expanded notion of motherhood.

But if women understood the need to earn a living, there was little public acceptance for taking a job, no matter what the economic need was—be it for essentials or "little extras." The onslaught of media and public messages women received regarding the negative impact of paid employment on their families could be daunting.[124] Women faced a genuine conundrum: "More household gadgets set more women free for employment, and more wives in paid employment increase the need—and provide the cash—for more and better appliances," noted sociologists Alva Myrdal and Viola Klein.[125] Many of the ten million working women in 1953 wanted "the things most Americans want: a home of her own, security and 'advantages' for the children, good food and clothes, a good car, a television set, and money in the bank," noted *Fortune*, adding that these women were "decent . . . with responsibilities at home."[126] But *Fortune*'s defense of working women illustrated the immense arguments against them.

Women's "Proper Place" and the Small Business Solution

The debate over women's roles garnered a public forum in national media. While the *Saturday Evening Post* and *National Business Woman* championed women's achievements in the workforce, Sloan Wilson, author of the *Man in the Gray Flannel Suit*, engaged in a *New York Times* debate with author Bernice Fitzgibbon about women's place being in the home.[127] Meanwhile, women's magazines touted women's firsts in politics and other fields while simultaneously layering on the guilt for leaving home. *Good Housekeeping* in 1951 featured an essay entitled "Why I Quit Working," where a former career mother comes to her senses and finds greater fulfillment baking cookies for her child than she ever found in her weekly paycheck.[128] But within six months, the same magazine printed a seemingly paradoxical article on why "every woman should learn a trade." Its rationale was this: "Today there is less reason than ever before for American women to depend on marriage for lifelong security. Divorce is ever more common." By learning and practicing a trade before marriage, the author argued, a woman could return to it "during family economic crises if necessary, and use it gratefully when home responsibilities [became] almost nonexistent and a life of dependence on married children [lay ahead for] her."[129]

At the same time, women faced other, equally public pressures to consider home their one and only vocation, as is evident in Adlai Stevenson's famous and widely published commencement address to Smith College in 1955: "[Most women were] destined for 'the humble role of housewife' whether they liked the idea or not. . . . When the time comes, you'll love it," he told graduates, linking women's containment at home to the triumph of the American way of life over the communists.[130] Similar speeches were made by Stevens and other leaders at other women's colleges and civic groups. Likewise, in his Kitchen Debates with Soviet premier Nikita Khrushchev, vice president Richard Nixon declared U.S. superiority based on the fact that Soviet women had to work and American women did not.[131] The rising juvenile crime rates—which kept pace with those for adults in the 1950s—nonetheless fueled a literature that attributed every childhood problem to bad mothering, in particular juvenile delinquency.[132] The more a mother was away from home—even if her job was needed for food and housing rather than extras—the more her bad mothering was blamed for family and youth problems.

Owning a home-based business became a simple, almost acceptable solution, particularly when women relied on commercializing the female skills of homemaking, beauty, or service. "We have found that a lot of women have developed skills while running their homes that are needed in operating a small business," said Helen G. Thompson, assistant deputy commissioner of the New York Commerce Department.[133] *Life* magazine offered similar advice in its article "Homemade and Hopeful," which highlighted the small business potential behind women's handicrafts and homemaking skills such as decorated trays, ceramic pieces, braided rugs, fudge, seafood sauce, tableware, dolls, aprons, and blankets. The pictorials illustrated women's home "factories" in full production but never promoted the idea that these and other women could compete in the manufacturing sector writ large. A photo captioned "Her Dining Room Is Her Plant" showcased Mrs. Robert Abrams surrounded by cloth dolls waiting, assembly-line style, to be sewn and stuffed in her living room.[134] Women's magazines also offered tips on stretching the budget by taking in work such as typing or babysitting, and they celebrated the stories of women who earned a whopping thirty to forty dollars a month for their families. One women's magazine, for example, suggested opening a charm school, running a neighborhood swap shop, or making sound recordings of weddings and parties—all highly feminine tasks.[135] While the occasional article focused on women in untraditional work, such as Lee Brown and her oil wildcat business, most of the women highlighted were those in traditionally feminine ventures.[136]

The numbers tell the story. In 1950 alone, women comprised 31 percent of the proprietors of apparel and accessories stores and 26 percent of eating and drinking establishments.[137] Roughly 43 percent of the women seeking business advice at the 1953 small business clinics in New York expressed an interest in service ventures, 17 percent in owning a shop, and 14 percent in "miscellaneous home business," which included raising animals or herb gardens or running a mail-order venture. Even the 26 percent who expressed an interest in manufacturing defined that category as the production of food items, arts and crafts, and needlework articles.[138]

Whether in magazines, business books, or government pamphlets, one element was central to the advice given to would-be women business owners: they could easily combine all their roles and responsibilities. "Miss Davenport feels that keeping both a successful home and business depends on learning to discipline one's time," noted an article profiling Thelma Davenport's ability to simultaneously run an insurance business and act the part of the "pretty blond wife."[139] Government booklets on beauty shops stressed that they provided women an opportunity to earn a living and still be home when the children return from school.[140] *Changing Times* ran a series from 1953 to 1954, advising women on "spare-time business" ventures that could be operated when their household duties were done, such as sewing, crafts, food, or garden products as well as services such as laundry, errands, shopping, or odd jobs. Taken together, the message was that motherhood and business could be harmoniously blended as long as motherhood came first.

Women were also admonished to remember their other familial role—that of wife—when launching a business. In its premier article on the topic, *Changing Times* underscored the recognition of the wife's subordinated status with this advice: "You should have your husband's whole hearted cooperation. That may not be so easy. The husband who thinks your big idea is a silly whim will probably not take kindly to your request for help with the bookkeeping later on." To convince him, the author advised, show him how the extra income from your "pin-money project" will help "run the home" and cover children's summer camp, family vacation, or "new draperies." Most of all, the author stressed demonstrating to the man of the house that "your duty to your family will have priority—no cold suppers, even when you have a deadline to meet, or at least not often anyway."[141]

Magazines also indicated an awareness that even with small children, women's work at home was not all-consuming. Articles advised female readers to parlay those "few spare hours" into typing at home, noting that businesses often needed extra, temporary help. Catering businesses were another frequent suggestion for women who needed to "earn her keep or at least her pin money," wrote *Good Housekeeping*, citing successes such as the Dallas woman who supplied chili suppers or women "all over the country selling their own tea sandwiches, casseroles, hors d'oeuvres, and complete dinners."[142] But no one more perfectly demonstrated the compatibility of home and business than Elinor Gene Hoffman, who made a living reading and writing scripts for two weekly West Coast children's radio programs. Noted *Good Housekeeping*, "[Hoffman] mixes family living and professional accomplishment so artfully it's impossible to tell where one stops and the other ends."[143]

Women sometimes embraced and helped propagate these ideas about the primacy of their domestic roles above all else. When Mary Crowley founded her direct sales company, Home Interiors and Gifts, on her Dallas, Texas, porch in 1957, she made the centrality of women's home duties a key component of her corporate policy. Crowley "urged her salesgirls to arrange their workdays to accommodate the needs of their families. Young mothers could stay at home with toddlers during the day and schedule parties at night, while moms with school-age children might prefer morning get-togethers that concluded before the dismissal bell."[144]

Crowley got the idea for her business when she was struggling to make a living as a single mother with two children. She had worked selling decorating and household products via home demonstration parties for the lucrative and popular Stanley Products, but she barely netted enough to make her efforts worthwhile. She decided to heed the suggestion of her friend, future cosmetics mogul Mary Kay Ash, to start her own business in the burgeoning direct sales field.[145] Home Interiors purchased home decor items and sold them at 100 percent markup, of which two-thirds went to the salesperson, another 10 percent to the division manager, and the rest to Crowley's firm. By the mid-1980s, Home Interiors had become a $400 million business where saleswomen earned as much as $75,000 to $200,000 a year.[146]

From the start, Crowley organized her firm around both her solid Baptist religious principles and her empathy for mothers who worked. She called herself a "Christian businesswoman" and was known for holding business meetings with a Bible on her lap. Her many books about her business featured chapters about God's role in personal success and women's mission to serve as an inspiration for their children while also providing a safe and happy home.[147] Female employees and sales agents were well aware of Home Interiors' corporate philosophy, and many shared its values of family, religion, and women's potential, including the notion that "home is the greatest influence on the character of mankind."[148]

As women's businesses and household roles were increasingly fused, articles and books showcased only those ventures that could be started with little or no money. In this way too, women's business ownership continued outside the mainstream economy and certainly beyond the purview of qualifying enterprises for SBA loans and programs. For example, none of Polly Webster's how-to books included pointers on convincing bank tellers or SBA officials to lend start-up funds. Instead, she focused on an array of businesses from sporting goods shops and house-cleaning or delivery services that could be started at home with very little money. Even just "$1 capital and an old English recipe for marmalade" could net big profits, she noted.[149] In a discussion of the catering business, she explained, "Small money-makers call for skill in cooking but almost no cash layout, no investment in equipment, no change in the house setup—and the return is almost immediate."[150]

For more extensive endeavors, women had to muster their creativity—and market their feminine roles—to raise start-up capital. Rose Totino, an Italian American wife and mother of two daughters, spent much of her formative years in economic hardship, and she and her husband Jim were determined to create a better life for their children. Like most postwar wives, Totino stayed home with the family while her husband worked in a local Minneapolis, Minnesota, bakery earning little more than eighty-seven cents an hour. But it was her mother's pizza recipe that would not only spark what would become the family enterprise in 1950 but also take part in a revolution in the packaged and frozen foods industry—if she could raise the funding.

For years, Totino had prepared pizzas for local PTA meetings or other community events, with those present raving about the unfamiliar concoction—which was still a novelty, particularly in the Midwest. Sometimes a friend would ask her to cater a party with her pizzas. But when soldiers returned home from World War II looking for the pizza they had enjoyed in New York, Italy, or California, Rose Totino decided it was time to open a shop of her own. The start-up costs were $1,500, far beyond her means. To convince the local bank to give her a

FIG. 2.4 Rose Totino making the pizza that would become the foundation of a frozen food empire. Courtesy of the General Mills Archives.

loan, she recalled decades later, "[I took] a pizza with me because a lot of people didn't know what a pizza was in those days. . . . I took a little portable oven with me. They had a lunchroom there and I plugged it in, cooked it and served it to the loan committee—maybe three or four people. They liked it and they gave us the loan." The bank also paid for the advertisement announcing the opening of Totino's.[151] By the end of the decade, the Totino's began selling frozen versions of "Mrs. Totino's" pizzas, becoming one of the leading frozen pizzas by the 1970s. Rose Totino sold her business to Pillsbury in 1975 for $22 million and a job as Pillsbury's first female vice president with an annual salary of $100,000 (equal to roughly $600,000 in 2024).[152]

For Themselves: The Rewards of Business Ownership

Women's business ventures may have started as a way to make ends meet, but to their owners, the pleasure of the work often added a sense of fulfillment that meshed with other, unaddressed ambitions they may have had. That was true even for single women: Chemist Hazel Bishop spent her days at Standard Oil Development, but at home at night, she used her scientific mind to develop a long-lasting lipstick in 1949 that would fuel her subsequent cosmetics empire. By 1954, the company she founded, Hazel Bishop, Inc., reported sales of $10 million.[153] While public norms may have frowned upon middle-class married women who worked outside the home, they nonetheless recognized women's hunger for achievement beyond the bounds of motherhood alone. *Woman's Home Companion* frequently offered tips to housewives on providing services to neighbors, and one article noted that women might feel "an inner urge to develop a sense of her own personal significance outside the round of home and social duties. . . . The check for her work is large enough to give her a sense of accomplishment."[154] Helen Hovey, who authored a popular advice manual for would-be women business owners in 1953, pointed out that juggling two roles—homemaker and employee—made women fill neither very well. "Yet women want to work—to raise the standard of living for themselves and their families, to find personal expression and satisfaction, and to contribute their best to community and national life," she wrote, noting that "small business enterprises in homes" enabled women to achieve these goals and more.[155]

Women took satisfaction not only from professional success but also from being adept at combining work and family obligations. Breag Cunningham, for example, who ran a real estate company, found great satisfaction in developing a streamlined system of making sales calls while doing household chores, and getting to know clients well enough to only show them houses selected for their needs. Though working forty hours a week at times, she found lessons for her children in their mother's labor. "If they're going to grow up believing that dancing lessons, cars and college are essential, they'd better learn to give a little as well as collect," she said in a 1958 *McCall's* article.[156] She started out, she said, for a little extra money to "meet emergency needs and buy the extras which her family [needed]." Over time, her business grew, with sales in 1957 topping $400,000.[157]

Similarly, for some women, business ownership provided a way out of bad situations. Rosemarie Simmons's handbag business empowered her to end her tension-filled marriage with her much older husband and proudly continue to provide a comfortable life for herself and her child. Years after her parents divorced, her now-grown daughter recalled that her mother's handbag business alone provided an upper-middle-class lifestyle for mother and daughter, complete with lavish vacations and her daughter's college education.[158] Similarly, although Shirley Konheim's success had its tensions, it may well have saved her marriage, freeing her musician husband from the burdens of providing a stable living and allowing him to pursue the music he loved.[159] And the income generated from Mary Smith's Philadelphia card and gift shop probably resulted in fewer rounds of domestic violence at the hands of her husband, recalled her daughter. Fiercely independent, Smith married late in life at age forty-four after having worked in a factory and earned enough money to buy her own home. Once she married, she had no intention of becoming dependent on a man, and that was certainly exacerbated by her husband's violent temper. "She started the business with money she had hidden away," said her daughter. "She didn't earn a lot—just some pocket money—and she had to close the store to be home in time to cook dinner. But, if she had her own money, she didn't have to ask him for money, and that meant fewer arguments."[160]

There were costs, however, as not all marriages (read: husbands) could make peace with the wife as businesswoman. Although Pauline Trigere's fashion house triumphed for decades, her marriage ended in divorce a few years after she started the company because her husband "did not want a wife who worked."[161] He walked out in 1947, leaving her with the business and their young children; she juggled both and continued to build and run her company until the late 1990s when she was ninety-three years old. While Hochberg hired her husband as president at one hundred dollars a week in 1954 and later gave him domain over her burgeoning wholesale and private label business, the couple drifted apart. "It was on a rainy day in March 1968 that I began to have serious doubts about my marriage," she wrote in her autobiography. "He looked at me as if we didn't belong to the same species. Then it hit me: perhaps we didn't. The entrepreneurial spirit was not in Sam. My drive and determination disturbed him."[162] Later that year, the marriage ended, and although the couple worked together for a year, Hochberg ultimately divided her holdings in what might initially seem unfair to her: Sam Hochberg took the thriving wholesale business, valued at $5 million, while Lillian kept the mail-order retail side worth less than $1 million. In the end, however, her business acumen won out, and within a few short years she began her steady sales climb to become one of the leading catalog businesses of its time.

The celebration of domesticity in the 1950s was not just constricting for women; rather, it could be used by women themselves as a legitimation for their extrafamilial activities. In fact, this linguistic shift is part of what makes the 1950s such an important decade in the history of women's business ownership. From this era forward, women's enterprises would be linked in large measure with their roles within the family—as something women did to combine motherhood with the need for an income. This forged a separate gendered identity for women's businesses distinct from those of their male counterparts.

Consequently, future generations of both women business owners and corporate leaders would let small business ownership become the de facto solution to the problems of increased pressure for additional household income and the need to address childcare concerns if women were to work. The 1950s justification of motherhood as a rationale for starting a business not only would solidify the link between home-based business and women's child-rearing duties, but in doing so, it dismissed questions about women's limited access to start-up capital as well as their legitimate claim to a place in the broader corporate economy. In effect, then, as the Cold War escalated, contestation over women's roles in the public and private realms, along with significant social and political trends, fueled a rethinking of women's business endeavors by the public and women themselves. Because they focused on areas that were considered "women's work"—even if they were doing it commercially—their ventures were not seen as a challenge to the idea of business as a male preserve. As a result, women's business ownership—while losing ground gained in the 1940s within the political and economic system—established itself on terra firma *outside* the system, a place it would continue to hold well into the 1970s.

The limitations of the 1950s domestic discourse fueled women's frustrations as they navigated economic inequalities. Those pent-up feelings would lead to new policy initiatives by the early 1960s and an emerging women's movement. At the same time, women who commercialized domestic skills would find that the rise of the service economy in the decades to follow would leave them well-positioned to lay claim not only to their share of the financial pie but also to the term *entrepreneur*.

3

"Doin' It for Themselves"

Gender, Race, and Women's Entrepreneurship in the Socially Conscious 1960s

It took many years, several applications, and endless perseverance before Mary Lou Redmond would secure the financing she needed in 1968 to start her soul food business.[1] A resident of Chicago's economically depressed, predominantly African American West Side, Redmond believed there was a market for, in her words, "a home-cooking place . . . especially the carry-out line like I want to start."[2] More important, she saw the business as a way to earn a living as a single mother. With six children to raise—one who faced severe mental disabilities—Redmond had been unable to work for nearly a decade and instead had little choice but to rely on government assistance (welfare) for support. She dreamed of moving from that complicated, often intrusive system to the independence, self-sufficiency, and flexible schedule of a business of her own.[3] Trained as a kitchen assistant, Redmond understood the food service industry, and she also recognized the vast market potential among the growing number of working mothers—specifically working-class women of color in her neighborhood—for prepared meals at reasonable prices. "There is no restaurant in the area to offer teen-agers [sic] good nutritious food, and young mothers sometimes like to pick something up at the end of the day," she said. Understanding too the value of affordability for Black families at the lower end of the socioeconomic spectrum, she added, "Kids don't get enough to eat today. I know what it is to take $1.05 and prepare a meal for seven mouths. My goal is to make good nutritious meals at prices people around here can afford to pay."[4]

But as someone who was poor, Black, and female, Redmond possessed none of the financial resources necessary to start a business, nor did she have access to traditional lenders, who typically preferred to make loans to white, male-owned ventures in categories they understood (i.e., that served predominantly white consumers). Instead, she turned to a new government-sponsored loan program for Black entrepreneurs via the federal Small Business Administration (SBA) designed to use business as a vehicle to address the racial disparities made visible by the civil rights movement. There too she faced biases. Much as banks did, SBA programs typically defined business in terms that favored men's ventures or what the often white men who ran these government initiatives regarded as viable business ideas, and they typically considered lending to women risky, especially women without husbands and women of color. Government programs such as Project Own that looked to Black capitalism to not only promote racial equality but also quell unrest were undoubtedly influenced by the widely publicized 1965 Moynihan Report with its bias against female-headed households.[5] As such, government Black capitalism initiatives focused almost entirely on aiding Black male entrepreneurs as potential family breadwinners and community leaders.

Nevertheless, Redmond and a few other persistent African American women did manage to secure funding through these government-sponsored initiatives, though their loans were usually small and sometimes required extra steps to obtain, such as reapplying multiple times. Redmond's application was rejected at least twice, and she spent two years volunteering at a hamburger restaurant without pay to prove her commitment to engaging in the food service industry before the SBA finally agreed to sign off on the $15,000 loan for her Soul Kitchen. In a short time, she was able to hire four employees and join an effort to reinvigorate the economically challenged and largely Black West Side. She was also part of a burgeoning new trend, the soul food segment of the restaurant industry—which white male officials at the SBA saw little promise in but Black women (and men) were successfully launching in cities nationwide throughout the civil rights era, most notably Sylvia's in Harlem, New York City, in 1962. By the 1970s, soul food restaurants became an industry mainstay, popular with Black and also increasingly white customers.[6]

By starting a business, Redmond was doing for herself what the labor market and government initiatives—even well-intentioned ones—failed to do: provide an opportunity, free of discriminatory wages and job options, to earn a living as a Black woman and a single mother. And she was not alone. In the 1960s, countless women of all races, classes, and ethnicities across America would similarly turn to business ownership in response to increasing pressure to be both mothers and earners in a rapidly changing social, political, and economic landscape, coupled with women's growing consciousness about and impatience with gender and racial inequality. For example, in 1966, Mary

FIG. 3.1 "Mary Lou Redmond" by Moneta Sleet Jr. (*Ebony*, September 1968). Shown here, Redmond is hard at work in her new soul kitchen business. *Credit:* Johnson Publishing Company Archive. Courtesy J. Paul Getty Trust and Smithsonian National Museum of African American History and Culture (made possible by the Ford Foundation, J. Paul Getty Trust, John D. and Catherine T. MacArthur Foundation, Andrew W. Mellon Foundation, and Smithsonian Institution).

Wells—a thirty-eight-year-old, white, divorced mother of two—left a lucrative advertising executive job and enviable $80,000 a year salary (roughly $771,688 in 2024, extraordinarily high wages for a woman in the 1960s) to start her own agency when her boss reneged on his promise to make her company president because she was a woman.[7] In the rural Blue Ridge Mountain town of McCaysville, Georgia, Bernice Ratcliff, Lorine Miller, and two other women turned workers' labor protests about conditions at the Levi Strauss plant into a competing textile business where women had greater flexibility, respect as workers, and increased earning potential.[8] And frustrated with the meager salary of her office job and minimal child support, divorced mother Ruth Fertel mortgaged her home to buy a steakhouse (Ruth's Chris Steak House) with the hope of earning a comfortable living so she could afford to send her growing sons to college.

Redmond's and many other women's stories illustrate the ways in which in the 1960s, individuals, activists, and the state would increasingly see in small business ownership a way to solve both personal and enduring social problems and inequities. For the history of women's business ownership, the 1960s marks a transitional and momentum-building period, serving as a bridge between the 1950s "momism" (chapter 2) and the feminism and racial equality activism that would infuse the explosive growth in women's business ownership in the 1970s and 1980s (chapters 4 and 5). In the 1960s, a wide range of social changes would forge a new relationship between women and business ownership: continued national prosperity, increased consumerism with its added pressure on household incomes, rapidly rising divorce rates and growing numbers of female-headed households, the shift from a manufacturing to a service-based economy with opportunities for commercializing women's domestic and other skills, increased civil and women's rights activism, Great Society programs, and a growing push for public policy and legislative changes to ensure equality of opportunity for women (read: white) and people of color (defined as Black and often male). In that context, when promising government initiatives such as Project Own / Black Enterprise / Compensatory Capitalism, the President's Commission on the Status of Women's 1963 report on women's unequal status, or Title VII of the 1964 Civil Rights Act failed to end job discrimination, increasingly frustrated women created solutions for themselves via independent enterprise, including companies like Redmond's or McCaysville Industries that focused on helping or providing services to other women. In business ownership, women saw the potential for a higher standard of living and better wages, ability to provide for their families, as well as control over the structure of their time and the meaning of work in their lives in ways the labor market did not. For those like Redmond, who faced the triple bind of gender and racial discrimination plus poverty, the dream of business ownership offered a way up and out of socioeconomic marginalization and, in some cases, the welfare system.

Media coverage of women's business ownership seemed to support these ideas. National publications in the 1960s increasingly featured women's ventures as either curiosities or, over time, symbols of progress (even if only on the surface or as tokens), though their stories typically appeared in racially segregated publications or described the women in sexist terms. Still, the growing attention to women in mainstream media created visibility, fostered social acceptance for these endeavors, and inspired countless others to see in business ownership a means to transform their personal circumstances. In effect, it encouraged them to buy into a reinvigorated Horatio Alger myth that muted the issues of race and gender—that is, continued discrimination in lending—that made starting a business for these groups challenging.

78 • She's the Boss

For women business owners, then, the narrow familial justifications for starting a venture that prevailed in the 1950s gave way to broader forms of legitimation in the politically and socially charged 1960s—while stopping short of the revolution and rise of activist businesses that would occur by the end of the decade into the 1970s (chapter 4). As such, the 1960s plays a more evolutionary role in the history of women's business ownership, creating the conditions that would draw more and more women to entrepreneurship in the decades that followed. The number of women business owners grew slowly and incrementally as the 1960s progressed, reaching just over 4 percent of all businesses by decade's end. But a focus on numbers alone misses a more important story: that without the foundational relationship forged between women and business ownership in the 1960s—a relationship that fused both a new "rights" consciousness with notions of individual action and responsibility—the surge in the number of women entrepreneurs in the 1970s, 1980s, and beyond may not have happened. By the end of the 1960s, a new synergy would emerge between women's quest for equality and their place in the economy as small business owners.

Rising Expectations, Limited Opportunities

By the time Mary Lou Redmond opened her soul kitchen in 1968, the country was in the midst of its longest period of economic growth. As the decade progressed, the heady optimism of the era would lead to such government initiatives as the War on Poverty and the Great Society with their wide range of programs to end social and economic inequality. For would-be entrepreneurs, the government's "Compensatory Capitalism" or Black Enterprise program that began in the late 1960s (discussed later in this chapter) sought to use business ownership as a tool for ending inequality. It would pave the way for the creation of both the Minority Business Enterprise in 1969 and Women's Business Enterprise programs a decade later—both designed to promote small business ownership and ensure equal access to government contracts for smaller, minority- and/or women-owned businesses.

Initially, though, what women of all races wanted was equal access to jobs and equitable pay; when that proved difficult, many turned to business ownership often as a way to bypass ongoing discrimination. In the years since World War II, increasing numbers of women—particularly married women—sought paid employment, only to find primarily limited, segregated, and low paid feminized options as well as a lack of available and affordable childcare. By 1960, women were 38 percent of the labor force, with more than 55 percent of them married, a trend that began in the post–World War II era. White women accounted for 40.3 percent, while women of color accounted for one of eight women who worked, and white women earned roughly 59 percent of white men's wages.[9] Significantly, women of color were still largely consigned to low-paid domestic or agricultural work. Even as more women, Black and white, sought college educations, they found few professional opportunities waiting for them after graduation. The juxtaposition of women's unchanging experiences of discrimination bumped up against the era's optimism and affluence, increasing women's frustrations. The election of John F. Kennedy, the nation's youngest president to that point with his promises of a New Frontier, led women of all races and their allies to expect that New Frontier would also be one for women.

Partly in response to women's demands, partly in gratitude for the role women voters—including women of color—played in his election, in 1961 Kennedy established his President's Commission on the Status of Women (PCSW). This was a two-year fact-finding collective of notable female leaders charged with studying the problem of gender inequality. The brainchild of assistant labor secretary and Women's Bureau director Esther Peterson, a longtime advocate for women's labor force issues, the commission began its work to much fanfare about its potential.[10] An early memo of endorsement promised, "The Commission would help the nation to set forth before the world the story of women's progress in a free, democratic society, and to move further towards full partnership, creative use of skills, and genuine equality of opportunity."[11] It was this last part—equality of opportunity—that drew women's attention and raised hopes. Women of color, who had rallied votes for Kennedy, were not only included on the commission but also a focus of study. With former First Lady Eleanor Roosevelt as chair, the commission included notable women of color such as Dorothy Height, president of the National Council of Negro Women.[12]

Two years later in 1963, the PCSW shared its data in an eighty-six-page report, *American Woman*, which validated women's mounting frustrations with the obstacles that blocked their advancement and the lack of safe, affordable childcare.[13] The report converged with the 1963 release of Betty Friedan's best-selling *Feminine Mystique*, and together they fed a simmering feminism and demands for change. The report, which received widespread media attention, noted imbalances in the types of work women did and the vastly unequal pay they received, and to this day it stands as a crucial moment in the history of public policy initiatives addressing gender inequality. It documented restrictive and biased hiring practices that led to the concentration of women in a few fields, the largest of which was clerical work, followed by service work as waitresses, beauticians, and hospital attendants, and at the professional level, nurses, teachers, and librarians.[14] The report noted that gender biases led personnel officers to "believe that women [were] less likely than men to want to make a career in industry, (as such) equally well-prepared young women [were] passed over in favor of men for posts that lead into management training programs and subsequent exercise of major executive responsibility."[15] It also noted that states passed the first equal pay laws in 1919 and that at the time of the report's publication, twenty-four states had such laws in place. Yet "women who [did] the same or comparable work as men" were still being paid much lower salaries;

women bank tellers saw wages that were five to fifteen dollars less per week than men's with the same employment histories.[16]

Even as it advocated that states establish laws ensuring equal pay, the report also reflected the tensions in the 1960s between old ideas about male bread-winners and stay-at-home mothers and the new reality of working women and single/working mothers. For example, the report simultaneously called for workforce equity while also maintaining the home and family as women's primary role: "Widening choices for women beyond their doorstep does not imply neglect of their education for responsibilities in the home," the report declared.[17] The commission also addressed the ways in which race added another layer of difficulty for women of color: "Negro women are twice as likely as other women to have to seek employment while they have preschool children at home," the report stated, adding that because of discrimination, "they [were] forced into low-paid service occupations."[18] Even as it called for eliminating the barriers posed by discrimination for all women, the report fostered the notion of freedom of choice that enabled and expected individuals in the United States to solve their own problems.

It was a fine line to walk—calling for progress while also maintaining a continuity of gender norms—but one that individuals, activists, and government officials saw as compatible. In part this was because they recognized the role of "mature women"—those whose children were already grown—in the labor force. According to the report, while more than half of all women workers were married in 1962, their average age was forty-one (in 1950, it was thirty-seven). Peterson and her team acknowledged that with women marrying at much younger ages in the 1950s and early 1960s (the average age of first marriage for women was 20.3 in 1960) and having children in succession, most would be in their thirties when their children were in school, leaving half a lifetime when they would need or want jobs.[19] For women business owners, the commission called for states to eliminate laws that imposed "legal disabilities on women" such as "restrictions on the rights of married women to contract, convey, or own real or personal property, to engage in business to act as surety or fiduciary, to receive and control her earnings."[20] Ultimately, this notion of individual responsibility coupled with the status quo regarding both gender roles and capitalism, would infuse women's decisions to shift from jobs into businesses of their own. About a month after the PCSW report was issued, Friedan attended a conference of academic and government leaders at the University of Washington to discuss how to implement the commission's recommendations.[21] At the conference, Friedan, whose book was an instant bestseller, assailed the limited role society offered women, asking, "[Are women are really] free and equal [if we are forced to choose between love and marriage and] devoting ourselves seriously to some challenge, some work of society, some interest that . . . would enable us to grow to our full individual potential, our human potential, which may or may not have anything to do with our sex role as women?"[22]

An immediate result of the PCSW was that the commission, feminists, and civil rights activists united in ensuring the passage of two crucial pieces of legislation for economic equality. The Equal Pay Act of 1963 was a direct outcome of the PCSW, followed a year later by Title VII of the 1964 Civil Rights Act. Both laws sought to legislatively eliminate job discrimination; neither would have the immediate impact activists wanted largely because both were passed via political compromises that diluted or eliminated enforcement power from the initial legislation.[23] The Equal Pay Act, for example, only guaranteed equal pay for women and men in the same jobs, an uncommon occurrence in the early 1960s. It did not include what many activists saw as a real safeguard to pay equity—comparable worth—which would have secured equal wages for men and women in similar types of jobs. The Equal Pay Act also had a deadline of 180 days from the start of the violation, after which there was no legal remedy.[24] Similarly, Title VII barred discrimination in employment on the basis of sex, race, religion, and national origin but did not gain the muscle needed to enforce these workplace rights until almost the end of the decade, driven by women's rights activists including Friedan.

In fact, ensuring the enforcement of Title VII's provisions inspired the founding of what would become the major arm of the liberal women's rights movement, the National Organization for Women (NOW). In 1966, Friedan, activist attorney and labor organizer Aileen Hernandez and civil rights activist and attorney Pauli Murray established NOW to put an end to the long practice of sex-segregated "Help Wanted" ads, which continued despite Title VII's sanction against them. From the start, NOW's focus was economic feminism; its mission, as noted in its statement of purpose, was to "bring women into full participation in the mainstream of American society now, exercising all privileges and responsibilities thereof in truly equal partnership with men." But much like the PCSW, NOW's mission statement walked the line between women's employment and household roles, seeking to "enable women to enjoy the true equality of opportunity and responsibility in society, without conflict with their responsibilities as mothers and homemakers." NOW stated, "We do not accept the traditional assumption that a woman has to choose between marriage and motherhood, on the one hand, and serious participation in industry or the professions on the other."[25] What NOW wanted was for *women* to have the freedom to choose motherhood or work—or a balance of both—and to have equal access to good jobs and fair pay. Of course, for this to happen, NOW also noted that society would have to implement "a nationwide network of child-care centers" and national training programs for women who seek to return to work after raising children full-time.

NOW's Statement of Purpose not only specifically called for "the excellent reports of the President's Commission on the Status of Women to be implemented," but it also exposed the lack of enforcement power for the PCSW's recommendations as well as the bans on employment discrimination in Title VII.

It highlighted that women of color faced the "double discrimination of race and sex." NOW noted that one-third of the early cases of discrimination came from women, including women of color, who were often consigned to the lowest-paid service occupations.[26] And it joined PCSW in exposing what would decades later come to be known as the gender pay gap, with women (presumably white women) earning 60 percent of what their male counterparts earned.

From the start, NOW was not only issuing a call to action to all women, an embrace of feminism as women's civil rights movement; it was also creating and mainstreaming an economic feminist language of equal rights and building on and borrowing from the civil rights movement to do it. Its mission statement—a recruiting document of sorts—argued, "Until now, too few women's organizations . . . have been willing to speak out. . . . Too many women have been restrained by the fear of being called 'feminist.' There is no civil rights movement to speak for women, as there has been for Negroes and other victims of discrimination. The National Organization for Women must therefore begin to speak." In its first year, NOW's membership grew rapidly to one thousand members in fourteen chapters nationwide; by 1974 that would grow to eight hundred chapters with forty thousand members, making it the leading feminist organization in the United States.[27]

Along with NOW, other women's and civil rights movements took up the challenges of inequality throughout the decade, though largely through seeking enforcement of existing laws or additional legislation to enable them to gain access to economic opportunities available to white men. In 1966, the Women's Equity Action League (WEAL) was founded by more conservative white women to ensure workplace equity as a single issue, detached from reproductive justice or the Equal Rights Amendment that NOW and other feminist groups supported. In the civil rights struggle, Martin Luther King Jr. notably shifted from emphasizing politics to economics, but for women of color, the most visible proponent of the potential for economics to bring social and political equality was activist Fannie Lou Hamer and the Freedom Farm Cooperative she began in 1969 (chapter 4). These and other activists not only showcased the power of economics—and in Hamer's case, of business ownership—to marginalized people, they also worked to ensure that Great Society initiatives, including Black capitalism, extended to women. All of this brought a language of rights/equality of opportunity that women of all races could and did tap into, even if they did not ally with these movements themselves. In many cases, it would lead more and more women to look beyond legislative or government policy initiatives to the private realm of business ownership as a solution to workplace inequality.

Women Helping Women—and Themselves—through Business Ownership

The PCSW report and the growing feminist and civil rights activism continued to expose discrimination for women who needed or wanted to work, but change was slow to materialize. As such, women turned to small business to provide opportunities for themselves and others like them. In doing so, they opted out of the problems of the workplace and into businesses of their own. They did so in the context of U.S. economic growth and a shift from a manufacturing to a service-based economy, something women were long familiar with. Many, like Redmond, started businesses designed to assist working women with domestic tasks they no longer had time to do, such as prepare meals. Others started companies to provide jobs and other services for women.

Felice Schwartz's foray into business ownership exemplifies the evolutionary, economy-centered approach taken by many women in the 1960s who saw in business ownership a chance to rectify gender disparities in corporate America. In her own life, Schwartz struggled to balance academic achievement and professional ambition with a desire for marriage and family. She interrupted her career from 1954 to 1962 to raise children, and when she wanted to go back to work, she experienced age discrimination, a bitter pill for a woman who had been successful from an early age. Schwartz graduated from Smith College in 1945 and immediately established the National Scholarship Service and Fund for Negro Students to expand opportunities for African Americans in colleges, particularly via financial aid. Over the years, she helped place 750 Black students in colleges where there had previously been few or no students of color.[28] Later, from 1951 to 1954, she took over management of a failing family metalworking company—her training ground for running a business—where she oversaw hundreds of employees and negotiated contracts with seventeen male shop stewards while pregnant with her second child.

When the youngest of her three children started school, she "met a huge number of women who had raised their children and were frustrated and very anxious about what they were going to do when their children went off to college," she would later recall.[29] This experience would prove transformative, inspiring the business she subsequently founded. Like the data in the PCSW report, Schwartz too found ageist biases that regarded these women as unnecessary and past their prime—even though many of them, including Schwartz herself, were only in their thirties or forties. With the average age of self-employed women between fifty-one and fifty-two—four years older than their male counterparts—many had bypassed discrimination by opting into ventures of their own.[30]

"I was shocked to discover how frustrated women were with their lives and even more so to see the terrible waste of talent," Schwartz explained.[31] Thriving as she did on problem-solving, in 1962, Schwartz moved her family from Cincinnati, Ohio, to the more visible New York City to launch a nonprofit company, Catalyst, Inc., to counsel women on reentering the workforce, study the difficulties they faced, and ultimately work for their professional advancement in the corporate world. Its mission was this: "To bring to our country's needs the unused abilities of educated women who want to combine work and family."[32] Run on a shoestring budget and with only one staff member, in the early days Catalyst did everything from helping women prepare resumes and find employment to slowly pushing for the value of "womanpower" to the nation's economic development.[33] Catalyst likewise set up 250 U.S. resource centers for women seeking careers.[34] Schwartz helped pioneer job-sharing programs that would allow women to combine motherhood with part-time employment by having two women split one full-time job. Schwartz convinced Boston, Massachusetts, city officials to let her firm implement job-sharing in its largely African American neighborhood of Roxbury, where Catalyst staffed twenty-five caseworker positions with fifty women.[35] Catalyst would go on to raise a $2.5 million annual budget for its research efforts from corporations and private foundations, including Sara Lee Corp. and the Mellon, Kellogg, Ford, Rockefeller, and Whitaker Foundations.[36]

In 1968 Schwartz turned her focus to the household dynamics that impeded women's quest for employment in her book *How to Go to Work When Your Husband Is against It, Your Children Aren't Old Enough and There's Nothing You Can Do Anyhow*. In the decades that followed, her firm would launch pioneering studies and programs for corporate day care, family issues in the workplace, parental leave, the problem of the glass ceiling for women's advancement to the ranks of executive and board members, and women's entrepreneurship. She would later stir controversy with her 1989 article—which critics dubbed the "Mommy Track"—in the *Harvard Business Review*. Contrary to its misleading nickname, Schwartz's essay argued for a corporate career path that allowed for both child-rearing *and* professional advancement.[37] At the time of her death in 1996, Schwartz and the company she founded had become the leading advocate of women's workplace issues.

Other women too fused their desire to increase opportunities for women with potential commercial markets—among the most obvious, employment services. While not embracing an activist agenda per se, in 1963 Audrey Cohen, age thirty, and Frankie Pelzmen, age twenty-six, teamed up to establish Part-Time Research Associates to help companies fill temporary staff needs and women find flexible work. "We act as a trained extension to a client's staff," Cohen told *Mademoiselle* magazine, noting that they had over one thousand "college-trained girls" ready to fill in on projects such as research reports for publishers, management consultants, and public relations firms. With rave reviews from clients, the firm had already "bailed out more than 125 married women."[38] The idea of temporary employment agencies, particularly for women, would continue to gain ground during the 1960s and 1970s.[39]

The problem of childcare would lead women to consider the flexibility of independent business ownership and inspire some to launch day care businesses. Books advising women on the range of part-time jobs and businesses proliferated throughout the decade, including *A Woman's Guide to Part-Time Jobs*, which was written by a man and published in 1963.[40] Similarly, the National Federation of Business and Professional Women's Clubs (BPW) held a series of "Forums for Breadwinners and Homemakers," guiding members on the types of companies open to employing women or the best businesses to start themselves. At a 1962 session, guest speaker Walter Parker of the Illinois State Employment Service advised, "As a whole, we in the employment service find smaller companies more receptive to women than the larger ones, with the exception of the hotel industry." Virginia L. Senders of the University of Minnesota Plan for the Continuing Education of Women told participants about the woman who turned her child care difficulties into a thriving cooperative, with a nursery on campus for women attending classes.[41] Some women began to open day care businesses, among them civil and later women's rights activist Dorothy Pittman Hughes in the mid-1960s. Along the same lines, Barbara Krohn, a book editor with Houghton Mifflin seeking to maintain her career even as she planned for maternity leave, saw in business a solution for her own and other women's needs. She founded a literary agency specializing in juvenile fiction among other book categories.[42]

From urban areas to the far corners of rural America, women began to help other women and to assert their political claims through their roles as business owners. In 1969, five women from the Appalachian / Blue Ridge Mountain region of McCaysville, Georgia, squared off against apparel manufacturing giant Levi-Strauss & Co. when they launched their own garment-making firm. Pooling their very limited resources, Lorine and Madelyn Miller, Bernice Ratcliff, and Eva Chancey opened a small piece-work factory. In 1966, these women joined many others in taking on the denim giant as part of a fourteen-month long wildcat strike over unfair labor practices. When it was over, they decided that returning to long days within a system many considered at best unfair and at worst inhumane was hardly a victory. Instead, they sought to build a garment business that spurred productivity by respecting the needs of female employees as working mothers and their integrity as human beings. Gone were restrictions on when women could take bathroom breaks or step away to phone home to check on children. McCaysville's founders also let employees make up missed work if they needed to care for a sick family member. Though they would face economic hardship and attempts by huge conglomerates to swallow up their company, these women were determined to make a go of their female-defined business—even if it meant some of these "mountain women" would have to supplement their meager earnings by raising hogs and keeping a garden for food.[43] They bought a building of their own a few years later—a former chicken hatchery—which they converted into their factory, and they secured contracts with major companies such as J.C. Penney and Sears.

But as garment production increasingly moved offshore in the late 1970s and early 1980s, McCaysville struggled. Still, Ratcliff especially fought to keep the business going because of what it meant to the women who worked there, recalled her daughter Linda Whittenbarger who worked for her mother when she was in high school and beyond: "They were paying everybody else, but they didn't get paid." By the early 1980s, "they were tired of fighting the battles, trying to keep the bills paid—it was just an uphill struggle, so they decided to dissolve the partnership and sold the business," Whittenbarger explained.[44] Although not a part of the women's movement, their business strategy of empowering and respecting women as workers ultimately proved the far-reaching impact of feminism. Their story was showcased in a feminist television show on PBS in the mid-1970s, and they were included in a book on the struggles, strength, and determination of rural Appalachian women.

The same year Friedan articulated the emptiness felt by a generation of women in her 1963 book, Mary Kay Ash saw in direct sales the opportunity for a beauty business for herself and flexible—and potentially lucrative—opportunities for mothers in need of an income. Ash had once been a single mother. Married as a young woman, her husband returned from World War II asking for a divorce, leaving Ash to support her three children by selling cleaning supplies at in-home demonstrations for Stanley Home Products.[45] There, she learned about the flexibility of the home-demonstration system for women who needed or wanted to generate an income.

Ash purchased the skin care formula she had used for years from a tanner's daughter, who formulated the cream from a treatment used to soften animal hides. It became the centerpiece of her Basic Set of a cleanser, freshener, and skin cream. When her second husband died a month before Ash was to launch her company, she hesitated until her son gave her both a gentle push and a loan for nearly $5,000 in start-up funds.[46] Within three years, her business grew from one small store into an $800,000-a-year direct sales venture. By 2001, she would have 475,000 sales associates, helping to generate retail sales of $2 billion. While Ash's business would face accusations of being a pyramid scheme in the 2010s,[47] in 2023, sixty years after its founding, the company was named the top direct-selling business in the United States by Euromonitor International, with representatives in over fifty countries and estimated sales in the billions.[48]

Ash succeeded early on because she effectively built the difficulties single and working mothers faced into her corporate philosophy. Wrote Ash years later, "So often a woman will join us who is in desperate need of hearing this message. Frequently, she is a homemaker who has been out of the job market for years. Perhaps she *never* worked outside the home; and now, because of divorce or widowhood she finds herself seeking a career . . . For whatever the

FIG. 3.2 Textile mill workers and owners (left to right) Bernice Ratcliff, Lorine Miller, and Eva Chancey, who worked to keep their McCaysville Industries garment factory running (circa 1980). Copyright © *Atlanta Journal-Constitution*. Courtesy of Special Collections and Archives, Georgia State University Library.

reason, she often needs to build her feelings of self-esteem and worth."[49] Her company motto, "You can do it!" was meant to inspire her recruits, as were incentives to top sellers from cars and cash to the company's signature diamond Bumble Bee pins.[50]

Making It on Their Own: The Single Mother / Divorced Woman Entrepreneur

As Ash, Schwartz, and other women were acutely aware, rising divorce rates and accompanying single motherhood provided its own rationale for both working women and especially would-be business owners. The divorce rate nearly doubled in a single decade from a total of 393,000 divorces and annulments in 1960 to 708,000 in 1970.[51] Many women found themselves in need of jobs for the first time since before they were married, only now they had children to support as well. Although many states had removed the antimarriage laws that blocked married women from jobs by the 1960s, hiring biases continued and were most pronounced against divorced women and single mothers. While still a small percentage of the population—the rates of single motherhood were also beginning to climb during the 1960s, with 9 percent of children living in single parent households compared to one in twenty a decade earlier. (By 1980, 20 percent of children would live in single-parent homes.)[52] Many became single mothers as a result of divorce or widowhood, but a growing number included women who never married. Raising children on their own, sometimes without financial assistance from their children's fathers, women struggled to find jobs with decent salaries. For many, given the typically feminized and low-paid job options for women, business ownership was a far better and more lucrative opportunity.

In 1958, when New Orleans, Louisiana, native Ruth Fertel's marriage came to an end, she reentered the job market, landing a $4,800 annual salary as a lab technician for Tulane University. That may have paid the bills, but Fertel knew it would not allow her to send her two teenage boys to college—even with financial contributions from her ex-husband. Instead, by 1965, she regarded independent enterprise as offering the solution to her approaching fiscal crisis. She combed the classified ads for businesses that were for sale and mortgaged her house to raise $18,000 to buy an ailing steakhouse. The thirty-eight-year-old had no restaurant experience when she took over as owner of Chris Steak House but trusted her instincts. "My attorney thought I was crazy for mortgaging my home," she recalled years later, "The first years were long hours, especially the first few months when I was learning everything, even the butchering."[53] In fact, the petite Fertel would use a heavy electric saw in butchering the sides of beef, laying on the floor to rest after each exhausting section.

Celebrity divorcees such as Sybil Burton added heightened visibility to business ownership as a survival strategy. Burton became the object of public sympathy when her actor husband, Richard Burton, abandoned her after fourteen years of marriage and two children for co-star Elizabeth Taylor in the early 1960s. But if mainstream America took pity on her, Burton was quick to prove the gesture unnecessary. In 1965, she was labeled both "heroine" and "Girl of the Year" by *Esquire* magazine for "triumphantly opening Arthur, the discotheque to end them all."[54] In the age of the jet-set, Burton hit on the right idea at the right time. More than that, she developed a clever financing scheme to get the business off the ground, one that also fueled media curiosity. In the months immediately following her divorce, Burton spent time at a club called the Strollers, and when it began floundering, she decided to buy it and convert it into the Arthur. She tapped celebrity friends such as Sammy Davis Jr., Julie Andrews, and Mike Nichols to become investors for $1,000 per share and raised the $80,000 necessary to renovate and redesign the space with an El Morocco motif. The club, which served British pub-style snacks and drinks, was such a hit that three years later in 1968, she was planning to expand nationally by selling franchises for $100,000.[55] But for Burton, who in 1965 married musician Jordan Christopher (more than ten years her junior), the Arthur enabled her to prove, as *Esquire* would point out, "that you don't have to be a combination of Scarlett O'Hara, Becky Sharp, and Cleopatra to survive a personal disaster."[56]

Whether divorced, widowed, or otherwise raising children alone, single mothers struggled to balance the need to make a living with the lack of widely available and affordable childcare, something the PCSW report noted as early as

1963. For many, small business ownership, especially ventures they could start and run from home, filled the void. June Harrison, for example, was widowed with nine children in the mid-1960s in suburban Palatine, Illinois, when her husband succumbed to a twelve-year illness. Taking an office job—or really any job with regular hours—proved difficult. She tried combining babysitting with taking in ironing, but when she advertised with a flier at the local supermarket, state officials told her she would need a license. Instead, she started a telephone answering service from her home.[57] Harrison found a community of women willing to help her; another woman with a nine-to-five answering service let her observe how her business was set up, for example. With no start-up capital at all, Harrison struck a deal with the Illinois Bell telephone company to lease the equipment she needed on the condition she agree to a five-year contract. Along with her high school daughter Mary Ellen, who Harrison considered her business partner, she hired several women to work the twenty-nine phone lines, collecting eight thousand messages per month. Customers paid a monthly fee for the first seventy-five calls and a dime for each message thereafter.

Gender sometimes dictated how women business owners recast themselves and their ventures during and after their marriages ended. Though married at the time she planned to start her direct sales cosmetics company, Mary Kay Ash tapped into her past as a divorced mother in the origin story of her business. Catalog magnate Lillian Vernon said her 1968 divorce made her a single mother; she later explained, "[In some ways this] gave me an advantage: I had a first-hand understanding of the needs of the women who worked for me." At a time when such moves were unheard of, she implemented policies that included flexible hours, work-at-home options, four-month pregnancy leave, and tuition reimbursement.[58]

A woman's status as a divorcee could, in fact, create a kind of economic, if not political, consciousness that shaped her relationship to and understanding of business ownership. Fertel, who built a business that by 1976 included franchises and had sales of $130 million by the mid-1980s, often attributed her success in part to the public's response to her status as a struggling divorcee. "I think maybe in the beginning that my customers, who were ninety-nine percent men, felt sorry for me," she repeated to reporters in several articles. "They knew I was divorced; they knew I had two teen-age boys. They saw me doing everything, butchering, cooking, waiting tables. They wanted me to succeed not only because I was working hard but because they loved my product. Because of that, being a woman helped."[59] It is impossible to say whether men really did treat divorcees more compassionately in business. But for women like Fertel—especially women newly alone after a divorce—embracing such notions undoubtedly mediated any insecurities they felt competing in the previously male realm of business.

Some men, seeing the difficulties divorced mothers faced, did become advocates of a sort. Jane Faul started first a secretarial service that quickly became a typesetting and printing business in 1965 after her divorce. Now a single mother, Faul needed to borrow money from a bank to keep her home and get the typesetting business going. She recalled, "[Loan officer Jack Collins] trusted me when I didn't have a job, had four children, had been ill, and I said to him, 'I'm going to start a business.'" Not only did he convince the bank's board to approve the loan, but when building inspectors saw that Faul was running the venture from her home—which violated local ordinances—they decided to look the other way: "They went into the kitchen. There were two ducks in a box there because it was a little early in the year and we couldn't put them out yet . . . the collie was sitting in the middle of the kids, and one of the cats brought in a snake. . . . After that, the inspectors turned friendly." Such kindness aside, a woman's status as a divorcee remained a liability, especially in the financial community in the years before the 1974 Equal Credit Opportunity Act. When Faul sought and eventually received a $700 loan for her growing venture, she said, "The bank where I had banked since I was 15 said, 'Let's see now, you're divorced.' It was ridiculous that they would begin with me being divorced, and it was very discouraging."[60]

Black Capitalism and Women's Business Ownership

As the 1960s progressed, policymakers increasingly embraced the notion that the "small business track" might lead to greater economic equality across racial lines. Influenced largely by the demands of both the civil and welfare rights movements, President Lyndon Johnson's administration initiated a number of antipoverty programs including the 1964 Economic Opportunity Act, which in turn spurred the Equal Opportunity Loan Program run by the Small Business Administration.[61] Beginning in 1964, the Small Business Administration (SBA) inaugurated what then-director Howard J. Samuels labeled a program of "compensatory capitalism."[62] The idea was to provide loans to help "the poor in depressed neighborhoods to become self-employed and to put struggling little firms on a sounder footing."[63] First, the agency raised the maximum loan from $15,000 to $25,000. Then the SBA focused on the larger goal of increasing the number of loans for Black businesses from 1,700 per year to 10,000 in the first year—which it did—and 20,000 the second year of the program, officially labeled "Project Own."[64] The goal was also to provide funding to those who might otherwise not qualify for loans because they lacked collateral.

Although not designed for women per se, African American women would nonetheless seek to benefit from SBA loan programs, as the case of Redmond noted earlier demonstrated. Before the mid-1960s, the SBA loan program had a spotty record, not to mention a clear bias favoring white men. In its brief history, the SBA rarely granted loans to women and almost never to African American women. Most women-owned businesses were started on a shoestring, typically using family savings or credit. But barely ten years after its 1953 founding, the agency underwent a transition that would shape its scope and social role for decades to come.[65]

Like most policymakers and reform-minded activists, Samuels fully believed in the potential of American capitalism to use prosperity to correct its past mistakes. While business held a strong symbolic position for Black Americans, they owned less than 3 percent of the nation's businesses.[66] Samuels saw room for improvement and toured the country to make speeches to local civic groups. He sought out the press, promoting the new loan program in magazines from the African American *Ebony* to mainstream business publications such as *BusinessWeek*.[67] He spoke openly about the agency's past imbalances. Upon taking the helm of the SBA, he said he noticed that "of the $800-million in SBA-backed loans the previous year, only $30 million had gone into black and Spanish-American businesses."[68] To Samuels, capitalism worked—it just needed to pull in wider segments of the population; increased financial wealth for minoritized groups would solve the problem of racial and ethnic inequality, or so the logic went.

Everyone, from civic leaders to journalists, saw the vast potential politically and economically from these business incentive programs. Whitney M. Young Jr., head of the National Urban League, wrote, "Wide scale support for black businesses—either of entrepreneurs or preferably of cooperative and community-run corporations—will help create an economically secure managerial class as exists within the white community. . . . There is a pride and dignity in ownership that must be satisfied within the black community as it is within the white."[69] Others, such as Mayor Richard Hatcher of Gary, Indiana, agreed about the importance of enterprise to bring previously excluded groups into the mainstream of the American economy: "What we must concern ourselves with is motivation . . . approaches that give the member of a minority group a meaningful stake in the system. America's a pretty good idea. Now it's time for us to try it," Hatcher told the *Saturday Review* in 1969.[70]

Cities and states also recognized the potential of assistance programs to would-be minority business owners. In New York City, the Bedford-Stuyvesant Restoration Corporation, co-founded by Robert F. Kennedy years earlier, had already helped thirty-two Black-owned businesses get started in fields ranging from manufacturing to a car dealership.[71] In 1969, San Francisco launched a minority loan program made up of funds jointly capitalized by a corporate sponsor and the SBA.[72] And in 1964, inspired by the SBA programs, Howard University's Small Business Guidance and Development Center became one of nineteen facilities aiding Black businessmen from poor areas. Women benefited from these programs as well, such as fashion designer Carrie L. Simon and beautician Delores Washington, who were among the women mentioned in press accounts of these initiatives.[73]

In Pittsburgh, Roberta Lewis was among those rare African American women, like Redmond, to receive an SBA loan under the agency's new mantle of openness. Trumpeted in a three-page article in *Ebony* as an example of the opportunities for economic independence via small business ownership, Lewis opened her specialty hors d'oeuvres shop in June 1967 with a $10,000 SBA loan and quickly became the celebrated doyenne of the local catering industry. Within months, this "sandy-haired grandmother" moved from catering local parties and selling at retail her Swedish meatballs, barbecued beef tips, and cranberry muffins topped with sausage to providing ninety thousand to one hundred thousand hot hors d'oeuvres a month to Allegheny Airlines for its in-flight cocktail hours. Working fifteen hours a day, Lewis and her team of eleven also sold hors d'oeuvres from her shop to passersby along with a wholesale allotment to the gourmet shop at Kaufmann's department store. The success of her business made Lewis something of a local celebrity: she was invited to speak and give food demonstrations at women's club meetings and was featured regularly as an expert in television shows and commercials. But missing from the fanfare that surrounded her was the difficulty she faced, largely as a result of ongoing racial bias, in securing SBA-backed funding and assistance.

Like Redmond, mentioned at the start of this chapter, it was Lewis's steadfastness—and *not* the obvious market potential of her venture—that eventually landed her the SBA loan she needed to start her business. "What impressed me most about Mrs. Lewis was the way she worked so hard to advance herself," noted C. L. Hapgood of the Pittsburgh SBA office, who approved her application. "She had spent 23 years perfecting her product and trying to get it on the market." Lewis had been a cook since she was twelve years old, working in hotel kitchens and catering gala events while honing her skills, later maintaining a marriage, raising four children, and contemplating how she might one day run her own business.[74]

For SBA officials, Lewis was in many ways the perfect example of what was possible with their loan program and, by association, the potential of business ownership to transform lives. But the way officials shared Lewis's story also revealed racial stereotypes and biases. In 1968, the Pennsylvania office of the SBA selected her as its "Small Businessman of the Year" from a pool of two hundred, describing her as both a person of integrity and a "classic example of disadvantage." In explaining her selection, Pittsburgh's SBA director Fern Thomassy hailed this respectable and elegant Black woman as someone who triumphed over "the disadvantages of poverty, a broken home, and lack of formal education" as well as "the additional disadvantages of sex and race" to put herself through hotel management school and become "a person of remarkable charm, poise, and dignity."[75]

These accounts did not share how Lewis turned experiences of racial bias into learning opportunities that would form the foundation of her catering business. As a teen working as a low-paid and poorly treated domestic in white households, Lewis said, "[I] learned everything I could on their grocery bill. And I learned I can talk to food and it answers me."[76] Also missing was the fact that she

FIG. 3.3 Roberta Lewis by G. Marshall Wilson (*Ebony*, March 1968). Lewis was one of the rare women of color to receive an SBA loan for her catering business and included a major airline among her clients. *Credit:* Johnson Publishing Company Archive. Courtesy J. Paul Getty Trust and Smithsonian National Museum of African American History and Culture (made possible by the Ford Foundation, J. Paul Getty Trust, John D. and Catherine T. MacArthur Foundation, the Andrew W. Mellon Foundation, and Smithsonian Institution).

had not yet been able to draw a salary for herself. Worse, despite her hard work and praise from the airline, within eighteen months, Allegheny offered its business to a national airline catering service, costing Lewis a sizable and important chunk of her business and forcing her to reduce her staff and cater weddings and private parties to survive.[77]

Most applicants for SBA loans did not receive the accolades—or the funding—that Lewis did. Even as it sought to provide greater assistance to people of color, the SBA at times resisted funding ethnically Black enterprises. It was far more difficult for an African American entrepreneur of any sex to obtain government loans for a soul kitchen, ethnic restaurant, or boutique than it would have been to open a traditional grocery store. When Redmond applied for the loan for her Soul Kitchen, she recounted, "They didn't like my idea at first—the idea of establishing a soul food place. SBA didn't think there was a need for a 'soul' restaurant in this neighborhood. Because I'm a woman, with no husband, they didn't think I could run it. . . . After I went through all this red tape, they still made me wait . . . and they still could have refused me." Some thought the SBA was influenced by white notions of what constituted a legitimate business and offered preferential treatment to whites seeking assistance or loans. In particular, Black people believed they were subjected to longer waiting periods between the application and acceptance of a loan, and their requests were scrutinized more closely. The lengthy SBA application, slow review process, and lack of assistance beyond financing engendered further distrust for the agency. "Black people feel these delays are a form of discrimination—especially since whites seem to get their money so much faster," said Bernetta Howell, program coordinator with the Chicago Economic Development Corporation, an SBA affiliate that worked with African American business owners. "Some people claim that the agency conducts a different kind of investigation for Negroes."[78]

People whose applications were rejected by the SBA charged the agency with catering only to the poorest of the poor or abandoning them after turning over the money. Eugene and Katherine Alexander were declined a $14,000 loan to expand their fledgling Parliament Recording Studio and Electronics Shop in Chicago. "We are the only Negroes in this city who tape and press records," they told reporters at the time. "But the SBA never even came to see our store. They never even had the courtesy to send us a letter of refusal." Instead, they averred, "SBA wouldn't give us money because they knew we would make it. They gave us the runaround. We know several Negroes who started grocery stores and had no trouble getting money. What happened to them? They failed. The whole theory behind SBA is 'See? We're trying to help these people, but they're just not ready.'"[79]

Making policy changes was one thing; opening the minds of the people who implemented them was another. Even Samuels admitted, "Some change in attitude is required. Not enough bankers know how to judge black loan applicants who come from a different world."[80] Redmond felt simultaneously cast adrift and under parietal control after her loan was approved. "The SBA has given me no guidelines," she lamented. "They put my loan money in the bank and in order to get one dollar of it I have to make a formal requisition. . . . There is so much pressure to running a business. I feel if the SBA would advise me more, I'd be able to go ahead. But I don't think they have faith in me because I am a Negro."[81] Redmond's Soul Kitchen grew in its first few years and even overcame lost revenue when 1966 racial protests in the West Side of Chicago caused a power outage for days and $1,500 in spoiled food. While the upheaval raised Redmond's consciousness about the links between economic success and civil rights, her business never reached her dream of frozen packaged foods. By the early 1970s, there were scant references to her business in the local press, and she was left out of a feature article in 1974 in the *Chicago Tribune* about the "new trend" for soul food restaurants—a sign that she may no longer have been in business.[82]

Despite its goals, the SBA's compensatory capitalism initiative struggled to have the desired effect on racial advancement. The program was hindered in part by a higher-than-expected failure rate, which inspired infighting and accusations. Leaders immediately placed the blame on both their own zealousness in granting capital to poor Blacks and the recipients' lack of training for such a weighty responsibility. After 33 percent of the $82 million in loans designed to turn poor Blacks into entrepreneurs ended in default, Samuels revised the program to focus on the "middle-class, college-trained Negroes with enough business experience to give them real potential for success."[83] Of course, this meant less funding for the neediest cases, where business ownership might radically change an individual's economic circumstances.

Still, efforts to spur "Black capitalism" would remain a central tenet of political agendas well into the early 1970s, although with adjustments along the way. Richard Nixon, for example, included racially oriented self-employment programs as part of his 1968 presidential campaign platform. Once elected, he inaugurated such initiatives as the Local Business Development Organization, Minority Enterprise Small Business Investment Companies, Business Resource Centers, and the Office of Minority Business Enterprise in 1969. This last, known as the Minority Business Enterprise (MBE) program, became the cornerstone of a kind of affirmative action policy for would-be and existing entrepreneurs when it was launched. Still in existence, the MBE required that the federal government set aside a portion of its lucrative contracts for businesses where a member of a minority held a 51 percent controlling interest. Hailing the MBE's mission and potential, Nixon said, "To foster the economic status and the pride of members of our minority groups we must seek to involve them more fully in our private enterprise system . . . not only as workers, but also as managers and owners." That meant removing such obstacles as access to credit and other assistance.[84] The Carter administration launched its gender-based counterpart, the WBE (Women's Business Enterprise), ten years later.[85]

Nonetheless, the SBA did launch some programs that appealed to would-be women business owners of all racial and ethnic backgrounds in the 1960s—even if they weren't designed with them in mind. The same year it revised its loan program, the SBA looked to enhance training initiatives. Started in 1964 and continuing today, the SBA's SCORE program (Service Corps of Retired Executives) was an elite group of volunteers who met with and advised would-be entrepreneurs about the marketing potential and growth strategies for their ventures. While the agency had no official charge to seek out women in particular, the programs were open and attended by potential and existing female business owners.[86]

These SBA initiatives no doubt accounted for at least part of the reason the BPW would urge its members in 1964 to consider the SBA a funding resource for their business ventures.[87] Though the agency's history of lending to women of all races was spotty, the BPW accepted the agency's claim that up to 25 percent of its loans had gone to women, with many starting as low as $6,000. The women's group used that figure, dubious though it was, to encourage its membership to apply for SBA loans to start or expand businesses.[88] In truth, the actual rate of loans to women was probably much lower, but such figures shed a positive light on the potential to finance a venture using government and institutional sources.

Staking a Claim in a Man's World

The changing political climate and the rising consciousness of civil and women's rights empowered many women to challenge the status quo in the 1960s—even if they preferred to work through capitalism to do it. The advent of the birth control pill in 1960 enabled more women to pursue college educations and professional careers first and have children later than in the previous decades. Whether married, single, widowed, or divorced, by the mid-1960s, women not only sought jobs in traditionally—and at times exclusively—male fields such as finance or advertising; they also launched businesses in these areas. Without question, the Equal Pay Act in 1963 and Title VII in 1964—along with ongoing and visible challenges to discrimination from NOW and other women's activist groups—empowered more and more women to feel they deserved the opportunity to work in any profession for which they were qualified, including traditionally male professions. They also expected to be fairly compensated and fairly rewarded for their efforts, and when that did not materialize, starting businesses of their own proved a viable and profitable option with potentially limitless possibilities.

Notable examples include Julia Montgomery Walsh and Phyllis Peterson, who broke a 116-year tradition in 1965 when they became the first women on the American Stock Exchange—one of the oldest in the United States—and Muriel Siebert, who in 1967 became the first woman to own a seat on the rival New York Stock Exchange (NYSE). Breaking in was one thing; moving up the ranks was another. Most faced limited mobility, lower salaries, and a chilly, often sexist or condescending reception from male colleagues and superiors—even when they generated big profits for their employers. "Six percent of the registered reps at the time were women," Siebert recalled of her early years in the male-dominated financial services industry. Rather than hail them as trailblazers, Siebert added that male colleagues "assumed that female brokers got their business from sleeping around."[89]

Even Walsh, who was hailed in *Time* magazine in 1966 as the highest-paid woman in America with her six-figure salary of $200,000 a year, knew she earned less than she would as a man.[90] What's more, articles described Walsh and Petersen's entry into the American Stock Exchange as "invading" a man's world or "crashing an exclusive party." Headlines also underscored that they were "moms" first, as was the case with the *Des Moines Tribune*'s "How Two Mothers Rose to the Pinnacle of Business Life."[91] The women's familial lives defied such traditional norms, however. "I have always felt more at home in the stock market than the supermarket," Walsh later recalled of her success.[92] Walsh in 1959 became general partner at Ferris & Co., the only woman to hold such a role at an NYSE company in D.C. By 1977, not only would she open her own firm, but she would call it Walsh & Sons, a moniker that was a twist on an old male mainstay.[93]

Siebert, an Ohio native who left college after two years when her father died, further challenged the white male preserve that was the New York Stock Exchange.[94] She decided to make this move after years of frustration with her low pay compared to that of her male colleagues. Seeking advice, she asked a male client and trusted friend, " 'What large firm can I go to and get credit for the business I am doing?' . . . he answered bluntly, 'There's no where you can go. Buy a seat on the exchange and work for yourself.' "[95] Though she would ultimately become the first woman to be seated on the exchange, the establishment was not eager to let that happen. First, she had to find a sponsor, and the men she approached worried that by assisting her, they would alienate their male colleagues. She was rejected by nine of the ten men she initially approached, and her former employer tried to block her admission by bad-mouthing her.[96] Her sponsors were then quizzed about her personal life with questions not asked about male applicants. After she had the necessary signatures, the stock exchange added a new condition. They told Siebert they would only consider her application if she obtained a letter from a bank saying it would lend her $300,000 "of the near-record" $450,000 seat price—something no man had been required to do.[97] But banks refused to commit to the loan until the stock exchange approved her membership, causing a stalemate that lasted several months until she found a lender.[98] "Whenever you break a tradition that's 187 years old, not everybody's going to love you," Siebert would later recount.[99] Still, Siebert gained a seat on the NYSE on December 28, 1967. Over the years, she achieved other firsts, including that of first discount brokerage owned by a woman, where she hired countless women who wanted to work on Wall Street and drew interest from widows with big inheritances who needed an adviser they could trust.[100] Siebert later served as New York State superintendent of banks from 1977 to 1985, one of the most trouble-filled times for the state's banks in decades.

For more than ten years, Mary Wells had ascended to the top ranks of the advertising world, and in 1966, she was working at the prestigious Jack Tinker & Partners in New York City. There, the newly divorced mother of two daughters earned a whopping $60,000 annual salary (equal to nearly $579,000 in 2024 dollars).[101] But after making a name for herself and her employer on such innovative national campaigns as Alka Seltzer, Wells wanted the big promotion to president, which her boss Marion Harper had promised her and she thought she deserved.[102] Instead, Harper offered her the salary and power of the president, but *not* the title. "It's not my fault, Mary," she recalled him saying. "The world is not ready for women presidents. You have worked so hard to make Jack

98 • She's the Boss

Tinker & Partners what it is, so many people are dependent on you for what the agency can become, you wouldn't want to limit the agency's future just for a title."[103]

Wells understood that no matter what she achieved, she would never advance further or make it to the executive suite at his company or, most likely, other advertising companies. So Wells quit her job and lured two of her best male colleagues (Richard Rich and Stuart Greene) to join her in starting a new agency, Wells Rich Greene, where she was both president and chief executive officer. Any anxiety associated with such a risky move was soon dispelled by a male mentor's accurate prediction that clients—particularly her biggest client, Braniff Airlines—would follow her with its $6.5 million account. Considered a pioneer in a daring new style of advertising, Wells had earned a reputation as the woman who turned the faltering Braniff around with a somewhat risky ad campaign—"The end of the plain plane"—that included painting its airplanes Easter egg colors. Stewardesses' uniforms were updated with a high fashion, Emilio Pucci–designed layered look featuring "apricot-colored outercoats and [sic] brightly patterned stretch pants with hats to match." Television ads described the outfits as "the air strip" for their versatility in going from day to evening—showcasing a mock striptease as a way to demonstrate.[104] With the Braniff account secured, Wells handily landed a $100,000 bank loan to get her business off the ground—a rare coup for a would-be woman business owner in the 1960s.[105]

In launching her agency, Wells managed to sidestep the discrimination she faced as an employee and prove Harper wrong. Businesses *did* want to deal with a woman president—at least a woman with Wells's track record for helping clients make lots of money. Her company rose to the top ranks of the advertising world at lightning speed, and she quickly became the darling of the national business media, appearing, as very few women had, on the business pages of *Newsweek*, *Fortune*, and *BusinessWeek*. Journalists seemed fascinated by the novelty of a successful woman with what they termed her blonde "bombshell" good looks who could keep pace with the big boys of corporate America—all while raising two daughters.[106] There was little mention of all the behind-the-scenes help with her children and boarding schools she could afford so she could focus on her business. Within six months, Wells landed several high-profile accounts, including Benson & Hedges cigarettes and Burma Shave, placing her company among the top fifty largest advertising agencies in the United States with total billings of $28.5 million—a figure that would triple by decade's end.[107]

In 1968, Wells took her company public at $17.50 per share, netting $3.5 million herself (equal to almost $31.7 million in 2024 dollars) by selling a portion of her shares. She would continue to earn fame by developing some of the best-known ad slogans of the 1960s and 1970s, such as the one-liner—"I love New York"—that recast New York City's bleak image as an economically bankrupt metropolis in the 1970s into a tourist haven in the years that followed.[108] The business Wells founded would dominate the industry well into

FIG. 3.4 Mary Wells at ease and in charge in the male-dominated world of advertising. *Credit:* Susan Wood, Hulton Archive, via Getty Images.

the 1990s, with its colorful leader gaining notoriety as much for her personal escapades—like marrying Braniff CEO Harding Lawrence a year after launching her business—as for her tough-as-nails business acumen.[109]

While many of these women understood their roles as trailblazers challenging gender norms, not all identified as feminists or joined women's liberation groups per se. In part, this may have been an expedient move, walking the line between breaking barriers and the pragmatism of working with men every day (gaining acceptance by seeming not to be radicals or feminists). "When I started to work, I had to succeed by my own talents and abilities, years before the women's liberation movement," Walsh later recalled. "The words 'sex discrimination' weren't in our vocabulary."[110] By the early 1970s, Walsh, a devout Catholic, began to make connections with the women's movement, inviting feminists Betty Friedan, Gloria Steinem, and others to a brainstorming session at her home. She also helped establish a business program at the all-women's Simmons College in 1975.[111] Siebert lived her feminism by blazing trails and supporting women's issues and groups; only later in life would she make clear her allegiance to feminist causes associated with women's advancement. All these women, though, by the 1980s would become symbols for that decade's careerist feminism.

The Woman Entrepreneur in the Press

In the 1960s, the press seemed to warm to women's ventures, portraying them as big dreams born of creative and ambitious minds—a sort of female Horatio

100 • She's the Boss

Alger (rags to riches) story. At the same time, however, there was a clear gender bias in coverage in both the language and description of their ventures, as if the writers were surprised or amused by women's achievements. Reporters also highlighted the appearance of the women in both flattering and unflattering terms according to standards of femininity. While women's businesses were sometimes discussed in mainstream and business magazines of the 1940s and 1950s, writers typically characterized their ventures as almost quaint, such as selling fruitcake or salad dressing just to buy those little extras. They were depicted as home-based and likely to stay that way, lasting only as long as a need existed, and they were covered primarily in women's magazines or women's/lifestyle pages of newspapers and mainstream magazines—with the exception of Tupperware's marketing genius Brownie Wise, who was the first woman on the cover of *BusinessWeek* in 1954.[112] But with the changing social climate of the 1960s, with more women like Wells and Siebert breaking into previously male bastions, the mainstream press not only started to cover women's accomplishments but, in doing so, also tacitly (or unintentionally) encouraged women business owners to have even greater ambitions for their ventures than previous generations. Although much of the focus in mainstream media was on white women business owners, some Black women also garnered attention. Here too there was a tone in keeping with racial and gender norms.

In mainstream newspapers and magazines, the often-white women business owners were dubbed "career-minded wives" and "budding tycoons."[113] The choice of these labels is significant both for the praise and visibility they offered their subjects and for the distance they maintained from full parity with men's businesses. Women's ventures were described in flattering terms and increasingly as having big prospects, like Wells's company. There were even references after the mid-1960s to business ownership as an alternative to the gender bias that kept women from advancing in the corporate world—labeled "the glass ceiling" decades later. One magazine described these new female business owners this way: "Many had jobs, and found dead ends and frustration in a man's world, where they were blocked out of top positions because they were *women*."[114] Nonetheless, the pairing of the words *career* and *wife* demonstrated a reminder of women's familial obligations. Labeling them "budding"—but not complete—tycoons kept women in a diminutive place, playing catch-up to the "real" (read: male) tycoons.

Still, even business magazines, which had long ignored women as business owners, began giving them a closer look in the 1960s. In 1966, for example, *Newsweek* ran a three-page spread entitled "Women at the Top." Among the female executives profiled was the enterprising wife and mother Constance Boucher, a "40-year-old platinum blonde who [ran] Determined Productions, Inc., a $2 million-a-year San Francisco novelty and publishing house." In truth, Boucher had spearheaded what would decades later become a mainstay of commercial wholesaling and retailing: licensing. Boucher built her firm on the hunch that children would want to have giant-sized coloring books and toys based on their favorite storybook characters. She paid $500 for the exclusive rights to market Winnie the Pooh merchandise and later arranged a royalty deal for exclusive rights to Charles Schultz's popular Peanuts characters.[115] Her hunch continued to pay off well into the 1990s.

In the not-yet-fully sensitized 1960s, appearance mattered in how the press and corporate world responded to women business owners: they favored attractive women like Wells and Boucher, whereas Jean Nidetch, who founded Weight Watchers International in 1961, received barely a mention in the mainstream press before the late 1960s. When they did begin to write about her, the often-male reporters had little to say about her business acumen. Instead, they were far more interested in describing how fat she had once been (214 lbs.), how much weight she had lost (72 lbs.), her ability to consume copious quantities of food ("stuffing herself with box after box of chocolate-covered marshmallow cookies"), and the fact that her firm's mission was to likewise help "other fat friends" overcome their propensity to overeat.[116]

Media coverage demonstrated that the progress of the 1960s existed within the context of gender norms. For example, the increasing public comfort with women as emerging business owners came in part from articles depicting them in partnerships with their husbands or in traditionally feminine categories, selling the services or products women had long provided their families for free. As debates raged on about women's work lives, husband-wife partnerships had the air of public acceptance that would elude the average working woman who took a job. In partnership with her spouse, a woman still outwardly represented her role within the family—she was a wife and helpmeet.

Black women's ventures gained visibility primarily in the Black press, though they also received a few lines in mainstream articles about Project Own and the SBA's compensatory capitalism programs. The Black press helped make the connections between business ownership and racial justice in discussions about SBA programs by showcasing success stories such as Roberta Lewis or fashion designer Ann Lowe (see chapter 2) or by highlighting the obstacles faced by Redmond and other Black men and women. Magazines such as *Ebony* and *Jet* that catered to Black readers similarly brought a gender and class dynamic to their coverage of women's business ownership. Both publications highlighted women's ventures that aligned with a politics of respectability. In 1964, Lowe was dubbed "society's best-kept secret" by the *Saturday Evening Post*, a weekly (and later biweekly) magazine popular with middle-class readers.[117] The subhead to the title noted, "Rich women pass her name among themselves—some have even cheated her. But few outsiders have heard of Ann Lowe, the only Negro to become a leading American Dress designer." Two years later, she was hailed as the "Dean of American Designers" by *Ebony* in a six-page article where Lowe shared her commitment to her craft in the face of challenges such as losing an eye to glaucoma, the death of her son and business partner, extreme debt, bankruptcy, and IRS troubles.[118] Even for women on the lower end of

102 • She's the Boss

the socioeconomic spectrum, *Ebony* pointed out that they too were worthy of respect. For example, in discussing Redmond's financial situation, *Ebony* noted, "Mrs. Redmond is proud. She didn't want her children to live under the stigma of welfare for the rest of their lives."[119]

In the 1960s, for women, Black and white, business ownership provided a way into a system that had long discriminated against them. For both groups, it was a work-around: a vehicle to bypass prejudice while they waited for the promise of new laws such as Title VII to safeguard workplace equality. Through a confluence of economic, social, and political changes, women's work and business ownership would take on new and important meaning in the 1960s. While the decade is often characterized as a time of dramatic upheaval on a national level, for women's business ownership, the era was more a germination period than a time of revolutionary change. That political leaders believed they could correct the ills of the past lent credence to women's decades-old lament about workplace inequality. The civil rights movement further prompted new questions and initiatives as well as greater visibility and importance for women business owners of color. The emergence of an organized feminist movement in the 1960s would prove the engine that drove the future of women's business ownership into the modern era.

Taken together, the 1960s emphasis on bringing political awareness to every aspect of life created the social consciousness necessary to move women's business ownership to its next and most critical decade, the 1970s. The promise of business ownership both empowered people and required the individual to take responsibility for changing their circumstances without addressing or altering the root social causes of economic or political inequality.

4

Sisterhood Is (Economically) Powerful

Civil Rights, Feminism, and Women's Business Ownership in the 1960s and 1970s

In the summer of 1973, two Columbia University academics, Kirsten Grimstad and Susan Rennie, set off on a thirteen-thousand-mile, six-week, cross-country pilgrimage to discover feminist America. The pair went looking for pockets of women's activism to pepper a directory they were creating of the nascent women's studies programs and women's centers nationwide. What they discovered were thousands of activist businesses all attempting to merge women's need to make a living with feminist visions of an egalitarian society *and* economy. They found feminist presses, art galleries, health centers, bookstores, credit unions, farms, restaurants, schools, and auto repair shops from New York to California in urban, suburban, and rural areas alike. "It was viral—everywhere we went, we were directed to another connection or piece of the network," Rennie later recalled, noting how each activist business owner they encountered pointed them to many more that they would then drive to meet.[1] What quickly came into focus was a vast, undiscovered patchwork of feminists who optimistically saw in business ownership the potential to make capitalism work for the good of those who, like themselves, faced discrimination in the mainstream

103

104 • She's the Boss

economy—women, people of color, lesbians, and the poor. "We felt as though we were part of a world-changing movement, that we were ending patriarchy," Grimstad explained. "It was euphoric."[2]

When they returned home to New York, Grimstad and Rennie took the brochures, business cards, mission statements, and photographs they collected and, in just six weeks, reproduced them as-is in a large-format ($11'' \times 15''$), 223-page book entitled *The New Woman's Survival Catalog* (*NWSC*), which bowed in late 1973. Wrapped in a bright red cover, the book enthusiastically encouraged readers to help build an alternative culture by supporting the more than five hundred feminist ventures and organizations highlighted within. "We . . . had a feeling that we were fostering these activities by making the information available in this immediate grassroots way," said Rennie.[3] Clearly, they were onto something: Readers nationwide heeded the call and gobbled up all one hundred thousand copies of the book, earning it a spot for a week on the *New York Times* bestseller list.

Such visibility, along with the growth of the women's movement, likely helped draw increasing national media attention to the rising number of women's enterprises, feminist or not, from such outlets as the *New York Times* and *Wall Street Journal* and the popular television talk show, the Merv Griffin Show.[4] Grimstad and Rennie produced a second, smaller-format book in 1975: *The New Woman's Survival Sourcebook*, which grounded its catalog of businesses in "the *ideas* of feminism."[5] The experience of seeing what might be socially and politically possible via business ownership also led the catalog's two compilers to relocate to California and launch a venture of their own, *Chrysalis*, a feminist magazine "of Women's Culture" that lasted from 1977 to 1980 and was part of the burgeoning feminist print culture. The *NWSC*'s cult following also inspired a reprint of the original big red volume in 2019—which, like its predecessor, sold well and garnered renewed interest in this unique moment in feminist history.

While the most visible, dynamic, and comprehensive example of activist women's attempts to link their economic activities with efforts for social justice and equality, the primarily white women in Grimstad and Rennie's catalog were hardly alone or the first to attempt to do so. Black women in the United States had long recognized the possible connections between the businesses they owned and their goals of civil and equal rights, using their ventures throughout history—sometimes at great personal and collective risk—as sites for community building, activist organizing, job-training, or to rally support for political candidates. One of the most notable early examples was Madam C. J. Walker, the first self-made African American woman millionaire, who in the early twentieth century used her position to promote upward mobility for other women of color by training them as entrepreneurial sales agents in her beauty products business. She also supported and helped lead organizations such as the National Association of Colored Women.[6] Ida B. Wells, Maggie Lena Walker, and other early twentieth-century activists of racial equality likewise merged their economic activities with founding or participating in movements to advance the race, Wells with the newspaper she owned and Maggie Lena Walker by starting St. Luke's Penny Savings Bank in 1903, the first woman in the United States to charter a bank.[7] As historian Shennette Garrett-Scott noted, Walker saw the bank both as a way to "take the nickels and turn them into dollars" and as a site of job opportunities for women.[8] In the late 1960s and early 1970s, civil rights and feminist activists increasingly saw immense transformative potential in fusing activism and enterprise in their individual and cooperative ventures. But unlike earlier women business owners, Black and white, the activists who launched businesses in the late 1960s and 1970s often did so *because* of their politics; that is, for many of these entrepreneurs, the idea to start a business was inextricably linked to and inspired by their activism. That differs from their predecessors, who often became successful business owners first and then connected or used their economic status to facilitate their activist goals.

As noted in the previous chapter, women turned to business ownership in the 1960s and 1970s for a variety of reasons: to bypass the sexism, racism, and homophobia of the job market; to fulfill personal or professional goals; to provide for themselves and their children after a divorce, or to combine motherhood with income-generating activities. But for activists in the civil rights, women's, and gay (in this case, lesbian) liberation movements of the era, business also had the potential to serve a larger social purpose: as a building block for the economic empowerment of previously marginalized people and, for a growing number, as the foundation for a social revolution that centered and celebrated the talents and needs of women and people of color while also, many hoped, ending U.S. white, patriarchal capitalism. As such, many of the ventures activist women launched were designed to make an incursion into categories that had long been the site of and helped maintain white patriarchal power: food, media (publishing, the arts, music), bookstores, and money. They also saw their businesses as both a visible manifestation of social revolution and a vehicle for funneling money back into the movement. For example, feminist credit unions required members to join a feminist group—a simple means to expand the women's liberation movement—while also using deposits to invest in feminist ventures. The Harlem Food Co-op offered job training that would lead to better paying jobs and a sense of ownership for its members.

Such lofty goals did indeed inspire a kind of euphoria, as Grimstad observed, among business owners and collectives, especially in the heady early years, but as time passed, merging activism and enterprise would prove challenging. First, maintaining adherence to a pure, anticapitalist politics became difficult as these ventures sought to sustain themselves and do business in and with the broader economy. Feminists too faced sharp internal critiques—and nasty public debates—from other movement activists who questioned whether one could engage with white patriarchal capitalism, the interlocking systems that oppressed women, and remain true to revolutionary egalitarian ideals. Women of color found that white women's liberationist ventures at times failed to include Black women or to center Black women's voices, inspiring them to launch feminist businesses of their own. Some businesses faced difficulties competing with bigger mainstream companies with their more expansive financial resources as well as efforts by outsiders and rivals who sought to close them down.

While many activist businesses would not survive past the late 1970s and 1980s, collectively they did increase the number of women-owned businesses. More important, they made a lasting impact on the relationship between marginalized groups and business ownership that continues today. In 1972, the first year the Census Bureau inaugurated an official tally of women's business ownership as a distinct and regularly tracked category, women owned 1.4 million businesses, just 4.6 percent of the nation's total.[9] By the end of the 1970s, however, that number would almost double, with women launching businesses at three times the rate of their male counterparts. Clearly these were not all activist entrepreneurs, but activists infused women's business ownership with a new sense of rights, empowerment, and mission for equality of opportunity that would be embraced by contemporary and succeeding generations whether they identified with any form of feminist or civil rights activism. That is, even those who distanced themselves from or completely disavowed movement activism would nonetheless embrace the language of empowerment and access to economic equality that activist entrepreneurs inspired.

Setting the Stage for a Revolution in Business Ownership

The changing social and cultural landscape of the late 1960s and early 1970s paved the way for the growth of activist-based business ownership, and that was especially true for women in both the civil rights and feminist movements. Since World War II, the nation had been in the longest period of economic prosperity in its history (1945–1973). That growth inspired increased optimism about the individual's ability to achieve as well as the belief that perhaps such affluence made it possible for the country to solve enduring socioeconomic problems such as poverty and inequality. In the early years, civil and women's rights activists looked to politics and legislation as the curative, such as the Equal Pay Act of 1963 or Title VII of the Civil Rights Act of 1964. But change was slow, and by the second half of the 1960s, many activists began to shift their strategies toward economic structures. New critiques of capitalism emerged in various social movements, among them youth movements such as the student left and counterculture of the 1960s as well as civil rights / Black power and women's liberation. Liberals balked at consumer exploitation; radicals, like members of the feminist group WITCH (Women's International Terrorist Conspiracy from Hell) took it further, staging theatrical protests, including one where they put a hex on Wall Street, the cornerstone of capitalist patriarchal power.[10] Some activists embraced socialism as the antidote to capitalism.

Others increasingly began to identify access to the economy as the way that both individuals and groups could gain a foothold within the system and, once there, effect wider change for all.

To be clear, economics had long been intertwined with movements for social justice; what was different in the late 1960s and early 1970s was the way activists saw business ownership as a vehicle for changing society. Civil rights leaders in the 1950s and 1960s such as Martin Luther King Jr. understood early on the power of the boycott in ending segregation, as evidenced by the 368-day Montgomery bus boycott. By the second half of the 1960s, activists increasingly saw the potential of economic initiatives such as Operation Breadbasket that encouraged people of color to support Black-owned businesses. They also hoped that the federal Project Own's efforts to provide start-up loans for Black businesses could enable some to gain independence and upward mobility through the existing capitalist system (see chapter 3).

Similarly, early feminists in the 1960s focused squarely on securing for women the same economic opportunities men had. Mainstream, or liberal, feminist groups such as the National Organization for Women (NOW) sought equality of opportunity and pay in the job market and an end to the "double discrimination" of gender and race.[11] But for radical feminists on the far left, the groups that emerged in the later 1960s, these correctives did not go far enough. They believed a social revolution was required. In the introduction to an anthology of women's liberation essays, feminist authors Deborah Babcox and Madeline Belkin wrote that women were kept economically dependent, "incarcerated in the split-level dream house" where they had to ask their "husband's permission to buy something."[12] Capitalism and patriarchy combined to keep women out of the best jobs, others argued, with marriage their only legitimate option, even though in reality, more than half of the women in America were sole breadwinners.[13] "Under capitalism, there could be at best token integration of women into the labor force," wrote Shulamith Firestone in her famous feminist work, *The Dialectic of Sex*.[14]

Like 1960s and 1970s countercultural groups, many feminists and civil rights activists on the left were increasingly disillusioned with the dehumanization and competition innate to the American system of capitalism and, more specifically, the way it isolated women from one another. They joined what others on the left called "a moral revolt against late 20th century democratic capitalism."[15] In lieu of unquestioningly playing the social roles that were expected in terms of work, goals, and interpersonal relations—entering "role prison"—these activists sought something different. They embraced what contemporary author Charles Reich defined as a "new way of life (that) makes both possible and necessary a culture that is nonartificial and nonalienated, a form of community in which love, respect, and a mutual search for wisdom replace the competition and separation of the past, and a liberation of each individual in which he is enabled to grow toward the highest possibilities of the human spirit."[16]

Business became the vehicle for creating that social change and possibly inventing an entirely new culture for many activists. Left-leaning and socialist activists created business alternatives, such as the counterculture's "free stores" where people could simply take what they needed (and leave something they didn't for someone else). Across the country, thousands came together to forge collective or cooperative ventures, pooling their resources to gain a competitive advantage that they might not have independently. Co-ops and collectives where all had a say in operations also provided an opportunity to reimagine the structure and nature of business itself, its social utility, as well as its relationship to workers as reciprocal. Some lived communally on farms, growing what they needed and joining with others in food co-ops to sell the rest. In fact, women in the counterculture launched thousands of food co-ops in cities nationwide in the late 1960s and 1970s. They also opened restaurants as communal and cooperative businesses and sites of community, among them Alice Brook's Alice's Restaurant in western Massachusetts and the Moosewood collective started by Molly Katzen in Ithaca, New York.[17]

The co-op trend was becoming so popular that in 1976, five hundred people gathered at the Third International Conference on Self-Management in Washington, D.C., to attend "60 panels exploring the possibilities for increasing worker participation, ownership, and self-management in the United States." The event was documented by journalist Daniel Zwerdling in a 1978 book of case studies to help would-be co-op groups get started, entitled *Workplace Democracy: A Guide to Workplace Ownership, Participation, and Self-Management Experiments in the United States and Europe*.[18] The notion of co-ops seemed so promising that the Ford Foundation made "hundreds of thousands of dollars" in grants to support this work, and the U.S. Senate passed a bill to "authorize the Small Business Administration to guarantee loans to employee-owned businesses and to employee organizations seeking to purchase their businesses."[19]

Hiding in Plain Sight: Early Links between Black Women's Businesses and Civil Rights

This politics of business ownership infused the ventures white feminists started, but for Black women whose lives were always tinged with discrimination, politics and economics were inseparable. Women who owned businesses to help support themselves and their families or to find a way to market their individual talents often did not see what they did as distinct from their roles in the community, their activism, or their hopes as citizens. Women of color opened a range of businesses during the peak years of the civil rights movement. While all were important, some such as beauty parlors, soul food restaurants, and bookstores also served as sites of community and organizing, even in regions of the country where doing so could trigger violent backlash. These spaces, then, often in segregated sections of cities and towns, became places where activists not only could come together to talk politics over lunch or a haircut but could do so under the cover of merely patronizing a business. They could, in fact, hide in plain sight their activist organizing from those in power who would seek to stop or harass them.

Without question, the beauty business served as a nexus of personal and political life for African American women and an alternative to a limited job market. In 1966, *Ebony* magazine pointed out that half of all Black women in the labor force did "domestic and menial work," and the median income for Black working women was 70 percent of what white women earned.[20] One in four Black families was headed by a woman, simultaneously heralded as a symbol of strength and racial pride and, at the same time, gently reminded not to advance so quickly as to negatively impact the spirit of Black men. Beauty businesses enabled women of color to provide for their families while also engaging in civil rights activism in various ways, including as leaders. In 1957, Martin Luther King Jr. addressed the National Beauty Culturists' League (NBCL), a trade organization for Black hairdressers, on "The Role of Beauticians in the Contemporary Struggle for Freedom."[21] Katie Whickham, for example, owned a salon, was president of the NBCL, and was elected the first female staff officer of the Southern Christian Leadership Conference (SCLC), an important civil rights group, in 1959. Noted SCLC leader Ella Baker praised Whickham, saying, "We believe that Mrs. Whickham will bring new strength to our efforts. The National Beauty Culturists' League, Inc., of which she is president, has strong local and state units throughout the South and voter registration is a major emphasis to its program."[22] As Bernice Calvin, a woman of color hairdresser who founded *Beauty Trade* magazine with her mother, noted, "Women got together in beauty parlors, and everyone knew how powerful that could be. When a person was running for office, he came into salon, offered his message, and tried to raise money. . . . It was the way to meet the most people in the shortest amount of time."[23]

Like Baker, these "beauty activists" were seen as "bridge leaders" for the power they wielded in their neighborhoods. The Black beauty trade press noted in 1961 that Tennessee beauticians organized to aid Black sharecroppers evicted from their farms, while fifty thousand Black beauticians were organized to help elect John F. Kennedy in 1960, with each one held responsible for securing four Kennedy votes.[24] They were also heavily involved with ensuring that new government programs reached African Americans in need. In 1965, the *New York Amsterdam News* highlighted the United Beauty School Owners and Teachers Association's (UBSOTA) five-point plan to help win the "War on Poverty" for African Americans.[25]

Even annual trade shows had a civil rights theme: the 1963 NBCL convention included a "panel on Beauticians United for Political Action."[26] Throughout the decade, as political activism intensified, these businesses would continue to serve multiple roles, providing an income to their owners, a source of racial pride for the community, and centers for organizing efforts for civil rights groups. "Some beauty shops we would use . . . to get (people) interested in voting and get them registered, and after getting them registered, try our best to get them to go out to the polls," stated Ella Martin, president of the Georgia State Beauty Culturists' League from 1946 to 1968.[27] In 1969, Whickham, still NBCL president, worked to strengthen professional development for Black beauticians via a $1,000,000 research center in Washington, D.C. She also encouraged salon owners and hairdressers to support the SCLC's Operation Breadbasket, described as "a creative employment and business program aimed at ending the economic indignities which lead to the spiritual destruction of the Negro People."[28] In support of Operation Breadbasket, Whickham's group wanted African Americans to "produce goods and services to sell to other blacks."[29]

Even those Black women business owners who were not activists per se had an understanding of their ventures that was still often intertwined with the movement. That was especially true for women who owned restaurants, which not only served up ethnic or soul food dishes but also were quasi-community centers and meeting places for civil rights activists all across the country. Soul food restaurant owners such as Sylvia Woods of Sylvia's in Harlem took pride in their businesses being at the center of civil rights organizing. A waitress, in 1962 Woods bought the restaurant where she worked with $20,000 obtained when her mother mortgaged her North Carolina farm.[30] "You had Malcolm X walking down the street," explained Tren'ness Woods-Black, granddaughter of Sylvia Woods and among the family members who continued to own and run the business after Woods passed away in 2012. "Our restaurant was in the middle of all the action that was happening, whether it be happy or sad." New York Democratic congressman Charles B. Rangel, who was first elected to office in 1971, added, "From the beginning, Sylvia's has always provided an opportunity for people to get together and be free to talk about how to be free."[31] Similarly, the restaurant Edna Stewart opened in Covington, Tennessee, in 1966 was a favorite of Dr. Martin Luther King Jr., where he met with Rev. Jesse Jackson to strategize the fight against housing discrimination.[32] Dooky Chase's New Orleans, Louisiana, restaurant, family-owned since 1941 and later run by Leah Chase, was not only a site of organizing, but the owners had a room on the upper floor set aside for that purpose. Chase recalled receiving threatening hate mail for engagement with civil rights. In May 1965, passengers in a car threw a homemade firebomb at the restaurant, damaging the building but injuring no one.[33] (It remains open as of this writing.)

The mainstreaming of the Black Power movement by the mid- to late 1960s, with its emphasis on the value of African American history and culture, undoubtedly inspired some Black women to start businesses and gave them a waiting clientele. Bookstores were the centerpiece of activist entrepreneurship for the Black Power movement, including those owned by women, as historian Joshua Clark Davis has noted. Like their male counterparts, women bookstore owners linked their need to make a living with the activist mission to feature the works of Black authors, particularly those writing about racial justice and Black Power.

They also featured Black history and stories for children—not often available in mainstream bookstores.[34] Their sense of political mission was so strong that it often dwarfed economic imperatives. Opening Liberation Books in Harlem in 1967 was "not a question of bookselling. . . . It's the raising of consciousness," said owner and longtime pan-African activist Una Mulzac.[35] Located on Lenox Avenue and 131st Street in the heart of Harlem, Mulzac's bookstore—which lasted until ill health forced her to close in 2007—became a site where activists, academics, and residents could come together to organize, debate political issues, and plan protests.[36] Like other Black-owned bookstores, Mulzac featured the works of well-known authors like James Baldwin alongside lesser-known authors and activist tracts by Black Power and Pan-African writers. The key, though, was reaching the widest possible audience by pricing books low enough that readers on the lower end of the socioeconomic spectrum could afford them.

In Washington, D.C., Drum & Spear Bookstore played a similar role. Cofounder Judy Richardson said the bookstore was started within two months of Martin Luther King Jr.'s assassination in 1968 and the urban uprisings that followed: "We had to walk through tear gas to get there. . . . For me, Drum & Spear Bookstore was a continuation of the work we had done in SNCC, expanding awareness of ourselves and our power to change the world."[37] Drum & Spear not only sold to individual readers; they aligned with colleges that had new Black studies departments. And they were acutely aware of the needs of children of color for books that featured stories and characters that reflected them, which led the bookstore's founders to launch their own publishing house.

Black Power politics influenced a host of other types of women's ventures including fashion. Hazel Rodney Blackman launched a Manhattan boutique specializing in African-inspired fashions, proudly attributing her success in 1966 to this: "I'm black and black is what's happening."[38] Born in Jamaica, Blackman came to the United States to study at age seventeen and lived with her uncle. She worked in the fashion industry for more than a decade before launching her own design and retail business dubbed Treehouse on New York's Upper West Side in the mid-1960s. There, she specialized in using African fabrics, saying, "Let others look to Paris for design inspiration, but I'll look to Africa."[39] Like many women business owners, she struggled to stay afloat. Still, she quickly rose in status within the fashion industry, especially as Black Power ideals such as "Black is beautiful" reached younger consumers who "believed they could perform their blackness through their clothing choices," as scholar C. Tanisha Ford has documented.[40] By the early 1970s, dashikis became the quasi "uniform" of Black Power, and designers and customers helped popularize these and other African-inspired fashions. Blackman was hailed in newspaper articles alongside more famous white fashion designers of the era such as Oscar de la Renta.[41] She was also aware about the ways racial and gender biases made her business challenging. "I've always had the problem of capital," Blackman told a reporter in 1970. "I could have gone much further if I had found backing when I was starting out."[42]

FIG. 4.1 Hazel Blackman by Moneta Sleet Jr. (*Ebony*, September 1966). The designer is surrounded by her African-inspired designs in her salon in New York City. *Credit:* Johnson Publishing Company Archive. Courtesy J. Paul Getty Trust and Smithsonian National Museum of African American History and Culture (made possible by the Ford Foundation, J. Paul Getty Trust, John D. and Catherine T. MacArthur Foundation, the Andrew W. Mellon Foundation, and Smithsonian Institution).

Sisterhood Is (Economically) Powerful • 113

For women activists in movement politics, race and gender intersected as motivations for starting a business. Dorothy Pitman Hughes, a longtime community and Black Power activist, began her entrepreneurial journey by starting a cooperative day care center in late 1960s New York City. A mother herself, Pitman Hughes understood the need for safe, reliable childcare; her daughter had been abused by a previous babysitter. She also knew what the lack of day care meant for other women of color during the Vietnam War era, when Black men disproportionately were drafted or enlisted, leaving mothers to provide for children alone.

In 1965, Pitman Hughes applied everything she learned as a community organizer to open a day care business in her apartment. Two years later, she obtained a federally funded community development grant and expanded, moving to two rooms in the Endicott Hotel on West 80th Street on the Upper West Side of New York City—at the time, labeled "a west side ghetto." Pitman Hughes made her West 80th Street Day Care Center work, renovating the space, recruiting volunteers to help, and securing every available grant. The center cared for thirty-five children at five dollars per week and included the revolutionary and egalitarian approach of making parents members of the board. She also made her space a community center and linked what she did in business to activism for free day care. Gloria Steinem, a journalist at the time, wrote an article about Pitman Hughes's work for *New York* magazine. Later, the two would become speaking partners advocating for feminism and racial justice.[43] The center continued well into the late 1970s and provided the foundation for her future entrepreneurial ventures in the 1980s.

Advertising whiz Barbara Proctor walked away from years of gender and racial discrimination when she started her own agency in 1970. Proctor, an award-winning rising star in Black advertising agencies, was frustrated by racist advertising and by constantly being assigned to "women's accounts" as a copy supervisor at the North advertising agency in Chicago. But the final straw came when Proctor was assigned to a hair product for women of color with an ad concept that mocked civil rights activism by showing protesting women demanding that product via a "foam-in" (a parody that mocked civil rights sit-ins). She refused to demean the movement and was fired. "That's when I learned that you really don't make decisions unless you are the boss," Proctor noted. She took her $2,000 severance, contributions from friends—including a band member with the Count Basie Orchestra—and within months launched Proctor & Gardner in Chicago, the first advertising agency owned by a Black woman.[44] Dubbed the "Black Mary Wells" (see chapter 3) for her high-power status among advertising professionals of color, Proctor secured an $80,000 Small Business Administration loan based solely on her industry credentials. Not only did she launch her firm at a peak moment—what scholar Judy Foster Davis has called the "Golden Age" for Black advertising—she positioned her firm to focus on respectful portrayals of people of color.[45] "Advertising is the highest form of persuasion," Proctor noted, "We mold opinions. . . . What I resist is the business opportunity to

114 • She's the Boss

sell questionable or stereotypical products to consumers, especially when there is evidence the product is detrimental or reinforces negative stereotypes."[46]

Proctor's business grew to $15 million in annual revenues by 1984—including national clients such as Sears, Alberto-Culver, and Kraft. She prioritized working with Black-owned media companies as a way to promote equity. "Racism and sexism were only challenges to me, not obstacles," she told *Ebony* magazine in 1982.[47] Later, as other firms entered the field and as the industry evolved, Proctor's firm found itself in a diluted market; she closed the business in the mid-1990s and retired from advertising.[48]

Power to the People: Pooling Resources in Black Women's Co-ops

To some—particularly those with economic resources—starting a business in the boom economy of the late 1960s and early 1970s seemed financially easier and far cheaper than it would be in succeeding decades, but for those on the margins, start-up funding remained elusive. Until 1974, banks could legally discriminate on the basis of gender, and the Equal Credit Opportunity Act passed that year excluded business loans. While rents were low, especially in poorer or racially marginalized sections of cities and towns, amassing the funds for a lease could still be prohibitive. As such, a growing number of activist entrepreneurs employed creative fundraising strategies (such as membership drives) and organized cooperatives that would bring in larger numbers of people as members and potential beneficiaries of the opportunities that ownership could provide.

In 1964, as Harlem withstood days of uprisings, local attorney Cora Walker sought to make sense of the devastation. "In talking to the people on the street, they felt they didn't have anything, they didn't own anything," Walker, the first Black woman to practice law in New York State, later recounted. She told them "that if they wanted to, they could own something on a cooperative basis."[49] A Republican and believer in the ability to use the system to right past wrongs, Walker turned to business, specifically to a community-owned supermarket, as the answer.[50] At the time, Harlem, like many predominantly Black areas, had one major supermarket—white-owned—that offered limited or subpar food at much higher prices than in white communities. Owners blamed the cost and quality differentials on the community itself, claiming that they had to pay heavy insurance costs to operate in what they called high-risk, high-crime areas. Walker shrugged that off as a fallacy. Instead, she believed that a community-owned business—a cooperative—would not only instill racial pride and empower the community, but it could also provide access to fresh, healthy, and affordable food; help train and provide a good income for workers; and potentially lead to continued business development there.

As a resident of Harlem who had unsuccessfully run for office twice, Walker was trusted by her community. By late 1966, when Walker began selling

Sisterhood Is (Economically) Powerful • 115

five-dollar shares—a figure she considered affordable to area residents—in the Harlem River Consumers Cooperative (what became the Harlem Co-op Supermarket), people eagerly responded. She even rode through Harlem on a sound truck, broadcasting to recruit neighborhood investors. "We . . . started out on 145th Street and 8th Avenue and said if you are interested in finding out how you can buy shares in a supermarket that you own, and we were flooded with people," Walker recalled, noting that Harlem residents embraced the potential to be part of a collective, to avail themselves of the prospect of upward mobility through jobs, and to enjoy a supermarket with better prices and food. She quickly raised $102,000 from 1,719 residents and added a few hundred thousand more from sponsors to get the venture off the ground.[51]

In June 1967, the Harlem Food Co-op opened with Black celebrities such as Ruby Dee and Ossie Davis photographed by the press shopping the aisles.[52] Walker took pride in the loyalty that the co-op inspired in the neighborhood. "The beautiful part was the stockholders," she later recalled. "They really loved that store. If they came in there and they didn't have salt, they didn't buy salt until we got some." In the first nine months, the store earned $2.8 million. Rival white-owned supermarkets were not happy about the food co-op's success and colluded to create labor strikes that brought negative publicity and other woes. Still believing that the tools of the system could be put to use, Walker brought suit. Although she won, it took years. In the meantime, the co-op struggled, ultimately closing and ending Walker's communal experiment.[53]

Not long after the Harlem Food Co-op opened, renowned voting rights activist Fannie Lou Hamer was similarly launching a cooperative that centered on food. A poor woman who worked as a Mississippi sharecropper, Hamer came to civil rights activism in 1961 when she attended a meeting about voter registration. Transformed, she dedicated her life to the cause of racial equality—initially voting rights—which cost her job, led to her arrest, and made her the victim of a brutal beating by white police officers in a Mississippi jail when she attempted to register to vote. Hamer would gain national attention when she helped form the Mississippi Freedom Democratic Party and sought to be seated at the 1964 Democratic National Convention. But by the late 1960s, she had turned her focus toward the potential for racial justice through the economy.[54] Toward that end and inspired by the antipoverty initiatives of President Lyndon Johnson's "War on Poverty," Hamer established the Freedom Farm Cooperative, designed to empower poor Black farmers in rural Mississippi.[55]

Hamer's vision for the Freedom Farm Co-op (FFC) was multilayered and built on her belief that such ventures offered freedom "from hunger, poverty, and homes that did not adequately protect needy families from the cold winds of 'Old Man Winter.'"[56] First, in association with the National Council of Negro Women, Hamer bought thirty-five female and five male pigs in 1968 to create a Pig Bank. The animals were loaned to local families, who could breed them and keep the offspring, later returning one or more to the bank to help other

FIG. 4.2 Cora Walker proudly demonstrating the Harlem Food Co-op supermarket she started to Bess Myerson, New York City Director of Consumer Affairs. *Credit:* New York Daily News Archive via Getty Images.

families. (Pigs reproduce eighteen to twenty piglets at a time.) By the third year, up to three thousand new pigs had been produced.[57] Then Hamer moved to her dream of a cooperatively owned and run farm where people worked together to improve the land. Only seventy-one of the thirty-one thousand Black people in her home of Sunflower County owned land. Hamer believed that with the economic stability of the co-op, people of color would then be empowered to participate in political life.

In 1969, Hamer bought the first forty acres of Freedom Farm for $20,000. Membership fees were one dollar; most of the 1,500 co-op members could afford to and did pay it. Freedom Farmers raised beans and collard greens for food as well as cotton and soybeans, which they boxed up and collectively sold. A popular speaker, Hamer toured the country and appeared on television to talk about Freedom Farm and raise money; every time she did, funds poured in. After speaking at various colleges, students held "Walks for Hunger" that collectively netted $200,000 for Hamer's initiative. In Hollywood, singer Harry Belafonte supported Hamer's effort with a fundraising letter endorsing the venture as an "example of initiative, racial cooperation and political militancy worthy of the support of all decent Americans."[58] Northern groups, including schoolchildren in marches against hunger, raised funds to support Freedom Farm: they sent $120,000 toward the purchase of farm machinery and an additional 620 acres. "For the first time in our lives, we will have a chance to control some of our own destiny," Hamer said.[59]

FIG. 4.3 Civil rights activist Fannie Lou Hamer and members of her Freedom Farm Cooperative, preparing to sell their produce. *Credit:* Fannie Lou Townsend Hamer Collection (T/102). Courtesy of the Archives and Records Services Division, Mississippi Department of Archives and History.

Hamer's FFC tackled a range of socioeconomic problems designed to facilitate the emergence of a fiscally sound Black economy. Projects included scholarships and an "African Fashion Shop" and "Afro-Botique" where local women could sell apparel they made. In 1969, the co-op purchased buildings intended for a sewing co-op and laundromat, and while it did ultimately open a sewing factory, it was forced to close after a year due to "marketing problems."[60] The farm even made loans to help start other small businesses in the area. During its history, Freedom Farm was ranked the third largest employer in Sunflower County, providing jobs for more than thirty-five people and food for thousands. It also supported a day care center and made women key members of the collective's board of directors. It tackled housing too, securing funds from the Federal Housing Authority mortgage programs in 1969 to build seventy affordable housing units by 1972 with monthly payments ranging from thirty-eight to one hundred dollars. The units were so well constructed that many are still in existence as of this writing. Freedom Farm continued to provide a vision of an alternative economic reality, but it struggled with debts and various reorganization plans before folding in 1976, a year before Hamer's death.[61] Despite its closing, the co-op helped countless individual families and, more importantly, represented the intersection of economic self-sufficiency with political and social equality.

The Feminist Revolution in Business

Much like civil rights activists, feminists saw in business ownership a chance to not only circumvent employment discrimination but also create businesses that would serve what they saw as the unmet needs of women—publishing companies that printed books by women authors and/or on topics that would empower other women; bookstores that would not only sell those books but also serve as possible sites for community building; record companies that recorded women's music; health centers and art galleries that showcased ideas and information important to women; and even feminist mechanics who promised not to lie to, overcharge, or talk down to women. They were also acutely aware of what business ownership had done for people of color. "You can draw some kind of rough analogy between what we're trying to do and black capitalism," feminist entrepreneur Jill Ward pointed out. "The blacks have learned that there is no substitute for economic power, that it is an important step on the road to equality and independence. Now women are beginning to discover that's true."[62]

The owners of feminist ventures, including those featured in Rennie and Grimstad's *New Woman's Survival Catalog*, ran the gamut in their relationship to feminism from liberal to radical. Those on the liberal side embraced their right to own a business just as men did; those on the radical left saw their enterprises as "counterinstitutions"—vehicles for creating an alternative, feminist, women's culture. But some were also in the middle, regarding their ventures as part of a mass movement of women staking a claim in the economy—and even as vehicles for promoting, recruiting, and making visible the feminist movement—but they were not troubled by engaging with capitalism to do it. Longtime civil rights activist and women's liberationist Susan Hasalo Sojourner (a last name she and her activist husband took to honor abolitionist Sojourner Truth) started what she called a "fe-mail order business," First Things First, in 1971 in Washington, D.C., selling women's movement crafts, books, jewelry, and ephemera.[63] Similarly, Ferne Williams started her business selling feminist bumper stickers, T-shirts, and jewelry, first as a fundraising boutique for her local New Jersey NOW chapter and as a means to support her children after a divorce. Soon, she branched off on her own, manufacturing 95 percent of what she sold and selling by mail, at conferences, or on street corners—even outside the Democratic Convention in New York City. "The things that I make are helping to raise people's consciousness, and so I really feel I'm helping the movement," noted Williams, whose business in the late 1970s had gross sales of $52,000.[64] In Brooklyn, New York, Rose Fontanella and Stephanie Marcus used $3,000 of savings to launch their feminist catalog, Liberation Enterprises, saying that they did so "with the belief that our products will give women the opportunity to express the spirit of the women's movement . . . and serve as consciousness-raisers by making the feminist spirit more visible." Their most famous (or notorious) item was an apron emblazoned with "F—k Housework!" (with that word spelled out), which the *Village Voice* refused to advertise.[65] NOW too had a catalog of feminist ephemera, "Financing the Revolution," featuring pins, handcrafted jewelry, and books. None of these businesses worried about ideological conflicts with capitalism.

While mainstream feminist groups continued to seek women's inclusion in the existing system, a younger and more radical feminist contingent emerged around 1967 that would not only provide the theoretical frameworks for understanding inequality but also seek to dismantle the existing system and create a feminist culture using business to doing so—even if their politics were anticapitalist and/or socialist. Opposed to the proestablishment agenda of mainstream feminism, these women founded their own groups, such as the Chicago Women's Liberation Union, New York Radical Women, and Boston's Cell 16.[66]

For these feminists, consciousness raising was an essential tool for bringing social change, including their efforts to launch movement-inspired businesses. Initiated by New York Radical Women, consciousness raising (CR) referred to the notion that by coming together weekly in small groups to discuss their individual experiences as women, they would not only end the isolation that all women felt but also learn that what they assumed to be their personal problems had broader social implications.[67] That, they believed, would lead to activism. Through experiences with CR too, they hoped women would develop self-determination, self-actualization, and self-awareness.[68] Many women in CR did gain strength to resolve dilemmas or take enterprising new risks.[69] At a ten-year reunion of her CR group, "Jeannette F" enthusiastically noted how it changed

120 • She's the Boss

her life. "I was in the process of getting a divorce, and right away I began to strip away the old ideas about myself and acquire new ones," she recalled in the late 1980s. "I remember saying to my lawyer that I didn't need alimony—I could work to make my own living. I remember thinking I could start my own business.... When I think about starting the business, it's very linked with feminism in my mind."[70]

In the late 1960s, without necessarily intending to enter the business world, radical feminists began self-publishing manifestos and other literature about the feminist revolution. Using mimeograph machines and selling printouts to cover their costs, groups and individuals published such leaflets as "Notes from the First Year," put out by New York Radical Women—typically selling to women at half the price offered to men as a way of underscoring their societal inequities.[71] Many of them embraced socialist feminism, which linked capitalism *and* sexism as the sites of women's oppression, as historian Linda Gordon explained. Arguing for a class consciousness among women, they published works such as "Class and Feminism," "Sex and Caste," and "Socialist Feminism."[72] Seeing capitalism and sexism as responsible for women's oppression, socialist feminists such as members of the Chicago Women's Liberation Union sought to, in their words, "wrest control of the institutions which now oppress us" and also create their own "counter-institutions" that would help build a feminist-inspired world. Some understood counterinstitutions as women's health or domestic violence centers and other efforts to provide assistance and community to women; perhaps ironically, others extended the term to include feminist businesses.[73]

For feminists who had been marginalized by society and the mainstream women's movement such as lesbians—dubbed the "lavender menace" by Friedan—business-as-counterinstitution provided a way to create community and jobs. In fact, lesbian feminists took the lead in the idea of business-as-vehicle for creating a feminist culture. According to Grimstad, many of the approximately five hundred businesses in *The New Woman's Survival Catalog* were owned by lesbians or lesbian collectives. In some cases, they lived and worked together communally. Some expected that not only would these "institutions" be controlled by members of the movement but "preference in hiring would be given to lesbians, lower and working-class women, Third World women, and women in need."[74] As a lesbian collective, Olivia's members lived and worked together in Los Angeles and later Oakland, California. Olivia's founders had belonged to the Furies, a lesbian collective that began in Washington, D.C.[75] The Furies published a newspaper during the D.C. years (1971–1973); afterward, some moved to California to start Olivia, and others, notably Charlotte Bunch and Coletta Reid, remained on the East Coast, launching a new feminist publication, *Quest: A Feminist Quarterly* (1974–1984), and a publishing collective, Daughters, Inc.

Publishing became a key business—and potential counterinstitution—for feminist activist entrepreneurs. Radical feminists launched publishing ventures and bookstores to not only take back control over the spreading of their message but also give a greater number of women a voice in print. Women writers had long struggled to be taken seriously by the publishing industry; as popular interest in feminism grew, large commercial publishing houses began selecting feminist books to reproduce for the mass market. To feminists, this meant that capitalism was in some way determining who the stars of the women's movement would be and thereby shaping feminism's course. This was particularly disturbing to a movement that disdained leaders of any kind, seeing all women as equal participants in the same goal.[76] "Freedom of the press, we learned by the early '70s, belonged to those who owned printing presses," recalled Carol Seajay, longtime editor of the *Feminist Bookstore News* and editor of various feminist newsletters in the 1970s: "So we established our own so that no man could ever again tell women what was true, what was relevant to our lives, or what we could publish and read."[77]

From 1968 to 1973, more than 560 new feminist publications were launched, and feminist presses began publishing what would become groundbreaking women's works, among them Rita Mae Brown's *Rubyfruit Jungle*.[78] In 1970 alone, journals such as *off our backs*, *It Ain't Me Babe*, and *Women: A Journal of Liberation* were launched within months of one another. Virtually every city, and many small towns, had their own feminist newsletters or newspapers.[79] In 1974, there were 123 women's publications.[80] Despite naysayers, the demand for the information they offered was real: *Ms.* magazine's circulation grew from 250,000 when it launched in 1972 to 400,000 two years later. Rather than deal with rejection or harassment from male-owned print shops, which often refused feminist materials, feminists began to launch their own typesetting shops, binderies, and print shops, including the Iowa City Women's Press and Diana Press. Feminist distribution companies such as Common Woman Distribution, Old Lady Blue Jeans, and Women in Distribution likewise assured that feminist publications found and reached their retail outlets.[81] "Heaven is earning your living as a feminist," wrote Paula Kassell, founder and editor of *New Directions for Women in New Jersey*, a feminist newspaper that existed from 1972 to 1993 and grew to circulation of 65,000 copies.

The outreach of feminist publishing was both diverse and widespread. The brainchild of English professor Florence Howe, the Feminist Press set up shop in Baltimore in 1970—with an original investment of just one hundred dollars—to publish books "restoring the lost history and culture of women in the United States and throughout the world," as one magazine tribute described.[82] In 1979, the press published the long-overlooked works of Harlem Renaissance writer Zora Neale Hurston and reprinted Charlotte Perkins Gilman's *The Yellow Wallpaper*.[83] Along with such classics, feminist presses uncovered new female talent with distinctive styles and perspectives. Lesbian poets, for example, found a far larger audience than would have been possible without feminist presses. Naiad Press, for example, was started to publish lesbian novels.[84] The Boston Women's

Health Book Collective, founded in the late 1960s and lasting until 2015, revolutionized women's health care with the landmark publication of its first book *Our Bodies, Our Selves* in 1971. Updated many times after, that book sold 250,000 copies in the first year.[85] In an age when male doctors dictated rather than listened to patients, *Our Bodies, Our Selves* sought to empower them as the experts on their own bodies. For example, *OBOS* taught women how to give themselves a pelvic exam using a speculum, advocated for the use of midwives in childbirth, and offered home remedies for gynecological and other health problems.

The eighty feminist publishers at the 1976 Women in Print Convention declared their goal "not to become a unified underground women's press, but actually to lead a feminist takeover of the nation's media."[86] Indeed, these companies' status as separatist publishing entities had a more revolutionary feminist agenda.[87] "Most of these women say they do not intend to stay 'separated' forever," wrote journalist Louis Gould in 1977, "only as long as it takes to change the world."[88] Feminists sensed that the establishment feared their influence in publishing. "In the early '70s social change was still very much an issue, and you had the feeling that it was something of a risk to publish," recalled Judy Hogan, who founded the women's press Carolina Wren in 1976: "The government was spying on small presses. I started meeting with the other feminist presses in '73, and they told us that they were getting their lines tapped."[89]

These ventures existed across the country and hoped for an outreach beyond their immediate region. In Pittsburgh, Pennsylvania, Ann Pride helped set up the publishing house KNOW, Inc., in 1970 to reprint and distribute feminist essays and articles—typically passed from hand to hand by feminists—on a wide scale. She later founded *Motheroot Writers Guild*, a quarterly review of women's small press books.[90] In 1969, a dozen members of a Chapel Hill, North Carolina, consciousness raising group formed a feminist publishing collective, Lollipop Power Press, to publish nonsexist children's books. By 1973, the company had published six "antisexist," multiracial children's books and sold twenty thousand copies, all in the "spare time" of collective members. Founded with just $1,000 in donations, the company would go on to win several awards in children's publishing. Titles included *Exactly like Me*, the story of "an independent girl who is proud of what she is," and *Jesse's Dream Skirt*, the tale of a young boy's beautiful handmade skirt and the courageous teacher who helps Jesse's teasing classmates understand why boys in skirts make them uncomfortable.[91]

In running their ventures, many white feminists tried to foster multicultural staffs and greater understanding of diversity within and outside the movement, with varying degrees of commitment and success. Businesses where white people were the majority often welcomed as friends and associates women from various backgrounds, typically African American and some Hispanic. Lollipop Power Press included books specifically for and about both Black and Latino children. *Ms.* magazine's largely white leadership included African Americans

Margaret Sloan and Alice Walker and staffers of various ethnic backgrounds. While Olivia Records recorded the music of some African American women, the primarily white collective was aware it lacked diversity and made an effort to recruit more working-class women and women of color.

In 1980, a group of Black feminists launched a press of their own, Kitchen Table: Women of Color Press. At the suggestion of poet and activist Audre Lorde, Barbara Smith—activist, writer, and member of the original Combahee River Collective of Black feminists in Boston—organized leading writers of the movement to establish the press.[92] It would go on to publish such path breaking works as Cherríe Moraga's *This Bridge Called My Back*. Smith, who was completing her groundbreaking *Some of Us Are Brave*, had mixed experiences when she published in feminist and lesbian journals. "Some of them were positive and some of them were negative, (but) none were women of color run," she said. "Kitchen Table Press began because of our need for autonomy, our need . . . to control the words and images that are produced about us. As feminist and lesbian women of color writers, we knew that we had no options for getting published, except at the mercy or whim of others, whether in the context of alternative or commercial publishing, since both are white dominated." Beyond books, Kitchen Table Press published pamphlets promoting Black feminist ideas and goals.[93]

Record studios, such as Olivia Records, also sought to give expression to women's power and pain in music, providing opportunities for employment in this exclusive male bastion. Such companies popularized female folk and rock artists and paved the way for the women in the rock revolution of the 1980s and 1990s.[94] "We decided to do a record company because we thought we could change the world through music," noted Judy Dlugacz, cofounder of Olivia Records, who pointed out that she saw herself as an activist first, entrepreneur second.[95] Ruth Bachelor, who had written lyrics for Elvis Presley, Mel Torme, and the Partridge Family, produced an album as a performer in 1971, "Songs for Women's Liberation" (under the Femme Records label).[96] The album featured such songs as "Drop the Mop" and "Stand and Be Counted."[97] Rock musician Joan Jett established Blackheart Records in 1979 after music industry executives said her records would never sell. They sold, all right, along with other female musicians on her label (roughly $40 million worth). "I couldn't believe that in America, people thought girls couldn't play rock and roll," Jett recounted years later, attributing her success to "being frustrated and pissed off."[98] Feminists also started speakers' bureaus and communications companies such as the Detroit-based Women's Radio Workshop; the Denver-based Women's Broadcasting Corporation; the Berkeley, California-based Pacifica chain of radio stations; and New York City–based Women Make Movies, which sought to distribute and publicize woman-centered films.[99]

124 • She's the Boss

Creating Feminist Spaces

In their efforts to forge a new social order, feminist activist entrepreneurs centered on the multiple roles their ventures could serve, including as the physical spaces or sites for organizing and building a feminist community. Bookstores, coffeehouses, restaurants—like those started by civil rights activists—as well as art galleries and more would prove vital to creating the feminist, woman-centered culture that activist entrepreneurs sought. Creating community not only helped the movement; it also helped owners share resources necessary to keep their ventures going. Collectives were especially important for providing community and a way to make a living for lesbian feminists on the margins. In some cases, as with the Olivia Records collective, members lived and worked together in the same space, often supporting their ventures by also holding part-time jobs.[100] These feminist community-centered businesses also provided a space where lesbian patrons felt safe to come out or be out.

Food-based businesses played a crucial role. Some were restaurants; others were coffeehouses and cafés, which could be started and operated at a lower cost than restaurants—pivotal in an era when women had limited access to start-up capital. Many were financed through personal savings, loans from friends, creative fundraising events, and by selling memberships. According to historian Alex D. Ketchum, "Every state at some point during the 1970s and 1980s had a feminist restaurant, cafe, or coffeehouse, with the exception of Alaska, Arkansas, North Dakota, West Virginia and Wyoming"—230 in total.[101] While other feminist business categories waned as the 1970s ended, restaurants and coffeehouses continued to open well into the 1980s.

In the late 1960s, lesbian feminists began to open bars, moving away from the discrimination they experienced in gay bars that historically served both men and women into new women-centered spaces of their own—a trend that would, like the growth of coffeehouses, continue to blossom in the 1980s.[102] Rikki Streicher opened the lesbian bar Maud's in the Haight Ashbury in the late 1960s, a staple until it closed in 1989.[103] Francine Logandise, a transgender woman, opened several bars in San Francisco beginning in the late 1970s, including the exclusively lesbian Francine's and Elaine's (her other bars were for a mixed gay/lesbian population, including transgender people).[104]

In 1971, two lesbian feminists, Dorothy Alexander and her partner Jill Ward, were looking for a place to eat late one summer night while driving back to New York City from the Hamptons, Long Island, and when they found nothing, the idea for a feminist restaurant was born. Dubbed Mother Courage after the Bertolt Brecht play featuring a strong feminist character, the restaurant was located in the meatpacking district and became a sort of salon.[105] In a *Newsday* article written by a self-proclaimed "befuddled male," Alexander explained that the restaurant would be "owned, operated, and staffed by women ... be pertinent to the women's lib movement," and serve a simple menu (initially the only planned item was spaghetti).[106] More than that, it would be a safe space for lesbian feminists and a hub for movement thought leaders, many of whom congregated there during the restaurant's seven-year existence: Audre Lorde, Kate Millett, and Susan Brownmiller, to name a few.

Not long after, in Bridgeport, Connecticut, Selma Miriam and Samm Stockwell launched the Bloodroot Collective, a communally run vegetarian restaurant and bookstore, as "a place where women would become more feminist, to meet with their friends, to encourage each other, just that we would supply the food and the context."[107] In 1980, the collective published a cookbook that merged recipes with feminist politics, *The Political Palate: A Feminist Vegetarian Cookbook*. Each recipe included a selection from a poem, work of fiction, or feminist tome—an excerpt from Robin Morgan's poetry accompanied a recipe for Rhubarb Custard Pie; a selection from Toni Morrison's *Sula* accompanied a quick description of how to make a wine cooler.[108] Bloodroot remains the only feminist restaurant still open in 2024, run by two of the original collective members, Miriam and Noel Furie.[109]

Women's bookstores were also crucial to creating feminist culture and emerged rapidly throughout the 1970s, spanning the nation from Manhattan to New Mexico and beyond. According to scholar Kristin Hogan, there were 130 bookstores in the peak years of the movement, providing books and resources focused on lesbian and gay themes that mainstream bookstores typically ignored.[110] Bookstores could be opened inexpensively, sometimes with as little as $400, as was the case for A Woman's Place Bookstore in Oakland, California. Some, like Minneapolis's Amazon (no connection to the internet giant of the same name), one of the earliest women's bookstores, began like many publishing ventures, in women's homes. In a kind of preinternet crowdfunding, it was not unusual for a bookstore to hold fundraisers to keep itself afloat. A Room of One's Own in Madison, Wisconsin, began in 1974 with $5,000 in donations and loans raised by the local women's community.[111]

Typically too, women's bookstores provided an entrée into feminism by serving as a kind of community center, with bulletin boards announcing local services and women's group meetings, talks, and readings. Recalled Seajay, "Many women who wanted the help or information that a woman's center could offer had been so intimidated by the media's portrayal of bra-burning, man-hating feminists that they were afraid to go into women's centers. Socialized to shop, they found women's bookstores to be a safer entryway into feminism." It is little wonder then, that bookstores outlasted many other women's liberation enterprises: nineteen of the sixty women's bookstores in existence in 1978 were still operating in the late 1990s.[112] That number dropped dramatically to just thirteen in 2014 due to competition from chains and the emergence of online retailer Amazon.com, but since 2017, amid book-banning controversies, there has been a bit of a resurgence, boosting the number of feminist bookstores to thirty.[113]

FIG. 4.4 Members of the Bloodroot Collective in Bridgeport, Connecticut, one of the longest-lasting feminist restaurants: Selma Miriam (center), Noel Giordano (left), Betsey Beaven (right). Photo by Robert Giard. Copyright © Estate of Robert Giard.

The vision for a feminist culture through business led some enterprising women to launch multipurpose buildings where different businesses could all be housed and where entrepreneurs could connect and possibly share resources and politics. In Los Angeles in 1972, feminist artists Judy Chicago, Miriam Shapiro, and a few others established Womanspace or the Women's Building, an art center for "women of all classes, races, and ages, a space in which women interested in the arts could exhibit, meet, perform and create a sense of community."[114] In 1973 in Detroit, members of the Feminist Economic Network (FEN), responsible for starting the first feminist credit union, sought to broaden feminism's reach by launching what would become the largest and most publicly visible feminist venture to date, the Feminist Women's City Club.[115] The group purchased a 1924 building that in its heyday had been a women's club but had fallen into disrepair. The idea was to create a space that could house a range of feminist businesses along with a club (including a swimming pool) and a cocktail lounge where women could gather and build community. It opened with a gala celebration in 1976, with Gloria Steinem as the guest speaker, but with heavy costs and infighting within the movement about it being elitist, it was sold two years later.[116]

Business Management—the Feminist Way

Feminists, especially radical left and socialist feminists, were conscious—at times even defensive—about how business could serve the cause of social revolution and which businesses could be considered truly feminist. That lent itself to the reasons a business was started, the way it was organized, the goals owners had for it, and especially whether they saw themselves as capitalists. Like other feminists, Coletta Reid, a member of the Furies and Diana Collective, made a distinction between those who were involved in ventures for the revolution and those who were in business for themselves, writing, "Feminist businesswomen are those who see their business as part of a multi-faceted strategy for gaining economic power for women as a group. . . . They are different from female capitalists who accept basic structures of capitalism as good but want women to be involved at higher levels."[117] As one newspaper article explained it, "They believe they are building the working models for the next critical stage of feminism: full independence from the control and influence of 'male-dominated' institutions—the news media, the health, education and legal systems, the art, theater and literary worlds, the banks."[118] They extended their theoretical analyses to point out "big business oppresses small business the way men oppress women."[119]

Feminists believed that by defining their businesses differently behind closed doors, they could influence the economic world beyond them—in effect remaining outside yet within the system. As a result, radical feminists—and sometimes liberals too—ran their businesses in highly unorthodox ways by conventional capitalist standards. Co-ops or collectives fit the anticapitalist vision by giving all members either a share or a vote in business operations, as was the case with *Chrysalis*. Many businesses balanced strategy meetings with feminist rap sessions, for example. At Olivia Records, one collective member noted that "business meetings (were) on Tuesdays; political discussions on Thursdays."[120]

Instead of profit, feminists organized their businesses according to their principles, pricing merchandise near cost—or at prices women could afford and channeling revenues back to the business or to other feminist start-ups. Some

128 • She's the Boss

even defined profit as a "women's issue": "Women could decide to be like the men who create, control and profit from this society, to adopt their practices and attitudes of success. . . . A profit-oriented consumption is profoundly alienating. It fosters competitiveness and the tendency to regard others as objects."[121] When there were profits, many feminist entrepreneurs used them to support the movement; Grimstad and Rennie shared 20 percent of the proceeds from the *NWSC* royalties with feminist groups; Those Uppity Women, a Florida jewelry business, pledged 10 percent of its gains to women's groups as well.[122] Bachelor made a contribution to NOW for every album she sold.

Feminists also reined in competition by adopting a nonhierarchical structure. In many of these ventures, there were no managers, no supervisors, no bosses. In pure socialist terms, there were admonitions against "divisions between white-collar/blue-collar work" and no separation between "thinking jobs. . . . (and) jobs in which you work with your hands."[123] Everyone shared work equally, and one enterprise made sure everyone got the same number of creative and noncreative tasks.[124] At *Ms.*, there were no secretaries—"everyone there was an editor." One of the founders in the early days explained it this way: "Sure it's easier to work in an office with a defined structure but it puts people down. This is true liberation."[125] *Ms.* staffers sat on the floor during meetings, and only the managing editor had a private office—at her insistence and in the name of efficiency. The same was true at KNOW, Inc., a Pittsburgh feminist publishing company, said founder Anne Pride, noting, "We work as a collective and don't have any titles." Carol Burris, who founded the feminist lobbying firm Women's Lobby Inc., added, "We're not trying to set up some male-type hierarchy where some women do the interesting work and others do all the [*sic*, expletive missing] work."[126] Unlike typical companies, at feminist businesses such as *Ms.* children were welcome and were even nicknamed "*Ms.* kids."[127]

When it came to salaries, socialism prevailed over capitalism. "Workers should be paid equally or nearly equally according to need," advised Reid, making an exception for weighing a woman's special needs such as children or health problems.[128] Although *Ms.* was not founded by those wedded to socialist ideology, it did apply similar principles regarding wages. Salaries were initially to be the same for everyone; only after some staffers objected did the publication form a three-tier wage structure that allowed for rewarding people for experience, talent, and professional development. It was not unusual for these businesses to offer little or nothing in the way of salaries, in part due to their perceived radical foundation and in part, of course, because they were typically underfunded. As such, volunteerism was a celebrated component of feminist business cooperatives or collectives. "What's more revolutionary," said Toni McNaron, a member of the Amazon Bookstore, "than to open a business and not pay anyone!"[129] Since most of the women involved in feminist enterprises worked at other jobs to support themselves, their contributions to movement-related businesses typically gave them an equal ownership share. They developed a philosophy of

FIG. 4.5 An editor working with her child—one of the "*Ms.* kids" (March 1975). Copyright © Maddy Miller.

nobility in working for something they believed in with little or no financial compensation: "Surviving voluntarily in poverty at once renounced capitalism and prepared one for survival in a money-free economy after the revolution."[130]

Even when their politics aligned, feminist politico-entrepreneurs ultimately faced the problem of simple economics. Self-sufficiency, even in feminist terms, meant that women contributors needed to earn a fair wage. As Beverly Fisher-Manick, one of the founders of the feminist quarterly *Quest* explained to readers, "We believe that feminist projects should support women at a decent living standard."[131] But that increasingly meant making more money and real profits, the very antithesis of the feminist take on the role of enterprise.

On another functional level for feminist businesses, there was the problem of supplies. The need to purchase the items necessary to print books, publish newsletters and magazines, or perform simple office tasks forced feminists to engage the mainstream economy and pay prices for goods as determined by the "system." These variables were beyond their control and did not often gel with feminist values for establishing the cost or worth of goods. Feminist publishers, for example, had to face a harsh reality when the cost of newsprint rose 200 percent from 1970 to 1981.[132] Like it or not, such factors would ultimately influence the success, failure, and long-term business strategy of feminist enterprises. Nearly bankrupt in 1978, Olivia Records traded survival for politics: the company cut its staff to eight, abandoned the collective in favor of a more traditional corporate structure, used male technicians at concerts and recording sessions, and developed a business plan to turn the red ink black again that kept

130 • She's the Boss

the company afloat well into the 1980s.[133] By the 1990s, Olivia had transformed itself into a financially successful lesbian cruise line and travel business, which still exists in 2024.

The Buck Talks Loudest

As women and people of color started businesses in growing numbers, they shared a common problem: limited (if any) access to start-up capital from banks and similar institutions due to widespread discrimination. In 1964, sports legend Jackie Robinson, known for having integrated baseball in 1947, gathered a small group of investors and activists including celebrated beautician Rose Morgan to establish Freedom National Bank in Harlem, New York City. The goal was to support economic development in the community and lending/credit opportunities for people of color. One of only two women among the eight founders, Morgan, a friend of Robinson's, was respected for her decades-long success as an entrepreneur.[134] Having faced discrimination in lending herself, Morgan started New Jersey Savings and Loan Association a few years earlier, which she later sold. When she built her beauty emporium in Harlem in the 1950s, she later recounted, she was turned down for a loan "because [of] the amount of money [she] needed. . . . They didn't loan black people that kind of money."[135] In the heyday of the civil rights movement, from the late 1950s to the early 1970s, seventeen Black-owned banks were established across the country, all with similar visions of providing access to credit for people of color.[136]

Freedom Bank's founders contributed money to secure the bank's charter and helped raise additional capital, including as Walker had done with the Harlem Food Co-op, selling shares to local residents. The bank opened with $15 million in assets, but as with other activist money-lending ventures, the bank faced the dilemma of whose money to accept and who to lend to. Though its founders saw the bank as providing financial services to the Black community (and 90 percent of employees were in fact Black), bank president William R. Hudgins averred, "Freedom National Bank is completely color blind. We invite business from everybody."[137] Critics claimed the bank served middle- and upper-class people of color, made large numbers of loans to corporations and to whites, and declined loans to lower-income Blacks.[138] For much of its history, the bank struggled to remain true to its politics of providing financial services to those underserved by larger banks while also attracting the large depositors—often from outside the community—that would keep the institution going. The bank faltered in 1974, began to show a small profit in the early 1980s, but by 1990 had closed its doors.[139]

Feminists too saw that access to and control of money was crucial in the battle for equality. In 1971, when Alexander and Ward launched their restaurant Mother Courage, they held a fundraiser for the $5,000 needed "because women [didn't] get loans from banks." Ward added, "My mother has been in businesses for years. . . . She has all sorts of business experience and all sorts of acceptable collateral, but she finds it almost impossible to borrow money from a bank."[140] Such stories of lending discrimination were all too common and the reason so many early feminist ventures used similar fundraising techniques before the Equal Credit Act was enacted and fully enforced.

As early as 1973, feminists founded and operated their own credit unions. The first, the Detroit Feminist Federal Credit Union (DFFCU), typified the goals and membership rules of the others that would follow: they were staffed entirely by women, and if they were not already a member of one of four feminist organizations, they paid initial dues to join one, plus made deposits to their accounts.[141] Like banks, the credit unions would reinvest deposits, but unlike banks, the credit unions would lend money for members' personal economic needs like auto loans or other projects or ventures, including feminist businesses. Members' deposits netted them an equal voice in electing the credit union leadership. As explained by a feminist credit union representative in Missouri, "[The credit unions were] based on the 'self-help' concept of women pooling our resources to develop some practical solutions to our common situations ... in this case, pooling our money in order that we may begin to provide ourselves with credit *and* information regarding the workings of the financial world."[142]

By 1976, eighteen feminist federal credit unions existed across the United States and Canada in places as disparate as Massachusetts, Houston, Washington State, California, New York, and Pennsylvania. They had at that time assets of roughly $3 million "and growing"—although few of them would survive into the 1980s due largely to internal strife over reinvestment strategies, management problems, and ever-changing regulations.[143] Many were nonhierarchical, most required members to adhere to a shared system of feminist beliefs, and all were dedicated to providing funds to help women. As one credit union brochure noted, "The goal of feminist credit unions is not to make profits, but to keep our money within the Feminist community; to withdraw our support from the banking establishment—and the government; and to keep our money in our Sisters' hands."

Unlike banks, feminist credit unions would make small, potentially risky loans, defying conventional banking norms about who and what to fund and opting instead to trust women. That meant women who needed money for a divorce or an abortion could successfully seek loans from feminist credit unions, even if they had no credit history or collateral. Politically speaking, feminist credit unions were about creating a separate women's financial services culture that would eventually have a trickle-down effect on the rest of the system. Setting themselves against and apart from the patriarchal power of traditional banks, one credit union brochure explained, "By supporting banks—any banks—we are supporting the repressive profit-oriented economic system which currently runs this country."[144] Changes in federal regulations, debates over lending policies and growth, along with conflicts over potential borrowers, contributed to the disintegration of the credit unions. The last feminist credit union in San Antonio closed in 2013, after its female director embezzled funds.

132 • She's the Boss

Liberal feminists took a different tack in countering lending discrimination—enacting equitable credit laws and establishing women's banks. In the early 1970s, around the same time feminist credit unions were getting off the ground, NOW worked to secure passage of the Equal Credit Opportunity Act of 1974 (ECOA) and to ensure banks' compliance. Implemented in 1975, the ECOA outlawed what had become standard bank practice: application questions about women's marital status and plans to have children as well as formulas that discounted a woman's salary by as much as 50 percent if she were married and of child-bearing age.[145] A married woman previously needed the signature of her spouse (or if unavailable, any man, including sons) to receive bank loans, mortgages, or credit cards, even if she was the primary wage-earner of the family. Prior to the ECOA, creditors did not need to give a reason when rejecting an applicant. Despite its flaws, the ECOA did bring change. A 1978 report by the Women's Equity Action League noted that as a result of the ECOA, "20 million two-income families find their buying power increased by fifty to sixty percent, and in some cases, much more."[146]

The ECOA, however, did not extend to business loans; that would not happen until 1988. In the meantime, banks could deny a loan without explanation, and their lending decisions and gender biases could limit business growth. Sue Little was initially one of the lucky ones: though in her early twenties in 1972, when she opened Jabberwocky bookstore in the small seaside city of Newburyport, Massachusetts, she secured a $2,000 bank loan to match her $2,000 in personal savings. Two years later, having repaid the debt in full, the bank rejected her request for a $4,000 loan to expand and move her thriving bookshop to a larger location. "She was told that as a young woman in the 1970s [sic] she'd be 'doing other things soon' and was declined," her son Erik Hoel later recounted. Those "other things" were code for having children and a family and ending her dalliance with business. Without the needed financing, it would be more than a decade before Little could expand from the 650-square-foot store to its subsequent 7,000-square-foot location, where it still was in 2024.[147]

Before the ECOA, one needn't be a feminist to understand what every divorced woman knew: that *he* got their credit history in the divorce, and *she* got the reputation of being too "emotionally (read: financially) unstable" to manage debt, as one NOW study noted.[148] NOW, along with *Ms.* and other women's magazines, received countless letters in the early 1970s from female readers complaining about their experiences with credit discrimination and seeking the right to credit separate from their husbands'. One angry Wyoming wife and business owner wrote to NOW in 1973, "For the first time since Women's Liberation started, I am in complete agreement with their cause." The woman, who sold her successful six-year-old beauty shop in 1972 for health reasons, was a year later eager to get back into business by leasing another salon for $2,500. When she went to the bank where she thought she had built a solid relationship, she was told she needed a co-signer. Even then, the bank only agreed

Sisterhood Is (Economically) Powerful • 133

to $1,200. When she picked up the check, the bank representative said they would require her husband's signature. She explained,

> They got my husband's signature. My husband doesn't know it though. In forging his name, I put myself in all sorts of jeopardy—including a jail sentence if discovered. In the meantime, I am adding to HIS credit rating. . . . They checked our credit rating. They did not discover several FACTS that I would consider under the same set of circumstances. 1. My husband is on probation. He cannot apply for or receive any loan without his probation officer's knowledge or permission. 2. My husband has never been in business. . . . 3. My husband has been unemployed from March of 1972. . . . I had managed my own business for three years, kept all business expenses and household expenses with the exception of a few groceries. . . . My son's father won minimum child support in our divorce because "I had a potentially greater income than he did." . . . I am tired of slavery. I want only what would have been mine if I were a man. I've earned it as a Woman.[149]

By 1975, mainstream feminists organized to establish women's banks; by 1979, there were nine women's banks from New York to California and eleven a few years later.[150] The pioneering First Women's Bank of New York, for example, was the brainchild of feminists *and* businesswomen, among them Betty Friedan, dress designer Pauline Trigere, and New York Federal Reserve Bank president Madeline McWhinney.[151] Like the feminist credit unions that preceded them, women's banks saw their mission to educate women about the complicated world of finances and serve as financial institutions by and for women.[152] Unlike the credit unions, the banks sought to provide financial services to "both men and women in a nondiscriminatory manner, and in fact men would come to comprise forty percent of the depositors at the Women's Bank in Denver."[153] The banks had greater assets than their credit union counterparts—the deposits at the Women's National Bank in Washington, D.C., topped $7 million in its first ten months, the First Women's Bank of California had $9 million in investments in 1978 after eighteen months in business, while Denver's Women's Bank's deposits increased 95 percent in 1980, its second year of operation, to $14.4 million.[154] They also had men on their staffs, and within just a few years of their founding some, including First Women's of New York and Connecticut Women's Bank, had male CEOs.[155] Little wonder then that feminists on the left, especially those who pioneered the feminist federal credit unions, dismissed the banks as too far "in" the system, operating with the same hierarchical structure and rules of business that capitalism imposed.

Almost from the start, the banks began to experience questions and backlash for being "women's" institutions. Some defended the naming, but by the mid-1980s, three of the remaining half dozen women's banks had deleted "women" from their titles. As early as 1978, stockholders at San Diego's Women's Bank voted four to one to change its name to California Coastal Bank—just two

FIG. 4.6 Employees, officers, and board members of the Women's Bank, Denver, circa 1978. *Credit:* Denver Public Library, Western History Collection (Call #WH2365).

years after its founding.[156] Some, like Connecticut Women's Bank, made it policy to "not pound the word 'woman,'" insisting employees use the bank's acronym CWB instead.[157] New York's First Women's Bank changed its name in 1989 to First New York Bank for Business. The Denver Women's Bank would be the last holdout in the name game, lasting until 1997, when it was retagged as Colorado Business Bank. Still feminist roots were hard for at least some bank leaders to let go of: When the Women's National Bank in Washington, D.C., changed its name to Adams National Bank in 1986, president and CEO Barbara Blum justified the new name by linking it to the second U.S. president's wife, Abigail Adams. "She was a feminist before anybody ever thought of the word," Blum bristled.[158] Perhaps, but Abigail was hardly the Adams who first came to mind when people heard the bank's new name.

The feminist attempt to regender money was short-lived. Ironically, the underfunded but highly politicized feminist credit unions would outlive the more moderate, mainstream, and fiscally sound women's banks. By 1987, only six of the eleven women's banks were still in existence. Some claimed the need for women's banks ended with the passage of the ECOA.[159] "When this women's bank thing started, the big banks were still unresponsive to women," Rita E. Hauser, a partner in a Manhattan law firm, told the New York Times in 1980. "But they finally woke up to the fact that they [had] a great clientele in women. . . . And a lot of women, even if they're feminists, think twice about putting their money in a small unknown bank"—despite the fact that they were all federally insured.

Roadblocks: Ideology versus Enterprise

While feminist activist entrepreneurs celebrated the potential of their businesses to create a new feminist/women-driven culture, others saw the ventures as at best incongruous with movement politics and at worst an absolute betrayal. Black activist entrepreneurs faced similar criticism, especially from those on the left who had concerns about co-optation of movement politics by engagement with capitalism. But the most visible and angry debates happened among feminists, waged largely in the feminist press, though even mainstream newspapers such as the *New York Times* covered the controversy. In part, this was fueled by concerns about commercialization—and, by association, trivialization of movement politics. Both Black Power and women's liberation were mass-marketed as fashion and pop culture—often by those outside the movements seeking to cash in on their popularity, though sometimes by those within the movement who sought to enhance its visibility or make a buck for themselves. To critics, the issue was ideological purity: business ownership was capitalist, which made it inherently classist, racist, and sexist—that is, antithetical to movement ideals. They worried too that the shift from activist politics to culture through business would dilute the movement. There were other concerns: among them, how the ventures were run, how profitable they were (which, the argument went, made them part of the system), who supported them, and whether they were making stars of some feminists.

The debate reached the 1973 annual NOW Convention in Washington, D.C., where a group of feminist entrepreneurs faced "shoddy treatment" for being entrepreneurs by the organizing committee and other feminists in attendance. They later met and produced a collection of essays defending the role of feminist enterprises in women's liberation, entitled "Dealing with the Real World: 13 Papers by Feminist Entrepreneurs," which "pointed up what each businesswoman had heretofore been suffering alone: the ambivalence and frequent hostility of movement women toward feminist business." The essays covered everything from defining a "feminist business" to "profit, that nasty ugly word" to the way other feminists' criticisms left them feeling "plagued by self-destructive fear and guilt about making profits."

In large measure, the debate speaks to the diffuseness of the growing women's liberation movement, which meant there was no one feminism, even among those on the left. It also reflected concern about who the real insiders were, and criticisms focused on loyalty or disloyalty to movement ideals. For example, in 1972, when Gloria Steinem and other activist women launched *Ms.* magazine, radical feminists accused them not only of practicing a watered-down feminism but also of being co-opted by the system, since $1 million of start-up funds came from Warner Communications, a huge media company, in exchange for 25 percent ownership. The feminist founders were also accused of trying to cash in on the movement themselves.[160] Joanne Parrent, Valerie Angers, and members of the Feminist Economic Network (FEN) were accused of seeking to profit themselves when they opened Feminist Women's City Club (FWCC) in Detroit in 1976. Others balked at its one-hundred-dollar annual membership fees, which seemed elitist to critics. Parrent later said she was both surprised and hurt by the accusations. She believed that they were driven by a combination of leftist anticapitalist ideology and jealousy over the visibility her involvement with the FWCC brought her and other leaders. She resigned from FEN and the DFFCU, and FEN was disbanded.[161]

Feminist entrepreneurs expressed resentment at having to defend their ventures and their loyalty to the movement. "We are torn by our two positions," wrote Susan Sojourner, owner of First Things First. "As businesswomen, we're tired of constantly being questioned about our profit (dirty, ugly word) motivations and our 'credentials' (how much free movement work are we doing?) Yet, as feminists we often look at other businesswomen with the same movement-protective attitudes: Why is she in this? Is she a movement woman? Or just in this for the money?"[162] The more visible a business was, the more susceptible it was to criticism, as was the case with Olivia. In a letter to *off our backs*, Ginny Berson, an Olivia cofounder, lamented, "Sometimes we feel that *oob* holds Olivia responsible not only for being perfect at all times, but also for making everyone else in the world perfect. We are doing our work—which we have defined very clearly over and over again, in the feminist press, in concerts, in articles, on records, in radio interviews."

Along with profits, feminists worried about co-optation of movement ideals, and like many other leftist groups, they feared infiltration by outsiders. One of the worst examples happened in 1974 when Olivia hired Sandy Stone, a "transsexual" (the term used at the time) as a recording engineer. In that era, both the women's and gay liberation movements often excluded transgender women and men. While radical feminists embraced and included lesbians, many feminists nonetheless reserved the term *woman* for those who had been assigned that way at birth. Within a year of hiring Stone, whose resume included working with Jimi Hendrix and the Grateful Dead, the collective received anonymous letters demanding that Olivia fire her as well as death threats leveled mostly at Stone. The letter writers considered Stone's hiring a betrayal because feminist businesses were supposed to be for women. "Sandy Stone grew up as a white male in this culture, with all the privileges and attitudes that that insures [*sic*]," said an anti-Stone letter in *Sister*.[163] At first, Olivia ignored the letters, but the pressure continued as the debate increasingly made its way into the feminist press. In defense of Stone, members of the Olivia collective first explained their hiring process and later why "transsexuals" should be counted among potential feminists, writing,

Because Sandy decided to give up completely and permanently her male identity and live as a woman and a lesbian, she is now faced with the same kinds of oppression that other women and lesbians face. . . . If she is a person who comes from privilege, has she renounced that which is oppressive in her privilege, and is she sharing with other women that which is useful? . . . Is she open to struggle around class, race, and other aspects of lesbian feminist politics? These were our yardsticks in deciding whether to work with a woman who grew up with male privilege. We felt that Sandy met those same criteria that we apply to any woman with whom we plan to work closely.[164]

Ultimately, the pressure and issues of safety led Stone to leave the collective; she later became a scholar and writer.

In April 1976, it was clear feminist business had mainstreamed when *Ms.* took on critics of feminist enterprises with a fifteen-page insert entitled "How to Start Your Own Business." The magazine advised would-be feminist entrepreneurs on everything from financing a venture to writing a business plan. Denouncing the "poor is pure" principle embraced by many feminist businesses, *Ms.* instead offered "six basic feminist principles of doing business that might be described as 'compassionate capitalism.'" The list included the following: "The product or service should fulfill a feminist need, advance a feminist cause or improve the quality of feminist life . . . [and] should not be overpriced. . . . The profit margin should . . . not be so large that one becomes a guilt-ridden profiteer."[165] The issue of profit also seemed to point at something else women struggled with: an insecurity about their worth. "Were we truly pricing our material at a price every woman could afford," wrote Pride in a separate collection of essays on feminist entrepreneurship, "or are we purposely keeping our prices as low as possible because we, in fact, were not completely convinced that anything we, as women, could produce was worth a higher price?"[166]

End of an Era?

In 1972, Claudia Jessup and Genie Chipps published what they titled "the autobiography of an outrageous business." The women, who four years earlier abandoned unsuccessful acting careers to try their hand at independent enterprise, began their book with a question: "What can a girl do if she chooses to think of herself as a total human being, and not just an appliance in the world of Man? The answer is: pretty much what she wants."[167] What Jessup and Chipps, both barely thirty at the time, wanted was to inspire readers with the tale of how, in just a few years, they had created Supergirls Enterprises Ltd., a kind of do-everything, girl-Friday business based in New York City in which these childhood friends got paid for services married women performed every day for free, taking on everything from the mundane (picking up dry cleaning, photographing prized pet Siberian huskies in the park or distributing menus for a new pizzeria) to the bizarre (promoting a new board game by playing it for two hours a day in a Manhattan store window).[168] They quickly gained widespread media

FIG. 4.7 The April 1976 issue of *Ms.* made women's business ownership the cover, with *Peanuts*' Lucy showcasing a wide range of entrepreneurial options. Courtesy of *Ms.* magazine.

attention, including from the *New York Times*, and *Time* and *Newsweek* fought over which magazine would profile them first.[169] Jessup and Chipps had several television guest appearances on *The Tonight Show*, *The Dick Cavett Show*, and *The Mike Douglas Show*, while network executives considered creating a weekly sit-com based on their business. They were also flooded with requests from women for advice on setting up an enterprise, and some sought to franchise the Supergirls operation in their hometowns.

The story of Supergirls is an example of both how visible women's business had become in the late 1960s and 1970s and how it had infused women's thinking about feminism and economics. Jessup and Chipps were not activists, yet in their memoir, they wrote about their emerging political consciousness and offered a feminist-inspired interpretation of the meaning of business ownership in their and other women's lives. "Women's liberation was telling us something about the changing times, particularly about the budding awareness in women," they wrote.[170] Certainly their ventures made some men nervous: a blurb on the back of *Supergirls* by conservative columnist Cleveland Amory labeled it "dangerous dynamite" and said that the authors were "almost the equal of men." By the end of the decade, Jessup's and Chipps's burgeoning feminist impulses made them proponents of the liberating potential of business ownership, and they authored a second book, *The Woman's Guide to Starting a Business* in 1976.[171]

As Jessup, Chipps, and countless women like them began to assert their right to stake a claim on entrepreneurship, the revolutionary feminist zeal that drove many into business began to fizzle amid ongoing challenges. Berson, one of the founders of Olivia, resigned from the collective in 1979, noting, "We could not be a revolutionary political/cultural organization and a successful business."[172] Other revolutionary feminist businesses were similarly facing the decision to reshape their businesses to survive in a capitalist system or close up shop. Feminists would continue to debate whether business ownership and movement ideals were incompatible at various moments well into the twenty-first century. Still Jessup and Chipps's story points to an important trend: whether they were feminist or not, a growing number of women in the 1970s and beyond were getting the message that business could be a source of women's empowerment.

5

Becoming "Entrepreneurs"

Women's Businesses in
the 1970s Recession
and "Go-Go '80s"

In early April 1984, President Ronald Reagan embarked on a speaking tour to various national organizations in the New York City area. Featured among his stops: giving the keynote address to the fifth annual Women in Business Conference. Reagan, who was in the midst of a reelection campaign, accepted the invitation as an opportunity to counter critics who disdained his poor record on women's issues and who saw him as thwarting women's equality, particularly through his opposition to the Equal Rights Amendment (ERA) and his stance on reproductive rights. While he pointed to his independent and successful daughters Maureen Reagan and Patti Davis as a sign that he valued women, Reagan sidestepped the question of legislative and political equality in his speech. Instead, he focused on the economy, noting that the recession of the 1970s and early 1980s "hit women especially hard. Elderly women living on fixed incomes found their purchasing power eaten up by inflation. Working women saw jobs become more and more scarce. . . . And the thousands of women who wanted to start their own businesses saw 21 1/2 percent prime interest rates slam the door in their faces."[1] Holding up a T-shirt the event's organizers had given him that boldly declared "Women Mean Business," Reagan, who took credit for ending the recession, further averred, "Economic growth will provide more opportunities for women than if all the promises made in the history of Washington, D.C., were enacted into law."[2]

140

FIG. 5.1 President Ronald Reagan proudly displaying a "Women Mean Business!" T-shirt at the 1984 Women in Business Conference in New York City. Courtesy of the Ronald Reagan Presidential Library.

A powerful and arguably overstated claim, to Reagan and the women at the conference, the economy in the form of women's business ownership—not politics or activism—was the solution to a host of gender-based inequality issues. Put simply: become successful, make money and gain the respect that comes with it, and equality will follow—especially if large numbers of women take this route. That is, with a successful business, women would garner the power needed to improve their own lives and potentially influence the policies that could improve the lives of all women—without the need for the ERA. The argument resonated with those present: while few women business owners were able to get loans—and therefore deal with the excessive interest rates Reagan cited—the women in the room did see entrepreneurship as the path to personal independence and proof of women's equality.

Politics aside, Reagan's presence at the Women in Business Conference pointed to several important factors shaping women's business ownership in the mid-1970s and 1980s: the impact of the recession and postrecession economic climate, the mainstreaming of women's business ownership and its growing economic and social importance, the changing relationship between women entrepreneurs and feminism, and the ongoing gender biases in lending. At the same time, the rise of women's networks proved vital to overcoming the obstacles to their advancement in the workplace (first dubbed "the glass ceiling" in this era) and to assisting women in starting businesses instead. In addition, women's visibility as entrepreneurs aligned with government officials' desire to expand small business in the United States during and after the recession, which led to increased government recognition of and support for women's ventures. In 1977, President Jimmy Carter established a task force to address the obstacles women business owners faced, and in the 1980s Reagan launched his own initiatives, culminating in the 1988 Women's Business Ownership Act. Media attention to a growing number of "celebrity entrepreneurs"—women whose business ownership made them famous—also facilitated the popularity of entrepreneurship as the key to women's empowerment, with or without any association with feminist politics per se.

Throughout the 1970s and 1980s, business ownership would move from the sidelines of women's options to the forefront of a growing consciousness of equality and self-determination. It also became a vehicle for women to fuse personal ambitions, familial obligations, and financial imperatives through business ownership. As such, women's business ownership surged by the end of the 1980s to nearly 30 percent of all small businesses nationally. Statistics, however flawed, paint a picture of the changing economic landscape for women via business ownership. Throughout the 1970s, the number of women-owned enterprises, which posted only slight increases in previous decades, increased.[3] In 1972, just over 1.4 million women owned businesses, a scant 4.6 percent of the nation's total.[4] The number of women-owned firms jumped to 2.1 million in 1979 and 2.3 million in 1981, an increase of 64 percent in just nine years.[5] Between 1977 and 1983, women opened businesses at twice the rate of men.[6] From 1980 to 1987, the number of women-owned businesses jumped 47 percent to 4.1 million businesses—a figure that the National Association of Women Business Owners publicly averred was inaccurate. According to NAWBO, the Census undercounted women's ventures by 1.3 million (bringing the total to 5.4 million) by not including companies that had started since 1987. NAWBO also noted that many self-employed women may not have identified themselves as such on their tax returns, the vehicle the Census used for its data.[7] Nonetheless, by the end of the 1980s, women were becoming self-employed at three to five times the rate of their male counterparts and launching businesses three times more frequently. Sales at women-owned firms also increased three times faster than those owned by men from 1977 to 1983, generating a total of $98.3 billion in 1983. NAWBO noted triumphantly that in 1990, women-owned firms employed nearly eleven million workers, and with employment rates dropping by three hundred thousand per year at Fortune 500 companies, NAWBO predicted women's businesses would out-employ men's by 1992.[8]

Like their predecessors in the 1950s, women in the 1970s and 1980s once again upheld the image of the independent business owner as men delayed or cautiously returned to small business. Women were also beginning to move beyond traditionally feminine realms—long a mainstay for women business owners—into a wider range of ventures including such male-dominated categories as construction and transportation.[9] But even with their growing numbers, by 1988, women's businesses generated barely 10 percent of all business revenues nationwide, due in part to the newness of their businesses, their size, and limited access to start-up capital. The number of businesses owned by people of color doubled from 1972 to 1982 yet remained 20 percent that of whites—who owned 63 percent of all businesses. As with white women, access to capital was a factor.[10] Nonetheless, in the 1980s, women of color increasingly looked toward business ownership to bypass ongoing racial biases in the workplace, sparking a trend that by the 2000s would have their rates of start-up outpacing both white women and men.

What corporate America had ignored for decades about working women's needs, their increasing forays into business ownership would help them address for themselves. In the process, these women redefined the very nature of what constitutes a business, forging new debates about gender differences in profit motive, firm size, and even management style that continued for decades thereafter. By the 1980s, women were proudly claiming the word *entrepreneur* for themselves, something earlier generations rarely or hesitantly did.

Last in, First Out: The Impact of the Recession

As the recession doused the optimism that had characterized the previous decade, the 1970s and early 1980s became a time of both hardship and ingenuity for women. The recession fueled high unemployment rates generally, and women were often hard hit, especially women of color. In 1975, for example, the unemployment rate was 8.5 percent nationally but was 7.9 percent for men and 9.3 percent for women.[11] By 1981, unemployment rates reached nearly 11 percent. Black women had an unemployment rate of 14.2 percent, while for Hispanic women, the figure was 11.5 percent.[12] The other group hit hard was professional women. Educated women who obtained MBAs after the passage of Title IX (1972) prohibiting discrimination in higher education often found themselves the first laid off as the recession gained steam. In 1974, women holding managerial and professional positions reached an all-time high at 17 percent. By the mid-1980s, however, that figure dropped to 11.9 percent.[13]

Fortune magazine tracked the career paths of eight thousand female and male MBAs over a ten-year period beginning in 1976. At the outset, women and men joined large corporations in equal numbers—about 69 percent. A decade later, 30 percent of the women versus just 21 percent of the men were self-employed, unemployed, or working part-time. Pace University MBAs graduating between 1976 and 1980 followed a similar path: in 1987, 21 percent of the women versus 1 percent of the men did not hold full-time jobs.[14] Even as late as 1990, the ratio of women to men on corporate boards of directors was less than one to eight. There were only three female chief executive officers of Fortune 500 companies, one of whom was Marion O. Sandler, who co-founded Gold West Financial Group with her husband in the 1960s.[15] As such, beginning with the recession,

144 • She's the Boss

many of these women turned to business ownership, particularly as the worsening economic climate conspired to further restrict women's access to better paying and managerial jobs in the workforce.

As unemployment spiked, one segment of the labor market grew: temporary employment, which saw increases of 9 percent annually. It also provided an important opportunity not only for displaced workers to find jobs but also for would-be women entrepreneurs to launch companies. Even when the economy stabilized, temporary employment growth rates were 17.5 percent compared to 1 percent for other workers. As historian Erin Hatton notes, by the end of the decade, "the size of the temp industry tripled, from 400,000 workers a day to more than a million."[16] The industry got its start after World War II, due to personnel shortages for shorthand and typing services. It was built on the nation's discomfort with the idea of women working full-time and became instantly feminized by providing office support services on an as-needed basis.[17] With the money companies saved on wages and benefits, by the 1970s, those categories continued in high demand, joined by technical professionals in accounting and engineering. In Colorado, Carol Grever (formerly Carol Grever Gray) cofounded Express Personnel in the mid-1970s; demand propelled the business into franchising opportunities nationwide that generated $425 million in sales by 1995. "The economy was not doing well, especially in Boulder, which was a small college town," Grever recalled. "But Denver is thirty-five miles away, and we had people eager to work and lots of jobs open in Denver. . . . Plus, one of the drives for women coming into temp services is that they can work when they want to . . . and it gives them an opportunity to try out a job before they take it."[18]

While temps could move in and out of the job market, full-time working women found themselves at the mercy of a gender-biased wage system. The number of female employees deemed underpaid according to the standards of the Equal Pay Act jumped from 960 in 1965 to 17,719 in 1970 and 31,282 in 1975.[19] While the Equal Employment Opportunity Commission (EEOC) was a product of the 1960s Title VII legislation, it was not empowered to bring suit against violators until the early 1970s, when concerns about affirmative action gained a political and legal foothold. Even then, women's groups spearheaded efforts to press the EEOC into action.[20] At the same time, women who remained outside the movement found it in their self-interest to become aware of feminism's role in ending gender inequality in the workplace. Mainstream women workers may not have been activists, but they increasingly understood themselves as beneficiaries of someone else's activism. Even as the economy improved in the 1980s and women, especially those graduating from college into a boom economy, found more and better jobs, they would continue to face biases in the workplace that limited how high they could climb.

Who Needs Feminism Anyway?

Feminist activist businesses may have jump-started the conversation about entrepreneurship a decade earlier, but by the mid-1970s and 1980s, women were increasingly doing exactly what Reagan nudged them to do in his 1984 speech—looking not to feminism but to their right to achieve as individuals. And they could do so without crediting the women's movement for making many of those rights possible or pushing legislators to see women as a key constituency. Feminism still mattered to many women, including women entrepreneurs, but what had changed was the 1960s and 1970s notion that business could be used as a tool for social revolution and for creating a woman-centered economy. Many of the businesses that started in the 1970s as feminist counterinstitutions closed up shop or reoriented themselves to a capitalist system. At the same time, the women's movement focused increasingly on legal and social equality, including the Equal Rights Amendment and protecting the gains made for reproductive rights via the Supreme Court's *Roe v. Wade* decision.

That does not mean that feminism's impact did not continue for many women business owners; instead, it points to a triumph of both liberal feminism and a rising number of women across the political spectrum who did not think they needed the movement at all. When Lucille Treganowan opened her auto repair business, Transmissions by Lucille, Inc., in an abandoned Pittsburgh, Pennsylvania, gas station in 1973, the media was charmed by the novelty of it. "The women's movement was getting a lot of publicity, and as a result, so did I," she said.[21] By the mid-1970s, media coverage, passage of new laws, songs like Helen Reddy's "I Am Woman," and the increasing visibility of women's businesses (whether feminist or not) helped mainstream the power and potential of women's individual achievement.

In effect, what won out was NOW's politics of inclusion into the existing capitalist system on equal terms with men and a more generalized belief by nonfeminist (those who were neutral) and even antifeminist women (vocal opponents) that they already had the ability to achieve whatever they wanted as long as they worked hard at it. What resulted was a kind of economic feminism without the "f-word." That is, women could embrace equality through the economy without crediting the women's movement for the gains that made this possible and without aligning with it (and in some cases, publicly opposing all things feminist). This also marked the beginning of what has come to be labeled "postfeminism," the notion that the problems women faced had already been solved. The idealism of the 1970s faded and morphed into the capitalist boom of what came to be dubbed "the go-go '80s." Women draped in man-tailored suits with floppy bow ties and strong shoulder pads not only believed they had a stake in the economy, but ironically because of the empowerment brought by the feminist movement, they also could be just as capitalist as men (for better or worse) without losing their femininity. They could bring home the bacon, as a famous perfume commercial of the era proclaimed, *and* they could fry it up in a pan, being the superwomen only capitalism allowed and promoted.

Where the movement's impact remained, it was more toned down and at times apologetic by the late 1970s and 1980s, with a growing awareness of what it took to succeed in the male-dominated economy. "I'm a lib woman; what do people have against that? No one else around here will say it, but I will," averred Ella Romera Rael, owner of a restaurant in Catron County, New Mexico, in a 1976 interview in *Ms*. Rael's decision to open Ella's Café was both a quest for autonomy and an opportunity to earn a living from her love of cooking Mexican-style specialties like tortillas hecho de mano and sopapillas.[22] Like Rael, many women business owners sought to balance their feminism with the day-to-day realities of commercial engagement. "I think everyone was influenced by the women's movement at that time," recalled Grever. "I didn't consider myself a rabid feminist by any stretch. I couldn't be; I was a woman working in a man's world, and I had to get along with male clients. I then and now consider myself more of a humanist than a feminist in that I want to help everyone reach their potential."[23] Others, who similarly operated in a "man's world," supported the movement privately. "I didn't have time to go marching but I gave money to NOW," said Marsha Serlin, who entered the all-male scrap metal industry in the late 1970s.[24]

Perhaps more common, there are countless examples of nonfeminist women business owners living by, yet remaining distant from, a feminist-inspired politics of equality—case in point, Sandra Kurtzig, who posed a challenge to the all-male computer industry when she founded ASK in 1972. Although started in her bedroom so she could spend time with her children and still make a living, the company rapidly grew to become an industry leader at $400 million in annual sales in 1991, complete with its own corporate headquarters in Silicon Valley, California, the center of the high-tech industry. Even as her firm broke through the technology boys' club, Kurtzig expressed discomfort with feminism. In 1987, she told author Diane Jennings that she agreed with the first half of the dictionary definition of feminism as seeking equality but disagreed with the second half, which she understood as promoting women's interests. "That's the thing I find offensive," she said. "I think if they're really equal, and they're comfortable with the fact that they're equal, they don't need to go waving the banner. They just need to go, and perform and be themselves."[25]

In truth, in the late 1970s and 1980s, there were plenty of women entrepreneurs who were philosophically aligned with some feminist issues but whose businesses were not built upon or governed by them. In this postfeminist moment, many too sought to embrace both femininity and women's empowerment, most notably Diane von Furstenberg. A Jewish immigrant who married a German prince, von Furstenberg parlayed her socialite standing into a fashion empire that generated sales of over $1 billion in the 1970s while she was still in her twenties.[26] The couple divorced in 1972, and two years later, her business grew dramatically when she introduced a simple wrap dress that traveled well, looked good on all body types, and was as feminine as it was professional. By the mid-1970s, she was producing twenty-five thousand of these dresses weekly (and millions since), making both the designer and her dress emblematic of modern femininity and liberation in media coverage and her advertising.

American women seemed to love the intersection of von Furstenberg's staunch independence with pure femininity, a kind of sexual revolutionary meets feminine/feminist heroine. Her ads, for example, featured a wind-blown von Furstenberg sitting on a white cube with her handwritten message: "Feel like a woman, wear a dress! Diane von Furstenberg."[27] Because of her marriage to Prince Egon von Furstenberg, her private, public, and business life netted regular coverage in *Women's Wear Daily*, the *New York Times*, and other publications. Reflecting on these times in her memoir, von Furstenberg recalled a constant struggle to seek her own identity separate from her husband and saw the business as a means to do so. Although she availed herself of his social contacts, she would not take financial help, and after their separation, von Furstenberg refused alimony: "I had the luxury and great satisfaction of being able to support myself and my children," she recalled.[28]

Even more, von Furstenberg relished her life on her own as a successful businesswoman and her ability to fuse independence with sexuality: "I loved playing the tycooness as I strode through airports wearing fishnet stockings and impossibly high heels with my dress in a shoulder bag. I was pleased that I could live a man's life and still be a sexy young woman."[29] Her business acumen won her the attention of the *Wall Street Journal* and *Newsweek*, landing her on the cover of both in 1976. She was also not afraid to use her femininity in business or to use her business to help political causes. She described her coup in securing a license with Sears for a home collection this way: "I don't think the men at Sears had ever done business with a woman before, especially one who looked like me. There were very few businesswomen at the time, and the few in management tended to play down their gender by dressing more like men than like women. For me, however, flaunting my femininity had always given me an advantage, even a weapon." But when it came to politics, she was seriously liberal, using her financial clout to host a fundraising initiative for Jerry Brown's presidential bid and participating in a benefit for the feminist group Women USA, where she was flanked by Bella Abzug and Gloria Steinem.[30]

Plenty of nonfeminist entrepreneurs relished what they claimed were the business benefits of being female. Debbi Fields, for example, was quite proud of cashing in on homemaking skills in 1977, when she parlayed the chocolate chip cookie recipe that won raves from family and friends since she was thirteen years old into a cookie empire, Mrs. Fields Cookies. Fields wrote in her memoir, "I can't really describe myself as a feminist—maybe a feminine-ist would be closer to the truth. I run my business in a very feminine way: my management decisions are often intuitive based on what I feel in my heart is the right thing."[31] Fields started her business at age twenty, driven in part by a

FIG. 5.2 Designer Diane von Furstenberg wearing a maxi-length version of the wrap-dress that drove her company's success (1976). *Credit:* Diane von Furstenberg Archives.

condescending comment from one of her husband's associates when she incorrectly said "orientated" instead of "oriented." His retort was "If you can't speak English properly, you shouldn't speak at all."[32] Fields was determined from that moment on to be more than an ornament for her high-earning, financial industry husband, ten years her senior. That meant ignoring detractors who thought her plan to open a cookie shop in a nearby mall in Palo Alto, California, was

FIG. 5.3 Diane von Furstenberg, circa 1976, in a company photo that captured the way she combined femininity with independence and take-charge business sensibilities. *Credit:* ARA GALLANT / Diane von Furstenberg Archives.

doomed to fail. Facing rejections for bank loans, Fields borrowed $50,000 in start-up funds from her husband, Randy Fields, who later also assisted her by serving as chief financial officer of her company. By 1984, Fields's business grew to three hundred stores and $45 million in sales and pioneered the inventory management systems used by similar businesses to this day.[33] In the late 1980s, the company had 425 stores in the United States and internationally, generating $87 million—all this while she raised five children. In the early 1990s, she sold the company for $100 million.[34]

Kurtzig thought being a woman helped get her computer business off the ground in the early days because "men always felt they had to pay for lunch. It helped with expenses," she recalled. "That urge to be helpful to women occasionally blinds male executives to legitimate competition from females, offering women the advantageous element of surprise. Men don't think women are a real threat.... They think you're cute and harmless.... Their real competition is that other male. So men are apt to help you more because, if you're successful, that doesn't take away from their ego."[35] And being a woman in an industry where men had earned a bad reputation had its rewards as well, as in the case of female auto repair shop owners. "Mechanics have the same reputation as muggers," claimed Susan Sasser, who co-owned with another woman a Washington,

FIG. 5.4 Debbi Fields baking up a batch of the cookies that launched her empire (with a carefully safeguarded recipe). Courtesy of Mrs. Fields Fabulous Brands LLC.

D.C., auto shop, Wrenchwoman, Inc., in 1977: "Many say I'm more trustworthy because I'm a woman. In some ways it's worked for me in that it has produced immediate recognition."[36]

Certainly there were scores of businesses run by avowed antifeminists, especially in the 1980s. Mary Crowley, who decades earlier founded the direct selling company Home Interiors, was by the late 1970s and 1980s branding herself as a Christian antifeminist entrepreneur. A Texas Republican, Crowley opposed most feminist issues, especially abortion rights. She was a member of the Eagle Forum, a conservative anti-ERA women's group founded by avowed antifeminist Phyllis Schlafly.[37] In 1984, Crowley employed thirty-nine thousand women who distributed her company's home decorating products by hosting parties or via home visits. Crowley also published several self-help books to inspire would-be women entrepreneurs with her mix of conservative Christianity and self-empowerment ethos under titles such as *Women Who Win: The Proverbs Way to Successful Living* (1979) and *A Pocketful of Hope* (1981).

Strength in Numbers: The Rise of Women's Networks

What feminism had taught women—even those who disdained the movement—was the power of organizing and sharing resources. As activist entrepreneurs faded from the landscape and with them their fervent feminist politics, they were replaced by women's networking groups, which would prove critical to the growth of women's entrepreneurship in the 1980s. Although decidedly careerist in focus, these organizations sought to stake a claim for women on the economy through resource sharing, training, and advocacy on laws and policies that would level the playing field for women business owners. The *New York Times* diluted the distinction between women's business networks and feminism when it wrote, "To survive, many of the feminist businesses must still rely on their ties to the women's movement, primarily through 'networking,' which includes referring people to other feminist businesses."[38] Women were hungry for the opportunities networking afforded: in 1977, the New York Association of Women Business Owners expected 250 women to sign up for its one-day meeting for aspiring entrepreneurs, but instead 500 signed up and another 750 were turned away.[39]

Founded in 1975, the National Association of Women Business Owners (NAWBO) was among the first organizations to assist women entrepreneurs. A year later it received a $20,000 grant from Equitable Life Assurance Society to publish a directory of one thousand firms in the Baltimore / Washington, D.C., area, where women were a small portion of business owners. That directory would be expanded and revised annually. From 1975 to 1979, NAWBO "worked hard to position the emergence of women business owners as a growing segment of the women's movement," noted former president Susan Hagar in the association's twenty-fifth anniversary tribute booklet: "Our multiple strategy was to demonstrate to the media, to lawmakers, to federal government agency chiefs, to the White House staff and to the business community that women business owners were indeed viable. We were a new and growing market and a new and growing constituency."[40] NAWBO also worked to ensure an accurate count of the number of women business owners.

As the decade continued, NAWBO was joined by other groups, including the American Association of African American Women Business owners (founded in 1982), the Committee of 200—a group of high-ranking women business leaders (founded in 1982) whose businesses had more than $5 million in annual sales—and the American Women's Economic Development Corporation (AWED). Bea Fitzpatrick launched AWED in 1976 with a grant of $124,000 from the Small Business Administration while working in the New York City mayor's office. AWED was a federally and commercially funded program that sought to train and counsel women entrepreneurs. Running seminars in the style of the women's clinics that were popularized in the 1940s and 1950s, AWED's programs taught women how to "mind their own businesses" and offered day-long workshops with famously successful women experts.[41]

Fitzpatrick aligned with what Reagan envisioned for women via the economy: "I was busy raising my three children and working out my own career, and I was hearing a lot about women's liberation," she explained, "but it seemed to me that liberation without money or a means of making it was incongruous. It occurred to me that economic development was the most important problem facing women."[42] With few programs addressing women's needs, Fitzpatrick started her own, training thousands of women well beyond the 1980s. AWED events appeared in national, regional, and women's publications, featuring laudatory comments from the women who benefited.[43] Its 1989 conference in New York drew 6,500 women from 1,081 cities nationwide who paid $150 each for two days of workshops and a chance to get advice from Oprah Winfrey, one of the many high-profile speakers. By the time of that event, AWED had a $2 million annual budget (primarily from private contributions) and had helped 62,000 women.[44]

Having It All?

In 1982, *Cosmopolitan* editor-in-chief Helen Gurley Brown published a book that helped popularize a new question about just how much women could expect from their lives: *Having It All: Love, Success, Sex, Money (Even If You're Starting with Nothing).*[45] Since then—and maybe before—feminists were blamed for promising women that they could indeed have everything they wanted, all at once, and as some incorrectly charged, effortlessly. In truth, feminists never made such promises; the movement had been about allowing women choices without legal or political impediments. "Even then," wrote the *New York Times*, "it wasn't so much a feminist mantra as a marketing pitch directed toward the well-heel 'liberated' consumer." Before Brown wrote her book, others were tackling the question of how to combine motherhood and a job, also using the banner "Having It All."[46] As women moved into careers, up the ladder, and into businesses, social mores about their roles within the home remained unchanged—adding to an increasing pay gap and struggles to juggle it all. Arlie Hochschild documented the problem in her best-selling book (and its sequels) *The Second Shift* (1989).[47]

Consequently, magazines began documenting a new phenomenon by the mid-1980s: women were leaving the corporate world, which made few moves to help them balance motherhood and careers.[48] While the term *mompreneurs* first entered the lexicon in the mid-1990s, its roots can be found in the 1980s when many women with children opted to start businesses—often from home—that allowed them to combine motherhood and making a living. It is little wonder, then, that the 1987 film *Baby Boom* was so popular. In that movie, J. C. Wiatt (played by Diane Keaton) goes from the "tiger lady" of the New York financial world to a struggling career mom when she adopts the child of a late cousin. Giving her almost no time to adjust, her male boss Fritz chides her that she can't have it all even though he does (because men have wives who make it possible). Demoted, she quits and retreats to Vermont where she establishes a successful gourmet baby food business—with a crib in her office—that her old firm then seeks to purchase. Declining the offer, she makes a speech that gives voice to the challenges of professional working mothers: "Fritz, do you remember that night when you told me about the things that I was going to have to give up and the sacrifices that I was going to have to make? Well, I don't want to make those sacrifices, and the bottom line is, nobody should have to."[49]

By the 1980s, there were new books for women on starting a business. In the mid-1970s, Claudia Jessup and Genie Chipps published a step-by-step how-to, *The Woman's Guide to Starting a Business*, which promised readers "everything you need to know to turn an idea into a profit-making venture"—something the authors had done years earlier with their girl-Friday business Supergirls. The book was so popular that there were three editions, 1976, 1979, and 1991.[50] Charlotte Taylor, who served as executive director of President Carter's 1977 Task Force on Women Business Owners, in 1980 published an authoritative guide—with a foreword from Secretary of Commerce Juanita Kreps—*Women and the Business Game: Strategies for Successful Ownership*. Taylor, who had owned a successful Washington, D.C., consulting firm specializing in business start-ups, wrote, "Just as immigrants have looked to business ownership as a way to increase their economic base and power in society, women, too are beginning to use this track." According to Taylor, two factors raised women's consciousness about inequality: the women's movement and women's experiences with the obstacles and gender biases that prevented their advancement in the corporate sector. Both, but increasingly the latter, made entrepreneurship especially attractive.[51]

Equally powerful, there were books showcasing stay-at-home mothers who started businesses, advising readers on how they too could combine these roles. *The New Entrepreneurs: Women Working from Home* featured biographies and how-to tips from forty women across the United States who pivoted from jobs to business ownership. While the majority started ventures in traditionally feminine categories such as designers, caterers / food proprietors, apparel, and retail, a few ventured into traditionally male realms, such as Patricia M. Goffette's general contractor business in Seattle, Washington. "I can build a fairly simple

154 • She's the Boss

home in about three and a half months," she said.[52] In 1984, author Phyllis Gillis addressed the issue head-on, publishing *Entrepreneurial Mothers: The Best Way in the World for Mothers to Earn Money without Being Tied to a 9-to-5 Job*: "The working woman has been over-pressured to succeed," Gillis wrote, noting that a growing number of women were caught in the push-pull between their obligations at work and home. But entrepreneurship could alleviate this pressure, she averred: "'I don't separate work and mothering. I love my children. I want to be home with them or be available when they need me. I also love my business—my work is an integral part of me. The two spheres play off each other, and I have the best of all possible worlds.' So can you."[53]

From "Glass Ceiling" to "Rubber Roof" to Breaking Barriers

By 1978, there was a new term to describe the limitations career women were experiencing as they attempted to climb the corporate ladder: the glass ceiling. The term would become a cultural mainstay in the postrecession 1980s and beyond. Marilyn Loden, a thirty-one-year-old human resources manager at New York Telephone Company is credited with coining the term during a presentation on women's advancement at the New York Women's Exposition, a feminist event. As one of the last speakers, Loden was frustrated by the stereotypes she heard used to describe and seemingly blame women for their inability to move into top jobs. Instead, she saw the problem as systemic, shaped by the lack of support for women, discriminatory attitudes by the men in charge, unequal pay, and few women role models—labeling these forces as the glass ceiling that held women and people of color back in the workplace: "Until that moment, it seemed we were relentlessly blamed for our lack of progress because, as women in a man's world, we didn't 'dress for success' or 'play games mother never taught us,'" she recalled years later. Loden went on to become a management consultant and authored a book in 1985 that was considered to be one of the fifty best business books, *Feminine Leadership, or How to Succeed in Business without Being One of the Boys*.[54] It would take fourteen years before the U.S. Department of Labor would study the problem with its Glass Ceiling Commission (1991–1995).[55]

No wonder then that when many professionals—feminists, nonfeminists, borderline feminists, and mainstream workers alike—hit their heads on the glass ceiling, they bounced out into private enterprise. Journalist Carol Smith dubbed this "the rubber roof."[56] Smith noted that as many as 85 percent of the women-owned business of the late 1970s and 1980s were started by older women who left the corporate world later in their careers after years of frustration with the glass ceiling. "The problem of the 1970s was bringing women into the corporation. The problem of the 1980s is keeping them there," commented one business leader.[57] Case in point, Patty DeDominic founded her Los Angeles employment agency, PDQ Personnel Inc., in 1979 after hitting the glass ceiling left her disillusioned with corporate America. Her firm, which would grow to $15.5 million in annual revenues, was also the result of her "quest for the perfect job." After leaving her job at a cosmetics company, DeDominic interviewed with an oil company, ad agency, and automotive supply company. She said, "I kept coming out the number two candidate, and I got tired of that," noting that inspired her to start a business to help women find jobs that matched their training and skill level. Her company generated revenues of $10 million in ten years and sales of $30 million by its twenty-seventh year.[58] She later served as president of NAWBO and sold her business in 2006.

While women remained stalwarts in traditional female businesses such as service and retail, by the late 1970s, they were moving into long-held male bastions. The number of women's service businesses jumped 38.2 percent from 1977 to 1987 and 32.9 percent in retailing. Women, such as former Peace Corps volunteer Ann Moore, found a fortune in domestic products and service, in her case the baby sling-carrier "Snugli." Others like Sandy Gooch had huge success in trendy variations on traditional themes, in this case natural and health foods.[59] Gooch, who suffered from debilitating allergies (many of them to food products), launched Mrs. Gooch's Natural Foods Market in West Los Angeles in 1977 with $92,000 of her own savings. It quickly became the largest of its kind nationwide and expanded to seven stores. By 1993, she had sold her business to Whole Foods Markets for $56 million.[60] Other women made dramatic strides in areas such as transportation firms where female ownership increased 125 percent, or in mining, construction and manufacturing, where women's business ownership grew 116 percent.[61] Mary Farrar used her $500 savings to start a steel contracting business in 1978. Katherine Moore, an African American woman going through a divorce in Wilmington, North Carolina, started a delivery service for "critical materials" for medical and industrial emergencies in 1977. "The idea of a black woman competing in this business was very unsettling to many people," she reported thirteen years later as her company continued to thrive.[62]

A year later and halfway across the country, Marsha Serlin, a mother of two in the middle of a divorce and facing foreclosure on her home, took her last $200 and with a rented truck launched a scrap metal company in Cicero, Illinois. At the time she started United Scrap Metal Inc., she was looking for a way to support her family and chip away at massive debt. She tried selling clothes and insurance; when she heard a male friend was earning a comfortable living—up to $300 a day ($1,481 in 2024)—in the scrap metal business, she wanted in.[63] She told him "teach me everything you know in 24 hours," and he did, while cautioning her about the gender barriers she would face in a male-dominated industry. "The first time I'd walk in . . . the guys would all call their controller, their CFO and president and say, 'Look what's here,'" noted Serlin, who has since made a pink hardhat the symbol of her business. "When I started. . . . I got on the back of the truck and unloaded the stuff by myself by hand, and nobody could believe a woman could do that."[64] She worked sixteen-hour days in those early years with her home doubling as her office.

Serlin also had to overcome the way the men in the industry colluded, meeting in steam rooms and other places where women could not enter to divide up the business among themselves. She persevered, meeting potential clients prepared with good prices and "showing them [she] knew what [she] was talking about."[65] A year later, Serlin got her first big client when, after much persistence, Del Monte foods hired her to clear its canning plant of debris after a blizzard.[66] By 1981, she was able to buy her first headquarters, an eight-thousand-square-foot building in Cicero, Illinois, just outside of Chicago. In an era of burgeoning interest in recycling, that metal salvaging venture would grow to nine locations in the Midwest and East Coast and earn Serlin over fifty national awards.[67] "The men in the business underestimated me," she recalled years later: "They thought I'd be gone in three months. I'm still here, and they're gone." Serlin has also focused on hiring and mentoring other women, and in 2018, for the company's fortieth anniversary, she gave each of her five hundred team members a bonus of two hundred dollars to follow their dreams, the same amount she used to start the business.[68]

As the 1970s progressed, women increasingly made their way into the privileged male worlds of high technology and finance.[69] Along with Kurtzig, Carole Ely and Lore Harp launched Vector Graphic, Inc., in 1976, marketing computer memory boards; and Janet M. Esty founded a medical-electronics firm in Boulder, Colorado, in 1971.[70] Twenty-two year old secretary Marcy Polier founded the box-office data collecting service in 1976 that the movie industry has relied on ever since.[71] Her firm, which collected data from more than 85,000 movie screens, covered 85 percent of the industry. She sold her business in 1997 to AC Nielsen, the ratings company, for estimates of up to $26 million.[72]

Moving from the Margins

For women on the economic and social margins—lesbians and women of color—the 1980s proved a transformative era. Lesbians, who had been active in the feminist entrepreneurial experiment of the 1970s continued to see in business a way to bypass discrimination and create spaces for women to come together. Some would join pioneers of the emerging New Age movement, with businesses that promoted spirituality and natural healing. Lesbian bars continued to be a growing category—in 1983 there were more than forty bars in Los Angeles alone—and with women earning more money, upscale bars became increasingly in demand. But in the later part of the decade, the advent of the AIDS crisis made separate spaces more challenging for gays and lesbians.[73] By the 1990s, lesbian and gay bars began to slowly disappear; where there were 206 in 1987, by 2021, there were reportedly only nineteen remaining.[74] New York had three; San Francisco's last bar closed in 2014.[75]

FIG. 5.5 Marsha Serlin took on the male-dominated world of scrap metal—and made a fortune doing it. She also made the pink hardhat a symbol of her ability to take on "the boys" and win. Courtesy of United Scrap Metal Inc.

For women of color, the picture was more complicated. While it was true that the total number of "minority-owned" firms doubled from 1972 to 1982, the ratio of their business ownership was 20 percent of whites. Statistics for both sexes show that in 1977, "whites owned sixty-three businesses per one thousand members of their ethnic group; Asians [owned] twenty-nine, Hispanics [owned] twenty, and Blacks [owned] nine."[76] Hispanic and Asian-American women combined owned barely 3 percent of all female sole proprietorships as late as 1987.[77] Black women would catch up to their white counterparts in the mid-1990s, when receipts for their businesses were comparable to those of their white female counterparts. By the new millennium, women of color would be the fastest growing group of new entrepreneurs. Native American women, though a small share of business owners in the 1980s, also saw potential for growth. In 1986, the First Nations Development Institute of Fredericksburg, Virginia, launched an outreach program to aid Lakota Sioux women in starting businesses on the reservation.[78]

Ethnic/racial and sexual discrimination in access to resources placed many women of color in a double bind. Programs targeting so-called minorities, such as the federal government's Minority Business Enterprise (MBE), typically focused on men rather than women. Counting mechanisms similarly reflected this social bias: not until the latter part of the decade did government studies consistently identify and track trends beyond race (Black and white). In private life too, some women, such as Hispanics, faced resistance to their independent ventures from within their families, typically from husbands.

Some, among them Ninfa Laurenzo in Houston, Texas, would pave the way for others to thwart ethnic bias through enterprise when she launched what would become a chain of Tex-Mex restaurants in the early 1970s. Laurenzo decided to go into business for herself after the sudden death of her husband. The couple, who met while he was an engineering student at MIT, previously owned a tortilla and pizza dough factory. With five children to put through college, Laurenzo—who called herself "Mama Ninfa"—opened a ten-table restaurant in front of the factory. Despite her existing business, she was rejected for bank loans and paired a $10,000 loan from a friend with funds from mortgaging her home for start-up capital. "There were five major obstacles in getting that loan in the bank's eyes," she later recalled. "First I was a woman, then I was a widow. I had five children. I was Mexican-American, and the risky restaurant business has a high mortality rate." The first day, she said, "We ended up with just $16 in the register," and nearly three weeks in, her restaurant burned down in a fire, but she rebuilt and pushed on.

Born in South Texas as one of eleven children, Laurenzo—who is credited with bringing fajitas to Texas—quickly earned a loyal following including "blue-suited anglo businessmen not usually seen in the barrio."[79] In 1975, she opened a second restaurant, and by 1978, she had a thriving business including cooking classes and catering, a team of her grown children and siblings at the helm, five hundred employees, and celebrity clientele including John Travolta.[80] By 1980, she had seven Ninfa's restaurants; by 1982, she had thirteen. A devout Catholic, she sought to give back: she worked with groups that helped teens stay off drugs and in school, gave money to help a high school build an auditorium, and paid a teacher to tutor at a neighborhood Spanish/English literacy center. She also became an adviser to President Bush on selecting minorities to serve on various committees and in judgeships and ambassadorships.[81] Later, the family expanded into other international cuisines—at its peak in the 1990s there were

FIG. 5.6 Ninfa Laurenzo stands proudly in front of one of the many restaurants she opened since starting the business in Houston. *Credit:* Ninfa Rodriguez Laurenzo Papers. Courtesy of Special Collections, University of Houston Libraries. Photo Courtesy of the Laurenzo Family.

fifty-five restaurants—took on more debt, and the business struggled.[82] After a reorganization, the company was sold in the late 1990s, but two restaurants, including one on the original site, continue in 2024.[83]

Some women of color saw their ventures as part of a broader economic agenda. In 1983, after years of running a successful community day care business, civil rights activist Dorothy Pitman Hughes launched Harlem Office Supply Inc., in Harlem, New York, which was profitable for fifteen years. Denied bank loans, her start-up funds came from paying her mortgage late. For Hughes, entrepreneurship was a political tool; she saw it as the key to empowering people of color—both the individual business owner and the people they might employ and train. "Collectively, we African-American businesswomen have generated millions of dollars in revenue for this community every year," said Hughes, in a nod to the fact that women owned a third of all Harlem businesses.[84] In the mid-1980s, she and four other Harlem businesswomen organized Women Initiating Self-Empowerment (WISE) to train other would-be women business owners. In the 1990s, as New York launched its Enterprise Zone Program to stimulate business development, Hughes spoke out both to ensure women were part of the plan and to express faith in what this could mean for women business owners in Harlem. Not everyone agreed; the development that occurred did not match Hughes's hopes. In the end, big corporate chains replaced local small businesses—including hers—as part of the gentrification of Harlem, which she railed against in a memoir.[85]

160 • She's the Boss

Emerging patterns in Asian immigration would also influence demographics surrounding women's entrepreneurship after the 1970s. Chinese and Japanese immigrants often relied on entrepreneurship as a way out of the poverty and discrimination many faced upon arrival in America. By the late 1980s, these groups had higher rates of self-employment than Americans generally. Where 6.8 percent of Americans were self-employed, 12 percent of Koreans, 7.9 percent of Japanese, and 7.6 percent of Chinese were.[86] Asian American women in businesses as diverse as food service, apparel, construction, importing, and farming overwhelmingly reported motivations that included providing educations for their children that the women themselves may have lacked. Similarly, they noted little resistance from their husbands, a problem that plagued white, Black, and Hispanic female entrepreneurs. In the late 1970s, researcher Ruth Finney profiled 230 women in Hawaii across generations and Asian ethnicities, demonstrating the ways in which their relationship to business ownership built on a long-standing tradition of women's agricultural work in Asian communities worldwide. Finney noted that in a farm society, women were a vital part of the family workforce. The shift to a consumer, service economy—with women as business owners—merely meant shifting women's traditional obligations onto a new plane.[87] A thirty-five-year-old Chinese woman who started a garment business in Hawaii in the early 1970s noted her struggle to convince her traditional family about the legitimacy of her venture. "My husband is very liberated, he teaches me women's lib," she recounted. "I was conditioned to be the obedient daughter but I found it hard to please both my parents and myself at the same time. . . . My husband teaches me independence."[88]

Celebrity Entrepreneurs and Entrepreneurs as Celebrities

By the 1980s, women entrepreneurs were becoming celebrities in their own right. For example, Martha Stewart was earning a "six figure salary" as a broker on Wall Street in the 1970s when she retreated to her Connecticut home to start a catering business and care for her young daughter. She took with her the lessons of big business in the decade that followed, becoming a celebrated cookbook author in the early 1980s, host of her own television show and editor-in-chief of her namesake magazine in the 1990s, and heading her own marketing, retailing, licensing and media empire worth over $200 million.[89] Part of a deliberate branding strategy based on homemaking, Stewart was one of the earliest women whose entrepreneurship made them a celebrity.

Fashion designers were another category where marketing strategies turned women business owners into public faces. Like Stewart, Josie Natori rose from stockbroker to vice president of investment banking at Merrill Lynch before leaving in 1977 to start the apparel business that made her famous. Trained to spot market trends, Natori was drawn to embroidered nightshirts she saw in the marketplaces on a trip home to her native Philippines. She brought some back, showed them to buyers at Bloomingdale's, and in a few months started the company that would become an $80-million-a-year lingerie, ready-to-wear, and perfume business twenty years later.[90] Like von Furstenberg in the 1970s, fashion designers in the 1980s and 1990s would launch businesses that made them as famous—and sometimes more famous—than the clothes they sold, especially as their companies grew, among them Liz Claiborne, Donna Karan (who left her job as a designer at Anne Klein to found her own company), and Eileen Fisher.

In the world of celebrity, few women wielded the power or played as important a role in career-making as Mitzi Shore, owner of the Comedy Store in Los Angeles. After a divorce, in 1974 Shore took over the business she and her husband launched, a nightclub featuring comedic performances. It became the training ground for would-be comics. Although comedy had been regarded as a "man's world," Shore decided who went on stage, who had real talent, and as such has been credited with launching the careers of renowned comics David Letterman, Jay Leno, Robin Williams, and Jim Carrey, to name a few. Timing was certainly on her side; *The Tonight Show* with Johnny Carson moved to Los Angeles as Shore's business was taking off. Carson's television show became a platform for many Comedy Store comics. Shore did not pay comics, considering the stage a career-making entrée to television, until they went on strike in 1979. "Mitzi was the queen," said comedian Marc Maron. "She determined your fate. All you wanted was her approval, and you were terrified of not getting it."[91] In 1981, on the other side of the country, Caroline Hirsch opened Caroline's in New York City, the club where East Coast comedians such as Billy Crystal and Stephen Wright practiced their craft by regularly performing.[92]

But the biggest celebrity-turned-entrepreneur of the era was Oprah Winfrey. In 1984, Winfrey moved her morning talk show to Chicago, renamed it "The Oprah Winfrey Show," and a few years later, launched Harpo Inc. (her name spelled backward) when she purchased her show. In doing so, she not only broke barriers; she challenged racial and gender norms about power in the media business. The company grew from her show to television and movie production—including the 1985 production of Alice Walker's best-selling novel *The Color Purple* with Winfrey herself in a starring role. By 1989, the media had labeled her a "mogul," citing her net worth at $40 million, and comparing her to perhaps the last megastudio celebrity-turned-entrepreneur when she was described as "an industry phenomenon reminiscent of Lucille Ball."[93] In the decades that followed, Winfrey became the entrepreneurial exemplar other celebrities (notably Suzanne Somers and Gwyneth Paltrow) would follow and a beacon for everyday women entrepreneurs as well. In 2003, Forbes magazine first listed her as a billionaire—the first African American billionaire.[94]

FIG. 5.7 Mitzi Shore, star-maker and owner of the Comedy Store in Los Angeles, with future megastar comedian/actor Jim Carrey. Photographer/Artist: Robert Knight via Getty Images.

Here, There, and Everywhere: The Woman Entrepreneur

All this business activity by women caught the eye of both the media and public policymakers. Business magazines, which first took note of women's ventures in the late 1960s, increasingly followed their pursuits in the 1970s and 1980s. The *Wall Street Journal* and *New York Times* both ran features on the links between feminist gains and women's business ownership, the *Journal* in 1974 and the *Times* in 1976, for example.[95] Books too increasingly staked a claim for women as business owners, some even borrowing from feminist politics in their titles, such as Helen Vanderburg's *Liberation through the Marketplace*. In 1976, the year of the American bicentennial, author Caroline Bird chronicled women's history as entrepreneurs and inventors since the 1770s, entitled *Enterprising Women*. For Bird, the book was inspired by a feminist desire to correct the historical record: "Enterprising men are often ingenious and perceptive rather than noble, and enterprising women have a right to be the same," she wrote. "Enterprising women have always been a part of the American scene."[96]

The woman business owner also became an increasingly visible fixture on the small screen. In 1975, *Ms.* magazine joined forces with the New York PBS affiliate to produce a woman-centered and feminist-inspired magazine-format show, entitled *Woman Alive!* Its fifth episode included a lengthy segment about women in business, showing the sensitivity of women business owners to the needs of their female staffs as well as the hardships faced by women-owned firms. The episode profiled the five women of rural McCaysville, Georgia, who worked hard to keep their textile company going for themselves and the women they employed. Two years later, New York filmmaker and independent entrepreneur Martha Stuart produced an even edgier documentary for her "Are You Listening Series." The show featured a segment on women business owners where several—from the barely surviving to the thriving—shared their stories. The group included Bette Nesmith Graham, founder of the lucrative Liquid Paper business in the 1950s; Carolyn Kelley, an African American woman who ran her own bail bond agency; and Ann Lello, who owned a struggling trucking business dubbed "Ann Lello & Son." The hottest topic, of course, was the roadblocks many of the show's guests faced in obtaining financing or sabotage by sexist competitors. Kelley, for example, described male counterparts sending her ten miles out of the way when she asked for directions: "There was so many awful things that would happen.... born out of the fact that here I was a woman, daring to compete in what they considered their world."[97]

Two new magazines spoke directly to working women and female entrepreneurs. Both *Working Woman* and *Savvy* magazines bowed in 1977, initially addressing distinct segments of similar markets. *Working Woman* at the outset was the more populist of the two, directed to every woman who worked from factory operatives to executives. Over the years, its focus shifted to the upper end of the female employment pool and entrepreneurs. It struggled in its first year, but a decade later, circulation soared to nearly eight hundred thousand copies. *Savvy*, on the other hand, always targeted the smaller and more lucrative executive women readers, and increasingly entrepreneurs, until the publication's demise in 1991. By the early 1980s, several urban markets would build on the interest in women entrepreneurs, launching city-based publications specifically targeting enterprising females, among them *Boston Business Woman* and, in New York, *Artemis: The Newsletter for Enterprising Women*.[98]

Academics also began to study the motivations, successes, and gender differences in approach, management style, and success rates of women entrepreneurs by the late 1970s. Doctoral candidate Nancy Flexman produced a study of the success and failure rates among self-employed women in 1976 and discovered that among her participants over 26 percent started businesses at home and part-time.[99] In 1977, Janice Demarest similarly wrote a dissertation on women entrepreneurs entitled "Women Minding Their Own Business: A Pilot Study of Independent Business and Professional Women and Their Enterprises."[100]

Several studies in the mid-1970s researched women as entrepreneurs in terms of the personality traits that led them into business ownership and whether entrepreneurship was the "new female frontier."[101] In 1978, the American Management Association produced a survey of women business owners that assessed both "the major problems they encounter and the major determinants of their success." Among the discoveries was that nearly half the women had fathers who were entrepreneurs (though likely some even could point to mothers as well) and, using mainstream feminist lingo, described "achievement and self-actualizing needs" as among their key motivations.[102] They also noted that a driving factor had been how men treated them in their previous careers. Among the comments cited in the study were the following: "Men don't take me seriously because they're not used to having women in executive capacities in male dominated business." And "You have to be better than men are because you have to prove yourself all the time."[103] Babson College, just outside of Boston, had a conference in 1982 on entrepreneurship in which Robert Hisrich and Marie O'Brien presented their study on "The Woman Entrepreneur as a Reflection of the Type of Business."[104] There were also studies of women's legal status as entrepreneurs conducted by the American Bar Association as well as women's groups.

In 1986, *Inc.* magazine ran an article entitled "Why There Aren't More Women in This Magazine." The answer, just below the headline, hinted that "maybe it's because women are creating a business world of their own." Noting that women owned more than a quarter of all businesses and were 17 percent of *Inc.*'s readers, the article explored what made women's businesses different from men's—and therefore too small to appear on *Inc.*'s pages as frequently as men's did. It noted that even "the prestigious Committee of 200—a national organization of women who own businesses with more than $5 million in sales—has only 236 members." The article discussed the lending barriers women faced, explored psychological differences between women and men, and ultimately concluded that women wanted something different from the businesses they started. "Many of these women are going back into the workforce after raising kids or getting a divorce," the magazine quoted Paula Manillo of Women's Economic Development in St. Paul, Minnesota, which had assisted over two thousand women at the time: "They aren't out to build the biggest companies." Instead, they wanted to support themselves and "bring balance and flexibility to their lives in ways that the corporate world can't. And won't."[105]

The U.S. Government Recognizes the Woman Entrepreneur

What became increasingly clear through all the activism, media profiles of women business owners, books and studies was that no matter how motivated, clever, or sound their business ideas were, the majority of women could not get institutional funding for their ventures. In a book highlighting the one hundred "greatest" entrepreneurs of the era—including those who had started companies that had become massive corporations—the vast majority used personal savings, loans or gifts from family and friends, or mortgaged their homes to come up with the cash they needed.[106] Joan Barnes started the megahit Gymboree (worth $493.5 million in 1994) with $6,000 in personal savings; Sandy Gooch used her retirement fund and "entire life's savings" to start her food market; Donna Karan used personal savings to launch what would become a fashion empire; and Lane Nemeth started Discovery Toys (worth $100 million in 1994) with $25,000 borrowed from family and friends, to name a few.

By the 1980s, the financing problem and faith in the rags-to-riches ideal of the Horatio Alger myth inspired what some called "the movement of low income women into self-employment"—or "the microenterprise movement." Microenterprise referred to tiny ventures, often run by a single person, with start-up capital as little as twenty-five dollars, and for those in the movement, the businesses were regarded as a possible way up and out of poverty. Pioneering women's groups in rural states such as West Virginia and in cities such as Minneapolis developed programs to train and help women start ventures, training them in everything from writing business plans to marketing and pricing goods. They also helped them obtain microloans.[107] Organizations such as the *Ms.* Foundation and the Ford and Mott Foundations assisted these efforts financially. Women such as the mother-daughter team of Sharon and Michelle Garza, who operated their Heavenly Dawgs hot dog cart in Denver, Colorado, and Lucille Barnett Washington, who owned F & S Auto Parts in Detroit, Michigan, were hailed as examples of what the microenterprise movement could do. Success stories aside, what became increasingly clear to individual women entrepreneurs, to networking groups, and to feminist organizations such as NOW, was that something had to change.[108]

Throughout the 1970s and 1980s, as women entrepreneurs' visibility and demands for equality grew, new legislative initiatives and government programs sought to address discriminatory practices facing women business owners. In 1972, the Commerce Department created an Office of Women's Business Ownership, extending its successful Minority Business Ownership affirmative action initiatives to women's firms, including—at least in principle—a share of lucrative government contracts. Equally important, the Census Bureau began officially counting women's ventures for the first time in 1972, inaugurating its Census of Women-Owned Businesses to be conducted every five years. While it represents the first time in U.S. history that the government sought to get an official tally, the Census figures relied on IRS tax data exclusively, and at times, oddly, they even conflicted with those findings, according to later reports by both the Commerce Department and Congressional Committees. For example, a report by the Commerce Department noted that in 1977, "according to the IRS, there were 1,900,723 female-operated sole proprietorships in non-farm industries. The census of women-owned businesses for that same year put the number at only 701,957, including 532,000 sole proprietorships. The discrepancy between the IRS and census figures exists despite the fact that the primary source of data for the 1977 census was the IRS."[109] Part of the challenge of accurate accounting had to do with the definition of a "woman-owned" business since various government agencies used different definitions. To the Small Business Administration, a business was considered woman-owned if it was "at least 51% owned, operated and controlled by a woman or women. . . . The Census Bureau considers a business to be women-owned if the sole owner of half or more of the partners are women, or, in a corporation, if 50 percent or more of the stock is owned by women." The IRS went only by the first names of tax filers in determining if a business was owned by a woman.[110] The challenge of getting an accurate count and definition would continue until the end of the decade.

Congressional hearings were held throughout the 1970s to assess the specific problems faced by women-owned firms, and in 1977 President Jimmy Carter created the Interagency Task Force on Women Business Owners to conduct a detailed analysis. The result was an extensive study, entitled "The Bottom Line: Unequal Enterprise in America," which outlined trouble spots in existing policies. On the simplest level, the task force defined for the first time what constituted a "woman-owned business," adopting the SBA definition. The study further outlined a range of problem areas, including the historical attitudes toward women that blocked their progress as well as their unequal access to capital to start or expand their businesses. In the task force's survey of women business owners, 67.3 percent said they were "initially capitalized by 'angel money,'" often meaning gifts or grants from family or friends. Only 10.8 percent received funding from government programs and 22 percent from banks or venture capital firms. The vast majority (82 percent) of women-owned businesses in the study were capitalized at $50,000 or less; just under 8 percent were capitalized at over $100,000. Even for larger firms—those capitalized at over $101,000—just 28 percent received bank financing.[111]

The Task Force suggested improvements for expanding a number of initiatives, including the loan program offered by the Small Business Administration, where women received a woefully small share. For example, in 1975, the SBA made 2,192 loans totaling $108 million to women-run businesses, up from the 1,945 loans of $90 million made a year earlier. Though seemingly impressive, it represented only 10 percent of the loans and 6.4 percent of the money distributed by the SBA in 1975.[112] Still, growing numbers of women applied for available programs: from January through September 1976, sixty-three thousand women attended SBA training programs nationwide—a figure that had already surpassed the preceding year. They sought more agency loans, receiving a total of $172 million in the first seven months of the year and far exceeding 1975 figures.[113] Among the immediate programmatic responses, President Carter issued an executive order to create the SBA's Office of Women's Business Ownership in 1979 to aid and stimulate women's business enterprise via mentoring and training programs and a flexible pilot loan program. The task force's report addressed the problems of loopholes in the Equal Credit Opportunity Act of 1974 that exempted business credit and allowed the discrimination women faced to continue. Although it proposed solutions involving the Federal Reserve Board, FDIC, and Federal Trade Commission, no change was forthcoming.

Increased activity began in the Reagan White House. In 1983, a short time before his speech at the New York Business Women event, Reagan issued an executive order creating an Advisory Committee on Women's Business Ownership "to review the status of businesses owned by women and foster private sector financial, education, and procurement support for women entrepreneurs." After meeting just three times, however, the committee was dissolved the following year. A few years later, in 1986, the Commerce Department issued a report—which it called an annotated bibliography—of women and business ownership, but it was much more. The 174-page document outlined ongoing obstacles women faced in business ownership from financing to education and training to family support and lack of access to "traditional business networks that provide contacts and assistance because these contacts are often found in clubs and associations restricted to men only." In a remarkable statement that marked the first time the government acknowledged the links between women's workplace experiences and entrepreneurship, the report noted that because of the discrimination women experience in the workplace, particularly as divorced women and single mothers, many "try to find success on their own by going into business for themselves."[114]

But the biggest change for women entrepreneurs came with the Women's Business Ownership Act of 1988 (HR5050), which the Congressional Committee called "the first legislative recognition of the importance of women entrepreneurs in our national economy."[115] As with all new legislation, the committee held numerous hearings in 1987 and 1988 and issued a report entitled "New Economic Realities: The Rise of Women Entrepreneurs."[116] Thoroughly researched, it noted the lack of accurate data about the number of women entrepreneurs and, most important, the obstacles—especially financial—that women business owners faced. It cited a survey in Michigan where 46 percent of women had business loans compared to 67 percent of men, and that 44 percent of the women had loans that were 2 percent above the prime rate, where only 12 percent of men did. On a national level, 68 percent of women believed they were discriminated against when they applied for loans, and 29 percent of women who received loans said they were on discriminatory terms. Many were asked for collateral worth 200 percent of the loan amount.[117] It also shared stories of two women, one who was denied a restaurant loan with claims that the bank was not making any such loans, yet soon after a man she knew applied and received a similar loan. The other: a nurse who sought to purchase a nursing home and "was told she needed 25% down payment and a co-signer, 'preferably a gentleman.' "[118] The commission's report defined women as crucial to the nation's global competitive advantage; women in 1988 owned 25 percent of all small businesses contributing $250 billion to the U.S. economy. The report also argued strongly that "remaining barriers to women's entrepreneurship be eliminated."[119]

The law that resulted closed the loophole of the ECOA by extending its protections against discrimination in lending to business credit and "eliminated individual state laws requiring women to have a male relative or husband to co-sign a business loan."[120] In addition, it codified the SBA definition of a woman-owned business, and required the Bureau of Labor Statistics, the Bureau of the Census, and the SBA to include data on sole proprietorships, partnerships, and corporations—effectively creating a single system for calculating the number of women-owned firms. It also identified the problems women business owners faced in gaining access to government contracts—a lucrative sector of the market. By way of example, the commission reported that in 1986, women owned businesses received 0.8 percent of the total $136,497,000,000, with the average contract to women amounting to $3,343, less than half of the average.[121] It charged the SBA with making what it termed "smaller loans"—those under $50,000—which would make SBA-backed loans potentially within reach and attractive to women business owners. To demonstrate the scope of the problem, the Committee noted that in 1984, women received a scant 10.7 percent of SBA loans; three years later, their share declined to 10.1 percent.[122] The law also authorized the SBA to provide matching funds for projects that benefited women business owners, such as training programs for start-ups. While most of these initiatives had a time limitation (many expired within three years), the law also established the National Women's Business Council—still in existence in 2024—to advise the president, Congress, the Small Business Administration, and the Office of Women's Business Ownership about the issues facing women business owners. The fifteen-member council included a chair appointed by the president, four members from each political party, and six members from women's business organizations and centers. No compensation was provided.

The Women's Business Ownership Act was as important symbolically as it was legislatively. It removed the final legal barriers women faced in lending and represented the first time the federal government made a major statement about their significance to the national economy and the nation's future. What's more, as a symbol of just how far women entrepreneurs had come, in 1989 President George H. W. Bush appointed Wisconsin representative Susan Engeleiter as the first woman administrator of the Small Business Administration, a position she held until 1991.[123] Her successor was also a woman, Pat Saiki, who had been chair of the Republican Party in Hawaii.

She's the Boss—and an Entrepreneur Now

In 1977, the New York Association of Women Business Owners changed the motto on its letterhead to read, "a collective voice for women entrepreneurs."[124] Decades, even years earlier, such a bold claim on the word *entrepreneur* would not have been possible. Women's businesses were widely referred to (even by women themselves) as simply "businesses." The term *entrepreneur* was reserved for what men did.

The social implications of women's appropriation of the word *entrepreneur* have been enormous and wide-reaching in the decades since the 1970s. For starters, it marked the articulation of a new vision, one in which women saw their businesses not as sidelines the way previous generations had but as full and equal participants in the economy. This created a ripple effect in reshaping the definition of entrepreneurship that had prevailed for centuries. First studied in the 1920s, by the end of the 1970s and in the years since, entrepreneurship has been expanded to include female-inspired notions of the nature of the entrepreneur and the place of businesses in society writ large. Among the first changes was a de-centering of the association with profit maximization. Where in the past, an entrepreneur was defined as one who takes a risk to bring a novel idea into a new and untapped market with the goal of profit maximization, since the 1970s, with the growth of women's entrepreneurship, the term has focused more on the initiative and conceptualization aspects and far less on the size of the firm or its profit margins.[125] Instead, the emphasis shifted to the innovation and "risk-taking" component of entrepreneurship, an area where women excelled. Because their ventures were often started with little capital, many women felt freer to take the risks associated with launching a business start-up; as one pundit noted, with less invested, they had little to lose. In the year 2000, the first encyclopedia of women entrepreneurs offered this retooled definition (note the declining importance of profit maximization): "Entrepreneurs are agents of change who take substantial risks—human, physical and/or financial—to initiate and develop an organizational entity and to participate in these endeavors even though there is no certainty of generating personal income. These innovators are catalysts for the American economic system."[126]

Further, the mainstreaming of these concepts was evident in some of the studies of female entrepreneurs in the 1970s. Among her research subjects, Flexman noted, "The high-powered, ruthless stereotype associated with entrepreneurs (which suggests a tendency toward unmitigated agency) does not seem to be compatible with the meaning these women attached to success. Rather, their concern for achieving goals seems to be balanced with their concern for other people." This reflected objectives that linked the success of the business to factors as diverse as the founders' own personal and familial relationships as well as her role as employer and visionary for her staff and corporate citizen.[127]

The ongoing reconfiguration of the definition of entrepreneur similarly raised new questions about gender differences in management style, triggering studies that argued for women's cooperative approach versus men's hierarchical corporate structures. Other questions, likewise unresolved, addressed whether the acquisition of corporate growth and power did not in turn lead to hierarchical tendencies in women entrepreneurs and whether women who opened businesses to merge their professional goals with child-rearing needs extended in-house childcare to their employees.[128]

However one defined it, in 1989, women's entrepreneurship had not only become an accepted aspect of U.S. life; it was also producing social changes. That year, *Ms.* ran a cover story about reversed gender roles; instead of male business owners bringing their wives into their firms as helpmeets, the *Ms.* article featured women who had made it big as entrepreneurs in their own right and then "recruited" or agreed to let their husbands work for their companies. But even with such radical change, upending traditional gender roles was not easily accomplished. The not-so-surprising conclusion: If *she* got to be the boss at work, *he* got to be the boss at home (because, as gender norms still dictated, *he* had to be the boss somewhere).[129]

Epilogue

Women's Entrepreneurship in the 1990s and Beyond

In early fall 2017, Kevin O'Leary, one of the millionaire investors on the popular ABC venture capital reality television series *Shark Tank*, made a bold pronouncement: "I prefer to invest in women-owned businesses." Although he initially made the statement at *Inc.* magazine's Women's Summit, an annual networking event in New York City, O'Leary was not just pandering to his female audience. Known for his bitingly honest, sometimes harsh commentaries since 2009 on *Shark Tank*, O'Leary—the man who dubbed himself "Mr. Wonderful"—would spend the next two years making the same statement to national television and print media. In every interview, O'Leary explained that the forty-plus women-owned companies he had invested in were far more profitable than the male-owned firms. As such, he said, he was moving to invest almost exclusively in women-owned ventures purely for "capitalist" reasons "because [he's] getting better returns."[1]

In his many national media appearances, O'Leary echoed two points: in terms of gender, he "has no political or social agenda"; it was simply about who was making him the most money, and that was women.[2] Second, in answer to an oft-repeated question by interviewers, he explained that women-owned ventures were more profitable because of what women do differently (read: better) than men: women set realistic goals, are disinclined to take unnecessary risks, and are more successful at retaining employees. Men, he said, chase "testosterone targets, crazy goals that they hit only 60% of the time." Women, on the other hand, he claimed, set achievable goals that they hit 95 percent of the time.

"When you meet your goals 95 percent of the time, you change the culture of your business," O'Leary explained. "People feel they're working in a winning organization. That's why women are doing better in business—they keep their people. The staff are sticky."[3] He also listed other gender-based assumptions he attributed to women's success, from skillfully juggling or multitasking (which he called the "busy mom" paradigm) to what he described as women's ability to listen without ego and adapt based on constructive feedback from both customers and employees.

Since it debuted, *Shark Tank* has helped to proliferate a modern version of the Horatio Alger myth of entrepreneurship as the great equalizer—that anyone willing to work hard (or "bootstrap it" in *Shark Tank* and contemporary parlance) has an equal chance to succeed—that entrepreneurial success could bypass or neutralize other biases. At times, the show embraces a "girl-power" feminism—without using the "f-word"—with female "sharks" Lori Greiner and Barbara Corcoran championing that women can do anything, even if the majority of "anything" on the show seems to be commercializing traditionally female products and services (food, fashion, cosmetics, baby/child items) along with occasional STEM-based companies. *Shark Tank* has painted a portrait of growing national interest in starting a business, even in the midst of the Great Recession of 2009 to 2010 or the COVID-19 pandemic. It does so two ways: by hitting hard the message that even in the worst of times, creative people can thrive as independent business owners and by profiling the rags-to-riches stories of its investor panelists—millionaires and billionaires who all came from humble working- or middle-class roots—along with the stories of would-be entrepreneurs who appear on the show.[4] The show's constant refrain is this: Everybody *can* be an entrepreneur, and entrepreneurship is an ever-growing segment of American society.

In truth, however, the overall rate of entrepreneurship in the United States has been declining for decades, with one notable exception: women. According to data from the U.S. Census Bureau, the Kauffman Foundation, and the Brookings Institute, the number of new companies has declined by 44 percent since 1978.[5] Only women's entrepreneurship has continued to increase, which O'Leary has clearly tapped into. What O'Leary did not say is that the greatest growth in women's business ownership since the 1990s has come from start-ups by women of color, who receive far fewer investments and in lower dollar amounts than other *Shark Tank* contestants. In the "real world" too they struggle more than any other would-be entrepreneurs to find start-up capital from traditional lenders or investors. Statistically, women's business ownership has increased 30 percent since 2007, and in the past fifteen years, their companies have grown at 1.5 times that of all other small businesses. In 2023, women collectively owned thirteen million businesses—42 percent of all U.S. businesses—generated $1.8 trillion in revenues, and employed ten million people, according to various sources including the Small Business Administration and National Association of Women Business Owners (NAWBO).[6] What's more, six million of those businesses were owned by women of color.[7] The number of white women's ventures has shown level growth; start-ups by women of color have skyrocketed. "Women of color account for 89% (1,625) of the new businesses opened every day over the past year," noted the business publication *Fast Company*.[8] African American women-owned businesses grew by 258 percent; Latina-owned ventures grew by 156 percent since 1997.[9] According to the SBA, 42 percent of newly created women-owned businesses are started by Black women, and 31 percent by Latinas.[10] The majority of women's businesses—85 percent—are owned by Baby Boomers and Gen X (55.7 percent and 29.9 percent, respectively), ages when women reach their peak frustration with discrimination and have acquired the training and resources to launch a venture.[11]

Even during the pandemic, when the nation shut down, women still saw a future for themselves in entrepreneurship. While their businesses were initially hit hard, by 2022, the growth rate resumed with women creating about half of all the new businesses. The acceleration in entrepreneurship for women of color is unquestionably a story of triumph, of those on the margins who are staking a claim for themselves in the broader economy. But it also points to a less rosy picture: those starting businesses are most likely to experience higher rates of discrimination in the workplace (the double-bind of race/ethnicity and gender) that entrepreneurship enables them to bypass.

The significance of women of color to the future of entrepreneurship is one of many areas worthy of future study and represents growing attention to the promise of business ownership for other marginalized groups as well, notably Native Americans and LGBTQ+ people. Since the 1990s, several other issues have emerged that have shaped and will continue to shape women's business ownership: the role of technology (specifically the emergence of the internet), continued difficulties accessing institutional start-up capital, limited access to government contracts, the role of the COVID-19 pandemic, increasing interest in social entrepreneurship, and the continued question of whether business ownership in and of itself is a feminist act. To fully assess the historical significance of all these issues requires a much longer view, but they do connect to the issues laid out in this book for previous decades. They also show that the challenges women faced in the past continue to be challenges they face in the present and the future. The unresolved issues of gender inequality endure even as the historical context itself has changed.

Beginning in the 1990s, several new trends pointed to business ownership as the tool for solving persistent social inequities in ways that the activism and social programs of previous decades could not. When the internet emerged as a global phenomenon in the mid-1990s, experts claimed it had the potential to be economically democratic, that the affordability of launching a web-based business would bypass the biases women and people of color faced in seeking institutional start-up capital. In the early, "Wild West" days of the World Wide Web, people could indeed start a website for very little money (maybe a few hundred dollars), and with little competition compared to today, they could hope to draw customers to their sites. New communities of women, such as iVillage, helped people from across the nation find one another, share resources, and even promote one another's businesses. While women did help shape the web's development to be more user-friendly than its early iterations, the promise of low-cost web businesses quickly evaporated. Launching a website can cost thousands or tens of thousands of dollars, including the need for SEO and other tools that attract customers. At the same time, megasites such as Amazon.com dominate the internet and can overtake the smaller, home-based ventures like those that early web pioneers started. Add those costs to other start-up expenses, and one estimate shows that would-be entrepreneurs today need roughly $184,000 to launch a business (including salaries for up to five employees).[12]

What's more, women receive a paltry share of institutional start-up capital—less than 3 percent of venture capital funding overall—and women of color have even less, under 1 percent. That said, in those rare occasions when women are the decision-makers in lending, women business owners fare better, which has encouraged the growth of women-owned venture capital firms. Even so, women remain just 8.6 percent of all venture capitalists. While 74 percent of women today launch businesses using personal funds—including credit cards and savings, loans from family and friends, and even mortgaging their homes—those with fewer resources are left out or leave themselves financially vulnerable. In terms of loans from the Small Business Administration, in 2023, of the $20 billion in approved loans, women received just 16.1 percent (a total of $3.25 billion). For Latinx-owned businesses, the challenge is even greater. Latinx-owned businesses have the lowest rate of using bank and financial institution loans compared with other groups and are less likely to get the loans they do apply for. The SBA has attempted to address the issue with new programs, including the Community Advantage Pilot Program (CA), which in 2023 granted 34.8 percent of its loans to women-owned businesses and 18 and 20 percent to Black-owned and Hispanic-owned businesses, respectively.[13] Nationally too in the 2000s, more corporations such as American Express, Bank of America, and Goldman Sachs all launched initiatives to help women entrepreneurs.

One way the internet has proven helpful to women entrepreneurs has been through crowdfunding, which emerged in the early 2000s as an alternative to traditional lending. Various crowdfunding websites such as Kickstarter and Indiegogo enable would-be business owners to make a pitch for funds to start or grow their ventures. According to one study globally, "22% of campaigns led by women reached their target, compared to 17% of those led by men." For women in the United States, the figures are even higher—"In tech, the success rate for women-led Kickstarter projects was 65% as opposed to just 35% for men."[14]

The rise of technology has also been a tool for those on the margins seeking to overcome workplace discrimination. In 2014, for example, Angelica Ross, a

Epilogue • 175

transgender actress known more recently for her role in the television series *Pose*, launched TransTech Social Enterprises in Chicago, "a training academy and creative design firm that contracts transgender workers, among others." As someone who lived through the hardships and workplace discrimination of coming out as transgender, Ross's vision for the company was to help other transgender people find work. Because the work was done remotely and online, the company could bypass discrimination: clients hired people based on experience only to complete the work they needed. Long before COVID-19 convinced corporate America that remote work was valuable, Ross knew what it meant for transgender people: "If you're able to telecommute, you can work through that time of gender transition and find balance as a freelancer. Most trans people are either violently removed or not welcome in many educational and work spaces. It gives people a place where there's no question that they belong and are valuable."[15]

Much as women in the civil rights and feminist movements of the 1960s and 1970s saw in business a chance to build a new world for themselves and their communities, recently other groups have expressed similar faith in the power of private enterprise. In the last decade, for example, the Gay and Lesbian Chamber of Commerce has built on the work of earlier lesbian entrepreneurs, encouraging its members to start businesses and do business with other LGBTQ+ entrepreneurs. In 2017, the National Gay and Lesbian Chamber of Commerce (NGLCC), released its first report on contributions made by LGBTQ+ Americans to the nation's economy. The study highlighted the following: that LGBTQ+ businesses contributed more than $1.15 billion to the U.S. economy; that they have an average revenue of just under $2.5 million, "with one LGBTBE reporting $180,000,000 in annual gross"; and that "average LGBT enterprises have been in business at least 12 years—far above the national average of ... (failing) in their first five years; and that non-white LGBT businesses continue to increase and constitute 17% of the total."[16]

Native American women too have focused on the potential of their ventures to empower themselves, their families, and their communities. Valerie Red-Horse Mohl has been one of the more visible examples, founding a film company—Red-Horse Native Productions, Inc.—in the 1990s to promote roles for and accurate representations of Native Americans in movies and producing films of her own. Red-Horse Mohl, who is of Cherokee descent, has run several businesses, including the highly successful Red-Horse Financial Group, which has raised and handled over $3 billion in capital for tribal nations.[17] Others too are beginning to make visible the importance of women's business. For example, in 2016, a study of indigenous women entrepreneurs in New Mexico highlighted the stories of eight women from the many tribal groups across the state whose businesses ranged from traditional (i.e., Zuni fetishes) to providing consulting and business services. Each woman's story showcased the need to overcome stereotypes as well as the centrality of their culture and of Native American history to business in the present and future.[18] In 2017, Native Women Lead was founded as a nonprofit to advocate, train, assist, and empower Native American women entrepreneurs. Its stated mission is this: "To . . . inspire innovation by investing in Native Women in business. We do this by co-creating with and convening our community to build coalition while honoring our culture, creativity, and connections." Since 2020, the organization has provided loans of $10,000 to $50,000 to women entrepreneurs at 3 percent interest via its Matriarch Restorative Funds.[19]

Younger generations of millennial and Gen-Z entrepreneurs have begun to impact the definition and role of business ownership. Though not activist per se, younger entrepreneurs embrace a vision not entirely dissimilar from their 1970s activist predecessors: that business can generate profits and benefit society. These "social entrepreneurs" contribute proceeds to environmental, microenterprise, or antipoverty initiatives. They also recognize that younger consumers like to be connected to such companies, which also benefits the bottom line.

Through all this history, the question first raised in the 1970s about the compatibility of feminism and capitalism never completely disappeared. In the late 1990s as feminist bookstores were beginning to fade from the landscape, movement women reminded other feminists that their survival depended on feminist consumer loyalty.[20] Beginning in the 2010s, new articles began appearing in feminist and business publications addressing with increasing intensity the relationship between feminism and entrepreneurship. Podcasts too highlight the stories, power, and potential of women in business. There have even been new streaming productions, such as Netflix's *Self-Made* and *Girl Boss*, that show how women entrepreneurs in the past overcame obstacles on the road to success, the former showcasing African American millionaire Madam C. J. Walker and the latter the story of Sophia Amoruso's blockbuster online apparel business, Nasty Girl.[21]

Celebratory tales aside, continued debates about whether entrepreneurship and feminism are aligned have ranged from the values at the center of the venture to the deeper questions of patriarchal capitalism versus humanistic feminism. Some argue that business can be feminist if it is governed according to principles of justice and equality, noting that entrepreneurial feminists "enter commercial markets to create wealth and social change, based on the ethics of cooperation, equality, and mutual respect." Examples include Lunapads, City of Women, the Safety Pin Box, and SheEO.[22] They triumph the notion of "gender equality through ethical capitalism," promising that "feminism can use capitalism as a tool for achieving female equality as well as to provide meaningful jobs"—an argument not unlike that of 1970s feminists (chapter 4). While some claim that the act of asserting one's right to own a business makes them feminist, others argue either that capitalism is "coopting and ruining" the feminist movement or that it "has done so much to liberate women" and is "the most feminist system."[23] By 2023, some writers—most of them female—touted the end of the "girl boss" era of the 2010s, gleefully bidding adieu to its "performative *You Go*

Girl! feminism," which they denounced as the commodification of the movement.[24] The conflict will likely never fully be resolved, but the tension between those who see business ownership as an act of self-determination (and therefore feminism) and those who worry about co-optation was best expressed in an article on the Stanford University Press blog: "Feminism seeks to address subordination. . . . Venture creation has become an effective means to gain power and to negotiate wider changes that redress gender inequality and discrimination. In some instances, it is perceptions regarding gender inequality that trigger women's entrepreneurial inclinations in the first place."[25]

The history of women's business ownership is a story of triumph and stasis. The triumph is self-evident: The number of women entrepreneurs has grown exponentially since World War II, with some claiming huge successes. The stasis is what that triumph obscures: that as women departed the labor market for enterprises of their own, they left unresolved the issues of discrimination, pay and promotion gaps, and childcare. Business ownership has been a de facto solution but really only for the individual women themselves, not for society writ large. What's more, by identifying "women" as a category of interest, government and other forces shaped postwar identity politics / feminism, encouraging women to focus on their own and/or community interests. It enabled the government to only address economic discrimination as it served the larger cause of American entrepreneurialism and only during pivotal economic moments. And discrimination does *not* vanish with business ownership: one third of women entrepreneurs report experiencing sexism.[26] Still, the appeal of private enterprise for women and those on the margins endures based on the belief that even if they cannot fix the public sector, they can at least attempt to control their own economic destinies.

Acknowledgments

In many ways, I can trace the origins of this book back to my early postcollege jobs. Long before I became a historian, I was a journalist, chronicling women's workplace issues for national publications. I was present at the 1989 conference of the American Women's Economic Development Corporation (AWED) for aspiring entrepreneurs mentioned in chapter 5, where thousands came to learn how to start businesses from experts including Oprah Winfrey. I had no idea then that it would put me on this path to studying and writing about the historic role business ownership has played in women's economic, social, and personal lives. That came over time and in part from the advice of many mentors along the way, starting with Marcia Ann Gillespie, the editor-in-chief of *Ms.* magazine (who I also met at the AWED conference) who guided a young writer to think about the social, cultural, and transformative potential of women's entrepreneurship and made me a better writer in the process. Later, during my graduate studies at New York University, I was further mentored on this path by the brilliant Marilyn. B. Young, Mary Nolan, Lizabeth Cohen, and Danny Walkowitz. Susan Ware—my first professor, adviser, and now friend—was especially influential in my path as a women's historian, helping me hone my skills and providing opportunities to showcase my work in her various projects.

I am most grateful to the women featured in this book. Every one of their stories is a treasure, as are those too numerous to appear here. They were trailblazers on whose shoulders every woman entrepreneur since stands. I appreciate those who took time to speak with me—notably Kirsten Grimstad, Joanne Parrent, Marsha Serlin, and Linda Whittenbarger—or who shared their stories in letters and emails. Throughout this project, I was moved by the kindness of strangers, people who responded to the appeals of a historian (and trusted that

180 • Acknowledgments

they were real, not scams) and rose to help. When I was looking to fill research gaps about one of my favorite examples in this book, McCaysville Industries, which was located in rural Appalachian Georgia, the Copper Basin History Preservation Facebook group not only accepted the invitation of this outsider but led me to Durinda Abercrombie. She then introduced me to her aunt Linda Whittenbarger, whose mother was one of the McCaysville Industries founders. Michelle Mariola put me in touch with Marsha Serlin and assisted with obtaining photographs, and Bonnie Morris helped connect me with Olivia Records. Similarly, responding to an email, journalist and author Carol Smith remarkably dug through her personal archives for the article where she coined the term *rubber roof*, which was essential for chapter 5.

Along the way, I have been fortunate to cross paths with scholars who proved helpful as I developed this project. At the Business History Conference, I met Joshua Clark Davis, who introduced me to publishers and later generously mentored me through the book proposal process. Special thanks also go to Pamela Laird, who offered important insights on the 1980s; Susan Yohn, who shared her collection of materials on Catalyst, Inc.; Mansel Blackford, who spoke with me about the history of the Small Business Administration; and Wendy Gamber, Angel Kwoleck-Folland, and Mary Yeager, whose insights into feminist business history have guided my work. Others whose insights have proven helpful include Christy Ford Chapin, Allison Elias, Mandy Cooper, Andrew Popp, Jennifer Fleischner, and Carla Golden. I am also grateful for the help of Roger Horowitz at the Hagley Museum and Library, who not only offered guidance but consistently provided opportunities to showcase my work (including my very first publication on this topic). He also introduced me to Katina Manko, who became my lifelong friend and women's history compatriot chronicling entrepreneurialism. Other colleagues who read very early versions of this work include Kathleen Barry, Neil Maher, Kirsten Ferminglich, Karen Krahulik, Michael Lerner, Andrew Darien, and Amy Richter. Stephanie Gilmore at Formore Editorial Services, whose feminist scholarship I followed for years, enthusiastically responded when I asked if she would edit the final revised chapters before I submitted them to the press. And at Rutgers University Press, I am similarly grateful for the assistance of Emma-li Downer and Daryl Brower and the encouragement, patience, and kindness of my editors, Kimberly Giunta and Peggy Solic. I also appreciate the meticulous work done by the team at Scribe, notably Hannah McGinnis.

This project was supported by Merrimack College, not just in resources but also in the enthusiasm that kept moving me forward. I would like to thank President Christopher Hopey, Provost John "Sean" Condon, Vice Provost for Undergraduate Education and Dean Steven Scherwatzky, Vice President of Research April Bowling, and members of the Faculty Development Grant Committee. Colleagues and friends also read chapters, shared insights, gave a gentle nudge, and helped me think through the publishing process, among them Zoe

Sherman, Ellen McWhorter, Kathleen Sills, Emma Duffy-Comparone, Sandra Raponi, Susan Marine, Simona Sharoni, Inès Ouedraogo, Anne Flaherty, Laura Marie d'Herete, Christy Potroff, Laura Kurdziel, Allison Seitchik, Ray Shaw, Jake Turner, and the "thirsty Thursday" crew of Gwyne White, Brandi Baldock, and Cinzia DiGiulio. Melissa "Mish" Zimdars not only helped me navigate the publishing process but also pointed me to Rutgers University Press as a perfect home for my work. Mentor and dear friend Gordene MacKenzie brought the magic that kept me believing I could do this; Marie Plasse offered endless assistance and encouragement; Jane Caputi and Raechel Anne Jolie provided wisdom; and my good friend Lisa Fuller generously listened whenever I felt stuck. Former students Catherine Hill and Meghan Demanchyk helped with some early fact-finding; all my students provided energy and optimism. And I truly cannot imagine including any of the photographs in this book without the help of the amazing Sofia Quinci, a graduate student in library sciences (and Merrimack College Honors alum) who provided additional research, organization, and good humor when I needed it most. Jenna Colozza, Katherine LaFlamme, and Lyena Chavez—the incredible research librarians at McQuade Library at Merrimack College—helped locate needed, and sometimes obscure, materials.

No historian can do their work without the assistance of librarians and archivists, and I am thankful for so many of them. The Schlesinger Library at Radcliffe provided access to a host of key manuscript collections, among them the letters to *Ms.* magazine, the records of the National Organization for Women and its credit committee, and the personal papers of several women entrepreneurs. Similarly, an early grant from the Henry A. Murray Center at Radcliffe afforded an opportunity to study data from research on women entrepreneurs conducted in the 1970s by scholars and business groups. The Hagley Museum and Library provided funding and access to primary documents and records from business organizations and individual female small business owners. Archivists at the Special Collections Department, William H. Perkins Library, Duke University, assisted with materials on feminist economic ventures and organizations in the South. Similarly, archivists at the Rare and Manuscript Collections of the Carl A. Kroch Library at Cornell University provided access to the papers of Jane Hedges Todd. Other notable assistance came from the Schomburg Center for Research in Black Culture at the New York Public Library; Michelle Asci at the Georgia State University Archives; Michael Pinckney at the Ronald Reagan Presidential Library (who aside from being helpful provided laughter on a tough day); Special Collections at the University of Houston Libraries; the Mississippi Department of Archives and History; the State Historical Society of Iowa; the Denver Public Library; and the archives of the National Federation of Business and Professional Women's Clubs. Early in my research, the National Association of Women Business Owners and the public relations team at Catalyst, Inc., also contributed copies of internal historical documents and histories for the purposes of enriching this project.

182 • Acknowledgments

Friends and family became the cheering squad I needed to reach the finish line. I am grateful for my mother, Camille Michals, who taught me never to settle, and my father, the late Peter J. Michals III, who reminded me that the road in life is up and down, never just up. When the end seemed so far away, there was my brother (my "nontwin twin"), Peter J. Michals IV, and his wife, Kelly, to clear the path and protect my time, and there was the promise I made to my long departed sister, Camie, that I would one day write a book. My aunt and uncle Nancy and Richard Samaria generously shared their Maine retreat when I needed a quiet place to work, and my aunts Gerri Schultz and Janet Tosto, uncle Anthony Samaria, cousin Barbara Walsh, and step-daughters Melanie and Sarah Antinoro never stopped believing in me. Treasured friends too listened and offered advice and the occasional distraction I needed, especially Elisa Agostinho, Faren Siminoff, Rona Wilk, Carroll and Andy Collins, Betsy Salerno, Rhonda Grady, David Chan, Mark Thompson, Aine Greaney, Jennifer Karin, Anthony Grace, Jose Dominguez, and Ena Chimelis. But no one has traveled this road with me more patiently than my husband, Mark Antinoro, who never let me forget who I am, who sacrificed endless weekends and evenings when I needed to work, who shared his immense graphic design talents, and whose boundless love makes everything possible.

Portions of chapter 1 were previously published in Debra Michals, "Toward a New History of the Postwar Economy: Prosperity, Preparedness, and Women's Small Business Ownership," *Business and Economic History* 26, no. 1 (Fall 1997): 45–56.

Notes

Introduction

1 "About Olive's," Olive's Coffee, last modified June 30, 2024, https://olivescoffee.com/about/; Debra Ball, Facebook message to author, June 24, 2024.

2 Wells Fargo, "The 2024 Impact of Women-Owned Businesses," 7, accessed June 1, 2024, https://stories.wf.com/iwob/.

3 Association for Enterprise Opportunity, "History Has Shown What Women Business Owners Can Do—Let's Not Ignore It," accessed April 1, 2024, https://aeoworks.org/history-has-shown-what-women-business-owners-can-do-lets-not-ignore-it/. See also American Express, "The 2019 State of Women-Owned Businesses Report" (New York: American Express, 2019).

4 "Harlem Wives Urged to Make 'Pin Money' through Marketing of Home Products," *New York Times*, October 3, 1946, 30.

5 "962,000 U.S. Women Set Up in Business, Not for Pin Money, But to Help Meet High Cost of Living, Miss Todd Reports," *New York Times*, September 18, 1948, 20.

6 Gabrielle Carpenter, "Expert Reviews: Small Business Statistics in 2024," National Association of Women Businesses Owners, accessed May 7, 2024, https://nawbo.org/expert-reviews/blog/small-business-statistics/.

7 Even government studies and task force reports show the disparity in statistics of women entrepreneurs due to varied counting mechanisms prior to 1972. Task Force on Women Business Owners, *Bottom Line: Equal Enterprise in America: Report of the President's Interagency Task Force on Women Business Owners* (Washington, D.C.: U.S. Government Printing Office, 1978), 5. This report shows that some studies showed women owning 4.6 percent of U.S. firms in 1972, while others showed them holding 5.7 percent.

8 Gaylord Nelson, *Small Business and the Quality of American Life: A Compilation of Source Material on the Relationship between Small Business and the Quality of Life, 1946–1976*, report prepared for the Senate Select Committee on Small Business, 95th Congress, 1st sess. (Washington, D.C.: U.S. Government Printing Office, 1977), ix.

9 Wendy Gamber, *The Female Economy: The Millinery and Dressmaking Trades, 1860 to 1930* (Champaign: University of Illinois Press, 1997). See also Sarah Deutsch, *Women and the City: Gender, Space, and Power in Boston, 1870–1940* (New York: Oxford, 2000).

183

184 • Notes to Pages 7–14

10 "Elizabeth Keckly Remembered as Dressmaker, Excluded as Author," *Smithsonian American Women's History Museum Blog*, March 5, 2024, https://womenshistory.si .edu/blog/elizabeth-keckly-remembered-dressmaker-excluded-author.

11 Charlotte Perkins Gilman, *Women and Economics: A Study of the Economic Relation between Men and Women as a Factor in Social Evolution*, ed. Carl N. Degler (New York: Harper & Row, 1966), 9. The book was originally published in 1898.

12 *Elizabeth Arden: Behind the Red Door*, 50 min., Great North Productions, Canada, 2000.

13 Maggie McGrath and Margherita Beale, "Why America's First Black Female Bank Founder Is Still Owed a Great Debt," Forbes, March 21, 2021, accessed April 1, 2023, https://www.forbes.com/sites/maggiemcgrath/2021/03/20/why-americas-first-black -female-bank-founder-is-still-owed-a-great-debt/?sh=16435a7d7fd3.

14 "Women Bankers in Home Financing Field Hear FHA Speaker," *Cleveland Plains Dealer*, January 8, 1935, in Lillian and Clara Westropp Papers, box 1, folder 2, Schlesinger Library, Radcliffe Institute for Advanced Study, Harvard University, Cambridge, Mass.; "The Women's Federal Savings Bank," *Encyclopedia of Cleveland History*, accessed February 26, 2019, https://case.edu/ech/articles/w/womens-federal -savings-bank.

15 Frank Futral, "Val-Kill Industries: A History," *Hudson River Valley Review: A Journal of Regional Studies*, Autumn 2009, 21–39.

16 *Imitation of Life*, dir. John M. Stahl, Universal Pictures, 1934.

17 Edith Sparks, *Boss Lady: How Three Women Entrepreneurs Built Successful Big Businesses in the Mid-twentieth Century* (Chapel Hill: University of North Carolina Press, 2017).

18 Discover Saratoga, "Hattie Moseley Austin, Founder of Hattie's Chicken Shack," accessed January 4, 2023, https://www.discoversaratoga.org/blog/stories/post/hattie -moseley-austin-founder-of-hatties-restaurant/. Ownership of the restaurant has changed hands in recent years, but it remains open in Saratoga, New York.

19 Angel Kwolek-Folland, *Incorporating Women: A History of Women and Business in the United States* (New York: Twayne, 1998), 97, 145–147.

20 Elaine Tyler May, *Homeward Bound: American Families in the Cold War* (New York: Basic Books, 1988), 49.

21 May, 145.

22 Mary A. Yeager, "Will There Ever Be a Feminist Business History?," *Women in Business* 1 (1999): 3–43.

23 Davis's chapter on feminist ventures includes my dissertation among its citations.

Chapter 1　From War Worker to Business Owner

1 "Harlem Wives Urged to Make 'Pin Money' through Marketing of Home Products," *New York Times*, October 3, 1946, 30.

2 "Job Bars to Women Decried by Dewey," *New York Times*, October 24, 1945, 24.

3 Lois Mattox Miller, "From Pin Money to High Finance," *Reader's Digest*, December 1948, 42; Laurie Johnson, "Women's Dreams Turned to Cash," *New York Times*, September 30, 1950, 14.

4 "Harlem Wives Urged," 30.

5 Tiffany M. Gill has written about the links between civil rights activism and African American beauty shop owners. See Tiffany M. Gill, *Beauty Shop Politics: African American Women's Activism in the Beauty Industry* (Champaign: University of Illinois Press, 2010); and Tiffany M. Gill, "'I Had My Own Business . . . So I Didn't

Have to Worry': Beauty Salons, Beauty Culturists, and the Politics of African-American Female Entrepreneurship," in *Beauty and Business: Commerce, Gender, and Culture in Modern America*, ed. Philip Scranton (Routledge, 2001), 169–194.

6 Box 2, folders 2–3, Jane Hedges Todd Papers, Rare and Manuscript Collections, Carl A. Kroch Library, Cornell University (hereafter Jane Hedges Todd Papers). The actual number was probably much higher, since much of women's business activities remains, as it always has been, largely undocumented.

7 "962,000 U.S. Women Set Up in Business, Not for Pin Money, But to Help Meet High Cost of Living, Miss Todd Reports," *New York Times*, September 18, 1948, 20; U.S. Department of Labor, Women's Bureau, *Changes in Women's Occupations: 1940–1950*, Bulletin 253 (Washington, D.C.: U.S. Government Printing Office, 1954); U.S. Department of Labor, Women's Bureau, *Status of Women in the United States* (Washington, D.C.: U.S. Government Printing Office, 1952).

8 Jane Hedges Todd Papers, box 8, "Scrapbooks."

9 "Bids Women Turn to Small Business," *New York Times*, August 12, 1944, 8. See also John Morton Blum, *V Was for Victory: Politics and American Culture during World War II* (New York: Harcourt Brace, 1976), 99–105, 127–130.

10 Bernice Milburn Moore, *Women after the War* (New York: USO Division of the National Board YWCA, 1945), 15.

11 Elizabeth Hawes, "13,000,000 Will Want Jobs," in *American Women in the Postwar World: A Symposium of the Role Women Will Play in Business and Industry* (New York: Newsweek's Club Bureau, 1944), 31.

12 Bess Furman, "'Domestic Revolution' Urged to Reduce Toil in the Home," *New York Times*, February 19, 1948, 1, 20. Other articles also predicted the professionalizing and selling of domestic homemaking skills in the future. T. Swann Harding, "Looking Ahead to 1950," *Independent Woman*, January 1947, 21. Harding noted, "The individual purchase, preparation and serving of food for each separate and individual family, often by a person having no taste or training for the job, is not only wasteful of time and labor but often of the food itself, or at least of many of its nutritive elements."

13 "Do You Expect War in Five Years?," *Woman's Home Companion*, July 1949, 14.

14 Dorothy C. Stratton, "Our Great Unused Resource—Womanpower," *New York Times Magazine*, October 1, 1950, 17.

15 William L. O'Neill, ed., *American Society since 1945* (New York Times Books, 1969), 3–7; Harold G. Vatter, *The U.S. Economy in World War II* (New York: Columbia University Press, 1985), 7–31; William Leuchtenburg, *A Troubled Feast: American Society since 1945* (Boston: Little, Brown, 1973), 4–7.

16 "Reconversion, US Style I," *Fortune*, September 1946, 4; Henry A. Wallace, *Sixty Million Jobs* (New York: Reynal and Hitchcock, 1945).

17 Susan Ware, *Holding Their Own: American Women in the 1930s* (Boston: Twayne, 1982); Caroline Bird, *Enterprising Women: A Bicentennial Project of the Business and Professional Women's Foundation* (New York: W. W. Norton, 1976).

18 Mildred Adams, "Wives Are People, Too," in "Business Wives or Housewives: A Debate," *The Forum*, September 1939, 125.

19 Mary C. Crowley, "Mary C. Crowley, President, Home Interiors and Gifts, Inc., Dallas, Texas," in *America's New Women Entrepreneurs: Tips, Tactics, and Techniques of Women Achievers in Business*, ed. Patricia Harrison (Acropolis Books, 1986), 75–76. When this book was published, Crowley's business had sales of $350 million.

20 The Window Shop Papers, Schlesinger Library, Radcliffe Institute for Advanced Study, MC427, box 1, folders 6–8; Ellen Miller, Ilse Heyman, and Dorothy Dahl, *The Window Shop: Safe Harbor for Refugees 1939–1972* (iUniverse, 2007), xiii, 31–33.

186 • Notes to Pages 17–20

21 "State of New York, Department of Commerce Press Release, July 18, 1945," Jane Hedges Todd Papers, box 4, folders 4–11, "Press Releases." According to Todd, 32.2 percent of those employed in New York war industries that year were women.

22 Dorothy C. Stratton, "Women after the War," *Independent Woman*, October 1945, 279.

23 "The Stake of Women in Post-War Full Employment," *Ladies Home Journal*, April 1944; A. G. Mezerik, "Getting Rid of the Women," *Atlantic Monthly*, June 1946, 83.

24 "Lady Beveridge and Mrs. Norton Divide on Women's Role after War," *New York Times*, June 7, 1943, 10.

25 Susan Hartmann, *The Homefront and Beyond: American Women in the 1940s* (Boston: Twayne, 1982), 77–78.

26 Margaret Culkin Banning, "Living and Working in the Peace-Building Years," *Report of the International Conference of the National Federation of Business and Professional Women's Clubs and the International Federation of Business and Professional Women*, 1946, 41, Archives of the National Federation of Business and Professional Women's Clubs, box BPW Publications, folder 1940s, Washington, D.C.

27 "Lady Beveridge," 10.

28 Hartmann, *Homefront and Beyond*, 68.

29 Hartmann, 22.

30 Cynthia Lowry, "Governor Dewey's Idea on Counseling of Grownups Pays Off for 6,000 Products Turned Out at Home," *New York Times*, January 18, 1948, Jane Hedges Todd Papers. See also "American Women in the Postwar World," 31–35.

31 Colston E. Warne, "The Reconversion of Women," *Current History*, March 1945, 202.

32 "News from Our Clubs: Offers Unique Postwar Plan," *Independent Woman*, May 1944, 142; "Bids Women Turn to Small Business," *New York Times*, August 12, 1944, 8; "Lady Beveridge," 10; "American Women in the Postwar World," 31–35; Hawes, "13,000,000 Will Want Jobs," 31–35.

33 "Bids Women Turn," 8.

34 This is evident from the ways in which women's ventures were described not only in the business books of the era or in newspaper articles but also in pamphlets put out by state and federal programs targeting women.

35 See chapters 4 and 5.

36 Warne, "Reconversion of Women," 205.

37 Mezerik, "Getting Rid of the Women," 82.

38 Harrison Smith, "Must Women Work," *Independent Woman*, December 1947, 342.

39 "Women's Job Needs after War Studied," *New York Times*, January 21, 1944, 1, 8.

40 "Lou Williamson Honored as 'Great Living American,'" *National Business Woman*, June 1959, 7.

41 P. D. Converse, *Should I Start My Own Business?* (Urbana: University of Illinois, Bureau of Economic and Business Research, 1945); Superintendent of Documents, *Check List of the Introduction of New Consumer Products*, Economic Series no. 41 (Washington, D.C.: U.S. Government Printing Office, 1945); Lew Hahn, *How to Start a Small Store* (New York: National Retail Dry Goods Association, 1945); *Establishing and Operating Small Businesses* (Washington, D.C.: U.S. Government Printing Office, 1945); U.S. Department of Commerce, *Establishing and Operating Your Own Business* (Washington, D.C.: U.S. Government Printing Office, 1945).

42 Edith Gordon (under the direction of H. B. McCoy), U.S. Department of Commerce and Bureau of Foreign and Domestic Commerce, *Establishing and Operating a Beauty Shop* (Washington, D.C.: U.S. Government Printing Office, 1946).

43 Lois Neuschutz, *A Job for Every Woman* (New York: H. W. Wilson, 1948), 61, 87, 176.

Notes to Pages 21–24 • 187

44 Vatter, *U.S. Economy in World War II*, 7–31. See also Sidney Ratner, James H. Soltow, and Richard Sylla, *The Evolution of the American Economy: Growth, Welfare and Decision Making*, 2nd ed., 492–512.

45 United States Veterans Administration, "The G.I. Bill of Rights," 1998, http://www.va.gov/benefits/Education/GI_Bill.htm.

46 U.S. Chamber of Commerce, *Freedom and the Free Market Inseparable: Post-War Readjustments*, bulletin no. 11 (Washington, D.C.: U.S. Government Printing Office, 1944), 3–4, in Chamber of Commerce Papers, Series II Publications, box 16, Hagley Museum and Library, Wilmington, Del.

47 "Consultation between Women Leaders and Business Managers on Home and Industry," Pittsburgh, Pa., November 15, 1945, 2, found in National Association of Manufacturers Papers (NAM Papers), NAM 1411, Series I Addendum, box 279, folder Committee on Home and Industry 1946 General, Hagley Museum and Library, Wilmington, Del.

48 NAM Papers. These meetings were held around the country on a regular and frequent basis, including in Louisville and several other locations. NAM also produced a newsletter for women on the program, as well as three films used to teach about the importance of small business to a free enterprise system.

49 See NAM and U.S. Chamber of Commerce Papers, both at Hagley Museum and Library, Wilmington, Del.; and Leuchtenburg, *Troubled Feast*, 37–39, 43.

50 Thompson, "Small Business and Women," 4.

51 Detailed descriptions of the mission of the Women's Program can be found in Jane Hedges Todd Papers. Also in the New York State Annual Report, from 1945 to 1971, available at the New York Public Library.

52 Jane Hedges Todd Papers, box 2.

53 State of New York, Department of Commerce, *Annual Report* (New York, 1944–1953).

54 List of New York Women's Council Members in Jane Todd, Papers, box 4, folder 4.

55 "Iowa City to Host Small Business Clinic," *Iowa City Press-Citizen*, November 7, 1953.

56 Jane Hedges Todd Papers. According to a year-end report produced by the Women's Program, an hour-long film was made about the small business clinics. The film itself does not exist in the Todd Papers holdings at the Cornell Library, nor does the New York State Department of Commerce have a copy of it. It remains difficult to say whether the film was ever distributed or completed.

57 Helen Thompson, "Small Business and Women," speech, November 3, 1945, in Jane Hedges Todd Papers, #2763, box 2, folder 2.

58 "962,000 U.S. Women," 20.

59 Jane Hedges Todd Papers, box 8, "Scrapbooks."

60 "Success Story #15," Jane Hedges Todd Papers, box 4, folder 4.9.

61 *Independent Woman*, the magazine of the National Federation of Business and Professional Women's Clubs, documented these efforts extensively in articles and news briefs from 1945 through 1954 (and later in some states). The BPW archives similarly contain notes made at the annual convention and annual meeting of the National Federation about the importance of the small business clinics and the group's efforts to urge state governments to adopt the New York model.

62 Jane Hedges Todd, "A Business Problems Program for Your State," *Independent Woman*, June 1950, 169–170.

63 This was accomplished with varying degrees of success. *Independent Woman*, the organ of the National Federation of Business and Professional Women's Clubs, frequently reported on club involvement with state efforts to replicate the New

188 • Notes to Pages 24-28

York Women's Program. Texas was the first to seek Todd's assistance; Ohio, Iowa, California, and others would follow suit. See *Independent Woman*, 1945–1957; and National Federation of Business and Professional Women Papers, Archives of the National Federation of Business and Professional Women's Clubs, Washington, D.C.

64 Though it only replicated the clinic model initially, Massachusetts eventually followed the New York model more precisely, launching its own women's division in the latter half of the 1950s.

65 Jane Hedges Todd Papers, #2763, box 2, folder 2; Miller, "From Pin Money to High Finance," *Reader's Digest*, December 1948, 42–44.

66 "Emphasis of Small Business Clinics Shifts to Conversion, Expansion Needs," *Independent Woman*, March 1951, 87; "Reports of National Standing Committees," *Independent Woman*, September 1950, 273; "Items of General Interest," *Independent Woman*, November 1953, 411; "Preview of the National Program, 1949–50," *Independent Woman*, March 1949, 75; "Mississippi Federation Holds First Small Business Clinic in Jackson," *Independent Woman*, July 1951, 206; "Fourteen State Federations Given Special Citations for Year's Work in Promoting Help to Small Business," *Independent Woman*, September 1951, 272.

67 *Proceedings: Mid-Year Meeting of the Board and Contents Committee Chairmen of the National Federation of Business and Professional Women's Clubs, Inc.*, January 20–21, 1950, Chicago, Ill., 41–42, found in the bound volumes at the Archives of the National Federation of Business and Professional Women's Clubs, Washington, D.C.

68 *Proceedings of the National Federation of Business and Professional Women's Clubs, Incorporated: Program Coordination Committee and Conference on Regional Programs*, New York, January 21–22, 1949, 51; *Proceedings: Board Meeting of the National Federation of Business and Professional Women's Clubs, Inc.*, July 1–5, 1949, Jacksonville, Fla., 27–33, both found in the bound volumes at the Archives of the National Federation of Business and Professional Women's Clubs, Washington, D.C.

69 Richard Moulton, "Just What Is Market Research?," *Independent Woman*, May 1949, 151–152.

70 Julietta K. Arthur, *How to Make a Home Business Pay* (Prentice Hall, 1949), mentioned in "Books You'll Want for Reference," *Independent Woman*, December 1949, 380.

71 Johnson, "Women's Dreams Turned," 1950; Miller, "From Pin Money," 44.

72 Jane Hedges Todd Papers, box 8, "Scrapbooks."

73 Helen Thompson, "Small Business and Women," 4.

74 "962,000 U.S. Women," 20; U.S. Department of Labor, Women's Bureau, *Changes in Women's Occupations: 1940–1950*, bulletin 253 (Washington, D.C.: U.S. Government Printing Office, 1954); *Status of Women in the United States* (Washington, D.C.: U.S. Government Printing Office, 1952).

75 Bess Furman, "Truman Bids Women Use Purse in Fight on High Cost of Living," *New York Times*, February 18, 1948, 1.

76 Laura Kozakiewicz, *Ladies Day at the Capitol: New York's Women Legislators, 1919–1992* (State University of New York Press, 2022), 53–54, 59. Kozakiewicz notes that Todd's victory on jury service was partial in that women were allowed to serve on juries as long as they stated their willingness to do so.

77 Mrs. Raymond Clapper, "The Women around Dewey," *Look*, September 14, 1948, 34, in Jane Hedges Todd Papers, box 3, folder 3.3.

78 Jane Hedges Todd Papers, box 3, folder 3.3. See also Carol Taylor, "Women Party Workers Tend House as Mama Votes," November 4, 1946, publication unknown, Jane Hedges Todd Papers, box 11.

Notes to Pages 29–31 • 189

79 "Dewey Called First Choice of Women for '48," *New York Tribune*, May 6, 1947; Jane Hedges Todd Papers, box 11.

80 Doris Ricker Marston, "Maine's Commissioner of Labor," *Independent Woman*, January 1952, 5–6.

81 Susan Ware, *Beyond Suffrage: Women in the New Deal* (Harvard University Press, 1981); Nancy Cott, *The Grounding of Modern Feminism* (Yale University Press, 1987).

82 Jane Hedges Todd, "Mobilization of Women War Power for Peacetime Endeavor," speech delivered at meeting of the Connecticut State Federation of Women's Clubs, New Haven, May 23, 1946, in Jane Hedges Todd Papers, box 2 Speeches, folder 2.2.

83 Selwin Thompson, "Good Cooks Make Good Politicians," *This Week*, November 4, 1945, Jane Hedges Todd Papers, box 3, folder 3.3. The end of this article told readers, "If you want Jane Todd's prize-winning recipe for mocha cake, send for our leaflet, 'A Politician Cooks,' which gives it and other of Miss Todd's good recipes." For other background on Todd, see "A Dial Daguerreotype: Jane Todd," *Club Dial*, Contemporary Club of White Plains, April 1941, Jane Hedges Todd Papers, box 3, folder 3.3; Meredith Whitener, "Miss Jane Todd," *The Empire Statesman*, November 1945, 12–26, Jane Hedges Todd Papers, box 4, folder 4.5; "Miss Jane H. Todd Retires as Deputy Commissioner of State Department of Commerce," press release, New York State Department of Commerce, June 27, 1960, Jane Hedges Todd Papers, box 4, folder 11. Various biographical sketches are found in Jane Hedges Todd Papers, box 2 Speeches, folder 2.10, and throughout her collection of papers.

84 Thompson, "Good Cooks."

85 Thompson.

86 Marston, "Maine's Commissioner of Labor," 6.

87 Papers of the Iowa Federation of Business and Professional Women's Clubs, Iowa State Historical Society, Des Moines. These papers include meeting minutes outlining the importance of the small business clinics and the women assisted as well as local newspaper articles.

88 "News from Our Clubs: Offer Unique Postwar Plan," *Independent Woman*, May 1944, 142; "Spotlight on Women Investors in Their Own Businesses," *Independent Woman*, March 1953, 90.

89 Tom Mahoney, "$49,000,000 Business in Round Figures," *Independent Woman*, October 1950, 310–311, 327.

90 Reader's Digest Books, *A Business of Your Own: The Reader's Digest Manual of Ideas for Small Business* (Reader's Digest Books, 1946).

91 Reader's Digest Books, 92, 121–128.

92 "The Screen," review of *Mildred Pierce*, Warner Bros., dir. Michael Curtiz, *New York Times*, September 29, 1945.

93 "The Screen: The Tale's the Thing," *The Commonweal*, October 5, 1945, 598; James Agee, "Films," *The Nation*, October 13, 1945, 38; "The Current Cinema: Ectoplasm and Plenty of Cain," review of *Mildred Pierce*, Warner Bros., *The New Yorker*, October 6, 1945, 87; "Suburban Badlands," review of *Mildred Pierce*, Warner Bros., *The New Republic*, October 22, 1945, 528; "The Fourth Joan Crawford," *Newsweek*, October 15, 1945, 102; Linda Williams, "Feminist Film Theory: *Mildred Pierce* and the Second World War," in *Female Spectators: Looking at Film and Television*, ed. E. Deidre Pribram (Verso, 1988), 12–30.

94 Karen Anderson, *Wartime Women: Sex Roles, Family Relations and the Status of Women during World War II* (Westport, Conn.: Praeger, 1981); Sherna Berger Gluck, *Rosie the Riveter Revisited* (New York: Twayne, 1987); Leila J. Rupp, *Mobilizing*

190 • Notes to Pages 31-35

Women for War: German and American Propaganda, 1939–1945 (Princeton: Princeton University Press, 1978).

95 The image of a woman struggling to provide for her family due to financial crisis or male absence was a familiar one in the context of the Depression and World War II, leaving critics to merely note offhandedly that as a businesswoman, Pierce was "fabulously successful." See "Fourth Joan Crawford."

96 Reader's Digest Books, *Business of Your Own*, n.p. Other books advising women on opening a business in the 1940s included Doree Smedley, *Careers for Women in Business* (E. P. Dutton, 1945); Maxwell Lehman and Morton Yarmon, *Every Woman's Guide to Spare-Time Income* (Harcourt, Brace, 1950); Polly Webster, *How to Make Money at Home* (Whittlesey House, 1949); Lansing M. Paine and Polly Webster, *Start Your Own Business on Less Than $1000* (McGraw Hill, 1950); and Neuschutz, *Job for Every Woman*. Books not specifically targeting women but suggested to them by the BPW and the Women's Programs included A. D. H. Kaplan, *Small Business: Its Place and Problems* (McGraw Hill, 1948).

97 Anthony and Diane Hallett, "Margaret Rudkin (Pepperidge Farm, Inc.)," in *Entrepreneur Magazine Encyclopedia of Entrepreneurs* (New York: John Wiley & Sons, 1997), 401–403. For a more complete discussion of Rudkin, see Edith Sparks, *Boss Lady: How Three Women Entrepreneurs Built Successful Big Businesses in the Mid-twentieth Century* (Chapel Hill: University of North Carolina Press, 2017).

98 Tom Long, "Polly Webster Was Columnist for Globe and Author, at 87," *Boston Globe*, March 8, 1995.

99 Neuschutz, *Job for Every Woman*, 61–62.

100 This is evidenced by much of the material in the Jane Hedges Todd Papers. The collection includes articles, brochures, press releases and small business clinic stories and materials.

101 Jane Hedges Todd Papers. See also State of New York, Department of Commerce, *Annual Report* (1945–1953).

102 Harding, "Looking Ahead," 21.

103 "Women's Dreams Turned into Cash," *New York Times*, September 30, 1950, 14.

104 Ruth Newburn Sedam, "These Mothers Make Money at Home," publication unknown, Jane Hedges Todd Papers, box 4, folder 4.5.

105 Ruth S. Finney, *Self-Employed Women in Hawaii: Their Work and Family Lives, 1977* (data set). These data were collected by R. Finney and are available through the archive of the Henry A. Murray Research Center, Radcliffe Institute for Advanced Study. Raw survey data were located in boxes 2 and 3. The names of the participants, as in many such sociological studies, are not available or included in the data files.

106 New York State Department of Commerce, Press Release, April 21, 1946; Jane Hedges Todd Papers, box 4, folder 4.11.

107 Jane Hedges Todd Papers, box 8, "Scrapbooks." Materials here include reports and press releases on the growth of and demand for the clinics and related pamphlets.

108 Jane Hedges Todd Papers, box 4, folder 4–7, 4–8, 4–9. These folders contain success stories as well as letters from and reports about assistance provided to would-be women business owners

109 "Women Called Good Credit Risks," *New York Times*, September 12, 1948, 26.

110 Nichelle Gainer, "Overlooked No More: Rose Morgan, a Pioneer in Hairdressing and Harlem," *New York Times*, April 10, 2018, https://www.nytimes.com/2019/04/10/obituaries/rose-morgan-overlooked.html; Gill, *Beauty Shop Politics*, 74–75; "House of Beauty: Rose Meta Is Biggest Negro Beauty Parlor in the World," *Ebony*, May 1946; Susannah Walker, *Style & Status: Selling Beauty to African American*

Women, 1920–1975 (Lexington: University Press of Kentucky, 2007), 115–141; Rose Morgan, "The HistoryMakers A2002.009," interview by Julieanna L. Richardson, January 28, 2002, HistoryMakers Digital Archive, session 1, tape 4, story 9, Rose Morgan talks about securing funds to expand her business in the 1950s, https://da-thehistorymakers-org.ezproxy.bpl.org/storiesForBio;ID=A2002.009.

111 Gill, *Beauty Shop Politics*, 74–75.

112 "House of Beauty."

113 "People You Should Know: Miss Rose Morgan," *Pittsburgh Courier*, December 18, 1954, 28.

114 Peter Brouillet, "Billions for Beauty," *American Magazine*, October 1946, 97.

115 Leonard Broom and John I. Kitsuse, *The Managed Casualty: The Japanese American Family in World War II* (University of California Press, 1973), 19, 32, 58–63.

116 Leonard Broom and Ruth Riemer, *Removal and Return: The Socio-Economic Effects of the War on Japanese Americans* (University of California Press, 1949), 203.

117 Broom and Riemer, 27, 65.

118 Precious Vida Yamaguchi, *Experiences of Japanese American Women during and after World War II: Living in Internment Camps and Rebuilding Life Afterwards* (Lexington Books / Fortress Academic, 2014), 41.

119 Yamaguchi, 47–48, 73.

120 Jaime Arellano-Bover, "Displacement, Diversity, and Mobility: Career Impacts of Japanese American Internment," *Journal of Economic History* 82, no. 1 (March 2022): 126–174.

121 Finney, *Self-Employed Women*, box 3.

122 T. Swann, "Looking Ahead to 1950," *Independent Woman*, January 1947, 21.

123 "Careen in the Kitchen," *National Business Woman*, October 1957, 8–9.

124 Esther M. Douty and Dorothy Virginia Lee, "First Ladies of the Laundry," *Independent Woman*, October 1950, 303–304.

125 "Women Clubs Vote Equal Rights Drive," *New York Times*, July 6, 1948, 26.

126 "Iowa City Group Is Host to Small Business Clinic," *Iowa City Press-Citizen*, November 7, 1953, Papers of the Iowa Federation of Business and Professional Women's Clubs, Iowa State Historical Society, Des Moines.

127 "Success Story #1: Mrs. Dorothy Orefice, Glamourette Baby Shoes," found in Jane Hedges Todd Papers, box 4, folder 4.8, "Success Stories."

128 Ruth Beeler White, "She Puts Personality into Houses," *Independent Woman*, June 1951, 168–170; Marion Rubenstein, "With the Greatest of Ease," *National Business Woman*, January 1959, 8–9; "First Woman to Become Mutual Fund Wholesaler," *New York Times*, February 17, 1951, 23. Annette Hyder's shipping business was founded in 1948.

129 Whitener, "Miss Jane Todd," 24.

130 "Women Clubs Vote," 26.

131 White, "She Puts Personality," 168–170.

132 Kathryn Brummond, "Are Wives People?," *Independent Woman*, November 1946, 330.

133 Eleanor Roosevelt, "Women at the Peace Conference," *Reader's Digest*, April 1944, 48–49; Judy Barrett Litoff and David C. Smith, "The Horrors of War and the Errors of Peace: United States Women Prepare for the Postwar World, 1940–1945," paper presented at the annual meeting of the American Historical Association, Chicago, 1995.

134 Academie Moderne Papers, *School Bulletin: 1941–42*, 4–6, box 1, folders 37, 38, found at the Schlesinger Library, Radcliffe Institute for Advanced Study.

192 • Notes to Pages 43–47

Chapter 2   Motherhood and Its Discontents

1   Lillian Vernon, *An Eye for Winners: How I Built One of America's Greatest Direct Mail Businesses* (Harper Business, 1996), 38; Russel R. Taylor, *Exceptional Entrepreneurial Women: Strategies for Success* (Quorum Books, 1988), 21–22.

2   Vernon, *Eye for Winners*, 36.

3   Taylor, *Exceptional Entrepreneurial Women*, 21–22. Born Lillian Menasche in 1927, her affluent Jewish family escaped Nazi Germany in 1933 for Holland in 1937.

4   Diane Jennings, *Self-Made Women: Twelve of America's Leading Entrepreneurs Talk about Success, Self-Image and the Superwoman* (Dallas: Taylor Publishing, 1987), 49.

5   Vernon, *Eye for Winners*, 38–39.

6   Jennings, *Self-Made Women*, 49. The company name combined her first name with a part of the name of the town where she lived and worked, Mount Vernon.

7   Jennings, *Self-Made Women*, 29–30, 49. In total, Lillian Vernon received 6,450 orders for bags and belts from her initial round of advertising.

8   Vernon, *Eye for Winners*, 62, 66, 97–99, 103.

9   Lynn Povich, "Lillian Vernon, Creator of a Bustling Catalog Business, Dies at 88," *New York Times*, December 14, 2015, https://www.nytimes.com/2015/12/15/business/lillian-vernon-creator-of-a-bustling-catalog-business-dies-at-88.html.

10   Not her real name. Simmons (daughter), interview with the author, telephone tape recording, August 1999.

11   Warren Thayer, "The Story of Rose Totino: From Pauper to Pizza Queen; Restaurateur," *Frozen Food Age*, February 1994, 1.

12   Martha Graham, "Hobby Town Meeting: Cakes for Students," *Profitable Hobbies*, September 1953, 38–39.

13   "Jane Todd Named State Commerce Deputy to Head a Program for Employed Women," *New York Times*, June 22, 1945, 10. See also "Dewey Completes Council of Women," *New York Times*, October 21, 1945, 32; and "Women in Business Hailed by Dewey," *New York Times*, October 11, 1946, 30. In 1950, Dewey further commented, "In New York State we have named more women to high public office than in any other state. In fact, it comes close to more than any ten states combined. It is criminal that the state should be deprived of the services of women who have made names for themselves in all phases of business and industry." "Women in Business Get Honor Scrolls," *New York Times*, March 17, 1950, 28.

14   Elaine Tyler May, *Homeward Bound: American Families in the Cold War*, 4th ed. (New York: Basic Books, 2017); William Chafe, *The Unfinished Journey: America since World War II, Third Edition* (New York: Oxford University Press, 1995); Joanne Meyerowitz, ed., *Not June Cleaver: Women and Gender in Postwar America, 1945–1960* (Philadelphia: Temple University Press, 1994); Brett Harvey, *The Fifties: A Women's Oral History* (New York: HarperCollins, 1993); Stephanie Coontz, *The Way We Never Were: American Families and the Nostalgia Trap* (New York: Basic Books, 1992).

15   Sherna Berger Gluck, *Rosie the Riveter Revisited: Women, the War, and Social Change* (New American Library, 1987); Eugenia Kaledin, *Mothers and More: American Women in the 1950s* (Twayne, 1984). See also May, *Homeward Bound*.

16   Natalia Molina, *A Place at the Nayarit: How a Mexican Restaurant Nourished a Community* (Oakland: University of California Press, 2022), 4–5, 65–65. The book tells the story of the author's grandmother and notes that the original restaurant opened in the mid-1940s, followed by two other locations, with the 1951 restaurant as a main focus.

17   The magazine *Profitable Hobbies*, along with *Independent Woman* and *National Business Woman*, frequently referred to women's businesses as "sideline," "bread and

Notes to Pages 47–51 • 193

butter," "pin money projects," and "profitable hobbies." Other mainstream magazines picked up use of the term as the decade progressed.

18 Libby Nicholson, "Plates Painted to Order," *Profitable Hobbies*, July 1954, 26.

19 Although the Lanham Act established the first and only federal day care system during World War II, women approached it reluctantly and regarded it as déclassé, and few took advantage of it. The program was disbanded by war's end.

20 Carol D. Briggs, "Have You Got What It Takes," *Woman's Home Companion*, September 1950, 11; Crockett, "She Humanized Bill Collecting," 24.

21 "Money Making at Home," *Woman's Home Companion*, December 1950, 8, 11.

22 Briggs, "Have You Got," 11.

23 Kay Bowe, "A Home Career in Handknits," *Profitable Hobbies*, March 1953, 24–25, 50–55.

24 Vivian Castleberry, "Ethics, people are liquid assets in her business philosophy," found in Martha Stuart Papers, 87-M126, carton 6, folder Women Business Owners, Schlesinger Library, Radcliffe Institute for Advanced Study (hereafter Martha Stuart Papers).

25 Tom Long, "Joyce Chen, Introduced America to Fine Mandarin Cuisine; at 76," *Boston Globe*, August 25, 1994, 37; Jack Thomas, "Joyce Chen: A Dynasty in Peril; Financial Woes May Cost Stephen Chen the Restaurant Business His Mother Built," *Boston Globe*, May 19, 1994, 63.

26 Arizona Women's Hall of Fame, "Mary Velasquez Riley (1908–1987)" https://www .azwhf.org/copy-of-jane-h-rider-1889-1981; Barry Richens, "Velasquez Riley Oral History" (interview of Mary Velasquez Riley), Arizona Memory Project, accessed February 18, 1977, https://azmemory.azlibrary.gov/nodes/view/162665.

27 National Manpower Council, *Womanpower: A Statement by the National Manpower Council with Chapters by the Council Staff* (New York: Columbia University Press, 1957), 17–18. Specific references to the large numbers of older women returning—or requiring a return—to the workforce were discussed at length in many of the womanpower conferences throughout the 1950s, as well as within Department of Labor publications. This document provides a summary of the trend and concern: "As recently as 1940, the chance that a woman would be in the labor force was almost one out of two if she was in her early twenties, but less than one out of four if she was around 50. Today, peak participation in paid employment occurs among young women of 18 and 19 . . . (after age 30) the percentage of women in the labor forces rises for each successive age group through to the early fifties. Currently, chances are about as good that a woman of 50 will be working as one of 20."

28 Alice K. Leopold, "The Earning Opportunities Forums for Mature Women," *National Business Woman*, June 1959, 4–7.

29 Annie S. Greenwood, "What Have You in Your Hand?," *Independent Woman*, September 1953, 308–310; Mary K. Pirie, "No One over Thirty-Five Need Apply," *Independent Woman*, February 1950, 42–43.

30 Greenwood, 309.

31 Maude D. Anderson, "Want a Business of Your Own?," *Independent Woman*, October 1954, 383.

32 Valera Tebben, "All about Aprons," *Profitable Hobbies*, July 1954, 40–41, 57–59.

33 Peg Tyndal Jackson, "Clothes That Doll up Any Doll," *Profitable Hobbies*, July 1953, 24–27.

34 Evelyn De Wolfe, "She Just Couldn't Stay Retired," *Independent Woman*, July 1955, 13–14.

35 "Pioneer in Freezing," *National Business Woman*, May 1958, 13.

194 • Notes to Pages 51-54

36 "A Telephone, a Typewriter, a File Case—and Determination," *National Business Woman*, July 1958, 23.

37 Florence Loba, "At Her Fingertips," *National Business Woman*, November 1956, 13.

38 Lillian Faderman, *Odd Girls and Twilight Lovers: A History of Lesbian Life in Twentieth-Century America* (Columbia University Press, 2012), 161–167.

39 Charlotte Coleman, interview by Steven Estes, Veterans History Project, Library of Congress, September 5, 2005, accessed June 2, 2021, https://memory.loc.gov/diglib/vhp/story/loc.natlib.afc2001001.43328/transcript?ID=sr0001; "In Remembrance: Charlotte Coleman," *San Francisco Bay Times* (date unknown), http://sfbaytimes.com/in-remembrance-charlotte-coleman/. See also Rebecca Jennings, "The Gateways Club and the Emergence of a Post Second World War Lesbian Subculture," *Social History* 31, no. 2 (May 2006): 206–225; Janet Kahn and Patricia A. Gozemba, "In and around the Lighthouse: Working-Class Lesbian Bar Culture in the 1950s and 1960s," in *Gendered Domains: Rethinking Public and Private in Women's History*, ed. Dorothy O. Helly and Susan M. Reverby (Cornell University Press, 1992), 90–107.

40 Sally Friedman, "Successful, By Design: 'The woman with the golden cut' comes to Philadelphia," *Jewish Exponent*, December 29, 1995, 54.

41 Susan Glenn, *Daughters of the Shtetl: Life and Labor in the Immigrant Generation* (Cornell University Press, 1990), 9, 13–14.

42 Bud Konheim, interview with the author, tape recording, spring 1998, New York, New York.

43 Vernon, *Eye for Winners*, 24–25.

44 Vernon, 26.

45 Vernon, 42.

46 For more on this tradition, see Booker T. Washington, *The Negro in Business* (Johnson Reprint Corp., 1970); and Marcus Garvey, *Aims and Objects of the Movement for the Solution of the Negro Problem Outlined* (New York: Universal Negro Improvement Association, 1924).

47 Bart Landry, *The New Black Middle Class* (University of California Press, 1987). Landry challenges E. Franklin Frazier and others on the timing of the emergence of a Black middle class. Landry sees the groundwork being laid in the 1950s for the class that comes to the fore in the 1960s. He differs from Frazier's *Black Bourgeoisie*, which dates the arrival of a Black middle class much earlier. Other literature discussing the class dynamics of the Negro race includes Mary C. Lynn and Benjamin D. Berry, eds., *The Black Middle Class: Proceedings of the Conference on the Black Middle Class* (Saratoga Springs: Skidmore College, 1980).

48 "Harlem's New House of Beauty," *Ebony*, June 1955, 62–68.

49 Rose Morgan's life was extensively covered throughout the Black press and within books on Negro business. For a sample, see "Beauty Culturist Appointed to Minimum Wage Board," *Opportunity*, April–June 1947, 113–114; "Rose Morgan-Louis Saunders Wed in Surprise Private Rites," *New York Amsterdam News*, January 6, 1960, 9; "Mrs. Joe Louis: Business and Beauty Queen," *New York Age*, May 10, 1956, 8; and "Rose Morgan," *Shoptalk* (summer 1982), 66–70.

50 "Beauty Culturist Appointed," 113–114.

51 Ethel Erickson, "Employment Conditions in Beauty Shops: A Study of Four Cities," Women's Bureau, Bulletin 133 (Washington, D.C.: U.S. Government Printing Office, 1939), 37–39; LeRoy W. Jeffries, "The Decay of the Beauty Parlor Industry in Harlem," *Opportunity*, February 1938, 50.

52 Vishnu V. Oaks, *The Negro's Adventure in General Business*, vol. 2 (Negro Universities Press, 1949); Claude McKay, *Negro Metropolis* (New York: E. P. Dutton, 1940);

Notes to Pages 54–59 • 195

Joseph A. Pierce, *Negro Business and Business Education: Their Present and Prospective Development* (Harper, 1947); "Economics Is Hope of Race," *Chicago Defender*, July 12, 1958, 21; Ronald W. Bailey, ed. *Black Enterprise: Historical and Contemporary Perspectives* (New York: Basic Books, 1971).

53 Vernice Marks, *First Edition to the History of the National Beauty Culturists League: 1919–1976* (Ann Arbor: Beauty Culturists League, 1977); Pierce, *Negro Business*; Marion Cuthbert, "Problems Facing Negro Young Women," *Opportunity*, February 1936, 47–49; "I've Tried to Show What the Negro Can Do When Given a Chance," *Beauty Trade*, November 1961, 30–31.

54 McKay, *Negro Metropolis*; Oaks, *Negro's Adventure*, 69, 87; U.S. Department of Labor, "Occupational Outlook Handbook," bulletin no. 1255 (Washington, D.C.: U.S. Government Printing Office, 1959).

55 Pierce, *Negro Business*, 78.

56 Marjorie Joyner, interview with the author, April 26, 1993; Bernice Calvin, interview with the author, April 28, 1993.

57 Tiffany M. Gill writes about the trip overseas and its coverage in the Black press in Tiffany M. Gill, *Beauty Shop Politics: African American Women's Activism in the Beauty Industry* (University of Illinois Press, 2010), 82–94; "Beauty Pilgrimage: Europeans Shower Honors on 195 Visiting Beauticians," *Ebony*, August 1954, 41; "Integration Comes to the Beauty Business," *Ebony*, August 1966 143; Bernice Calvin, interview with the author, April 28, 1993.

58 Julia Faye Smith, *Something to Prove: A Biography of Ann Lowe, America's Forgotten Designer* (Julia Faye Dockery Smith, 2016), 89. Society women held as a close secret the names of their dress designers to avoid having to compete with other women for their services in the future.

59 Judith Thurman, "Ann Lowe's Barrier-Breaking Mid-Century Couture," New Yorker, March 22, 2021, https://www.newyorker.com/magazine/2021/03/29/ann-lowes-barrier-breaking-mid-century-couture. Ann Levin, "An Uncredited Career," Princeton Magazine, http://www.princetonmagazine.com/an-uncredited-career/.

60 U.S. Department of Labor, Women's Bureau, *Womanpower Committees during World War II: United States and British Experience*, Bulletin No. 244 (Washington, D.C.: U.S. Government Printing Office, 1953), 3–31, 34–48, 55–72.

61 May, *Homeward Bound*, 23.

62 National Manpower Council, *Womanpower: A Statement by the National Manpower Council with Chapters by the Council Staff* (New York: Columbia University Press, 1957), 46.

63 National Manpower Council, *Work in the Lives of Married Women: Proceedings of a Conference on Womanpower* (New York: Columbia University Press, 1958), viii.

64 Alice Leopold, "Womanpower in a Changing World," Address before the Purdue University Faculty, Townspeople and Students, March 3, 1959, 5–6.

65 "Education and Vocations Committee Work Plans," *Independent Woman*, May 1951, 148.

66 "Massachusetts Members Win Commerce Women's Division," *National Business Woman* November 1957, 23. The state's women's division would become active in promoting programs for women in the 1960s and 1970s, but these tended to be less focused on training in business ownership and more of an assortment of women's concerns.

67 New York State Department of Commerce, *Women's Program*, 1953, 11–16.

68 "To All Clubs and Members," *Iowa Business Woman*, November 1958, 10, Papers of the Iowa Federation of Business and Professional Women's Clubs, box 20, Iowa State

196 • Notes to Pages 59-60

Historical Society, Des Moines. Earlier documents note men among the hundreds in attendance at clinics, including "Small Business Clinic," from "The Thirty-Third Annual Meeting," May 15–17, 1953, Papers of the Iowa Federation of Business and Professional Women's Clubs, box 21.

69 "Small Business Clinic," *Ohio Business Woman*, January 1958, found in Elva Chandler Papers, Hagley Museum and Library, Wilmington, Del.; Ina Wickham, "'Ideas Into Dollars' Is Theme of Iowa Business Clinic," October 27, 1954 (publication unknown), found in Scrapbook V, 1951–1966, Papers of the Iowa Federation of Business and Professional Women's Clubs, box 13, Iowa State Historical Society, Des Moines.

70 "Club Committees' Pages," *Independent Woman*, February 1954, 70.

71 Margery E. Martin, "Small Business Clinics," *Thirty-Eighth Annual Meeting of the Iowa Federation of Business and Professional Women, Inc.*, May 16–18, 1958, found in Papers of the Iowa Federation of Business and Professional Women's Clubs, box 21, Iowa State Historical Society, Des Moines; Beverly Quinn, chairman, "Small Business Clinic," *Thirty-Fourth Annual Meeting of the Iowa Federation of Business and Professional Women, Inc.*, May 14–16, 1956, 26, found in Papers of the Iowa Federation of Business and Professional Women's Clubs, box 21; "Proceedings of the Thirty-Fifth Annual Meeting, of the Iowa Federation of Business and Professional Women's Clubs," May 13–14, 1955, 85–86, found in Papers of the Iowa Federation of Business and Professional Women's Clubs, box 21, Iowa State Historical Society, Des Moines; "Annual Reports of the Iowa Federation of Business and Professional Women, Inc., 1955–56," 30–31, found in Papers of the Iowa Federation of Business and Professional Women's Clubs, box 5, Iowa State Historical Society, Des Moines.

72 The pages of the BPW magazines *Independent Woman* and *National Business Woman* are filled with stories promoting and encouraging small business clinics or discussing their outcome. For a sample, see: "Small Business Clinics," *Independent Woman*, November 1954, 431; "Reports of the National Standing Committees," *Independent Woman*, August 1953, 281; "Education and Vocations: For the Record—Small Business Clinics," *Independent Woman*, May 1955, 193. Many of these brochures no longer exist, since boxes were lost or destroyed when the National Federation relocated its headquarters, but references to them exist throughout their publications. See "Work Materials for the 1949–1950 Program," *Independent Woman*, October 1949, 320; "Education and Vocations," *Independent Woman*, May 1951, 142; "From Your National Committees: Education and Vocations," *Independent Woman*, March 1956, 22; and "Items of General Interest: Congratulations Pennsylvania," *Independent Woman*, May 1955, 191.

73 "Ideas for Live-Wire Programs," *National Business Woman*, March 1959, 26; "Ideas for Live-Wire Programs," *National Business Woman*, July 1958, 26; "Federation News, Views and Know-How," Independent Woman, January 1955, 24; "BPW Sets Career Clinic Next Sunday," newspaper article dated April 26, 1959, in Papers of the Iowa Federation of Business and Professional Women's Clubs, Inc., Scrapbook V, July 10, 1951–1966, box 13, Iowa State Historical Society, Des Moines; "Davenport (Iowa) Business and Professional Women's Club, Summarized Annual Report for 1958–1959," 2, in Papers of the Iowa Federation of Business and Professional Women's Clubs, Inc., box 16, Iowa State Historical Society, Des Moines; "Annual Reports, 1956–1957, of the National Federation of Business and Professional Women's Clubs, Inc.," July 6–10, 1957, 20–21 found in Records of the National Federation of Business and Professional Women's Clubs, Inc., box: Conventions, Washington, D.C.

74 Ben Seligman, *The Potentates: Business and Business Men in American History* (New York: Dial, 1971), 329.

Notes to Pages 60-61 • 197

75 Chamber of Commerce of the United States, "Small Business Its Role and Its Problems" (Washington, D.C., 1953), 11, found in Records of the U.S. Chamber of Commerce, COC Series II, Publications, box 20, Hagley Museum and Library, Wilmington, Del.

76 James Gilbert, *Another Chance: Postwar America, 1945–1985* (Dorsey Press, 1986), 8–9.

77 William L. O'Neill, introduction to *American Society since 1945* (Chicago: Quadrangle Books, 1969), 10–11.

78 May, *Homeward Bound*, 175–176.

79 William E. Leuchtenburg, *A Troubled Feast: American Society since 1945* (Little, Brown); O'Neill, *American Society since 1945*, 19–20.

80 Leuchtenburg, *Troubled Feast*; O'Neill, *American Society since 1945*.

81 Irving Kristol, "The New Forgotten Man," in U.S. Senate, Select Committee on Small Business, in Gaylord Nelson, *Small Business and the Quality of American Life: A Compilation of Source Material on the Relationship between Small Business and the Quality of Life, 1946–1976*, report prepared for the Senate Select Committee on Small Business, 95th Congress, 1st sess. (Washington, D.C.: U.S. Government Printing Office, 1977), 57, excerpted from *Wall Street Journal*, November 13, 1975.

82 "So You're Going into Business" (publication date not available but appears to be either 1959 or 1960), found in Chamber of Commerce Records, Series II, box 21, Hagley Museum and Library, Wilmington, Del.

83 U.S. Chamber of Commerce, "Survey of Local Chambers of Commerce" (Washington, D.C., 1951), 42, 49, in Records of the U.S. Chamber of Commerce, box 19, Series II Publications, 1951, Hagley Museum and Library, Wilmington, Del.; U.S. Chamber of Commerce, "Survey of Local Chambers of Commerce" (Washington, D.C., 1954), 57–58, box 22, in Records of the U.S. Chamber of Commerce, box 19, Series II Publications, Hagley Museum and Library.

84 U.S. Chamber of Commerce, "Women in the Chamber of Commerce" (Washington, D.C., 1957), found in Records of the U.S. Chamber of Commerce, Series II Publications, box 22, Hagley Museum and Library, Wilmington, Del.

85 "Women's Role in U.S. Economy Underlined by NAM Approach," *Christian Science Monitor*, February 23, 1957, found in Records of the National Association of Manufacturers, #1411 NAM Series III, box 223, folder: Women's Clubs General, Hagley Museum and Library, Wilmington, Del. Other articles claim women held as many as 74% of the titles to suburban homes. See "Women's Stake Gains in National Economy," *New York Times*, October 21, 1950, 9.

86 Louise Bushnell, "Beauty at Your Doorstep," *Idea Workshop Bulletin*, National Association of Manufacturers, in National Association of Manufacturers Records, #1411, Series III, box 223, folder Women's Clubs, General 1958–1959, 60–62 and 1963, Hagley Museum and Library, Wilmington, Del.

87 Alice K. Leopold, Careers for Women in Retailing, U.S. Department of Labor, Women's Bureau, Bulletin 271 (Washington, D.C.: U.S. Government Printing Office, 1959), 38.

88 Robert L. Aronson, *Self-Employment: A Labor Market Perspective* (Ithaca: Cornell University Press, 1991), 4–5.

89 Numbers vary depending on the counting mechanism used by a given government agency. See U.S. Department of Labor, *Handbook of Labor Statistics, 1972*, bulletin 1735 (Washington, D.C.: U.S. Government Printing Office, 1972); Frieda Miller, *Women as Workers: A Statistical Guide*, U.S. Department of Labor, Women's Bureau, D-65 (Washington, D.C.: U.S. Government Printing Office, 1954); and Alice

198 • Notes to Pages 62–65

Leopold, *Handbook on Women Workers*, U.S. Department of Labor, Women's Bureau, found in Jane Hedges Todd Papers, box 4.

90 Aronson, *Self-Employment*, 4; U.S. Department of Labor, *Handbook of Labor Statistics, 1972*, 38.

91 *The Small Business Act of 1953*, P.L. 163-83, title II, section 202, as cited in Anthony G. Chase, "Federal Support of the Vital Majority: The Development of the US Small Business Administration," in Deane Carson, ed., *The Vital Majority: Small Business in the American Economy, Essays Marking the Twentieth Anniversary of the US Small Business Administration* (Washington, D.C.: U.S. Government Printing Office, 1974), 5; Mansel G. Blackford, *A History of Small Business in America* (New York: Twayne, 1991), 77–81.

92 Chase, "Federal Support," 6–7.

93 Jonathan James Bean, "Beyond the Broker State: A History of the Federal Government's Policies toward Small Business, 1936–1961" (PhD diss., Ohio State University, 1994), 235, 255–256.

94 Blackford, *History of Small Business*, 78.

95 Business women were certainly encouraged by what the new SBA might mean for them in the long term. Marjorie L. Temple, "Uncle Sam and Retirement Plans for the Self-Employed," *Independent Woman*, November 1952, 335.

96 Miller, *Women as Workers*, 58.

97 Bean, "Beyond the Broker State," 255.

98 Henry C. Dethloff and Keith L. Bryant Jr., "Entrepreneurship," in *American Business History: Case Studies*, ed. Henry Dethloff and Joseph Pusateri (Boston: Heath, 1987), 5, 7–21.

99 Emphasis added. Gilbert Burck, "So You Want to Make Money," *Fortune*, June 1953, 115. The article is filled with male-only models of success and the ideal of the entrepreneur.

100 Burck, 115.

101 Dethloff and Bryant, "Entrepreneurship," 5, 11.

102 Kathy Peiss, "'Vital Industry' and Women's Ventures: Conceptualizing Gender in 20th Century Business History," *Business History Review*, 72, no. 2 (1998): 219–241.

103 Dethloff and Bryant, "Entrepreneurship," 11–12. It is interesting that a 1989 book studying the specific problems and relationships of women to the companies they owned used the term *entrepreneur* within its pages but chose as its title *Women-Owned Businesses*. Oliver Hagan, Carol Rivchun, and Donald Sexton, *Women-Owned Businesses* (New York: Praeger, 1989); The Entrepreneurship Institute, "How to Create and Manage Your Own Business," flier, found in Martha Stuart Papers, folder Entrepreneurship Institute; William McCrea to Martha Stuart, letter, July 10, 1978, in Martha Stuart Papers, folder Entrepreneurship Institute. See also David McClelland, *The Achieving Society* (Princeton, N.J.: Van Nostrand, 1961).

104 Vernon, *Eye for Winners*.

105 Thomas V. DiBacco, *Made in the USA: The History of American Business* (New York: Harper & Row, 1987), 262; Gilbert, *Another Chance*, 59.

106 Gilbert, 261.

107 May, *Homeward Bound*, 165.

108 Gilbert, *Another Chance*, 254–255.

109 Paul A. Carter, *Another Part of the Fifties* (Columbia University Press, 1983), 39.

110 Carter, 36.

111 Carter, 39; *Wall Street Journal* article as cited in Carter, 39.

112 "Women's Role in U.S. Economy." See also "Women's Stake Gains in National Economy," *New York Times*, October 21, 1950, 9.

113 Julie A. Matthaei, *An Economic History of Women in America: Women's Work, the Sexual Division of Labor, and the Development of Capitalism* (Schocken Books, 1982), 246.

114 Lee Rainwater, Richard P. Coleman, and Gerald Handel, *Workingman's Wife: Her Personality, World and Life Style* (Oceana Publications, 1959), 176, as cited in Matthaei, *Economic History of Women*, 246.

115 Lizabeth Cohen, "From Town Center to Shopping Center: The Reconfiguration of Community Marketplaces in Postwar America," *American Historical Review*, October 1996, 1073; Lizabeth Cohen, *A Consumers' Republic: The Politics of Mass Consumption at War's End* (Vintage Books, 2003).

116 Leopold, *Handbook on Women Workers*, vii.

117 Rainwater, Coleman, and Handel, *Workingman's Wife*, 176.

118 Matthaei, *Economic History of Women*, 248–251. See also Dee Dee Ahern with Betsy Bliss, *Economics of Being a Woman* (New York: MacMillan, 1976).

119 Lillian Breslow Rubin, *Worlds of Pain: Life in the Working-Class Family* (New York: Basic Books, 1976), 173, as cited in Matthaei, *Economic History of Women*, 249. Other works express a similar tension, though this tendency cut across class lines. See Mirra Komarovsky, *Blue Collar Marriage* (New York: Random House, 1964).

120 "Expanding Occupational Opportunities for Women," *Monthly Labor Review*, no. R. 2093, April 1953, 1.

121 Department of Labor, Women's Bureau, *Changes in Women's Occupations: 1940–1950*, bulletin 253 (Washington, D.C.: U.S. Government Printing Office, 1954), 29.

122 Konheim, interview with the author.

123 Konheim, interview with the author.

124 Joanne Meyerowitz, "Beyond the Feminine Mystique: A Reassessment of Postwar Mass Culture, 1946–1958," in *Not June Cleaver*, 229–253.

125 Alva Myrdal and Viola Klein, *Women's Two Roles: Home and Work* (London: Routledge, 1968), xi.

126 Katherine Hamill, "Working Wife, $96.30 a Week," *Fortune*, April 1953, 158, 162.

127 "Editorial: It's Too Late to Send the Working Woman Back to the Kitchen," *Saturday Evening Post*, January 24, 1959, 10; "We Talk about Women," *National Business Woman*, July 1957, 3; Sloan Wilson, "The Woman in the Gray Flannel Suit," *New York Times Magazine*, January 15, 1956, 15, 38, 42; Bernice Fitz-Gibbon, "Woman in the Gray Flannel Suit," *New York Times Magazine*, January 25, 1956, 15, 34–36; "That Woman in Gray Flannel: A Debate," *New York Times Magazine*, February 12, 1956, 26–27, 30–32.

128 Jennifer Colton, "Why I Quit Working," *Good Housekeeping*, September 1951, 53, 177–180.

129 Elsie McCormick, "Every Woman Should Learn a Trade," *Good Housekeeping*, April 1952, 51, 154–155.

130 Edith Evans Asbury, "End Conformity, Stevenson Urges," *New York Times*, June 7, 1955, 36. This speech is also well covered in May, *Homeward Bound*.

131 May, *Homeward Bound*, 16–18.

132 May, 18.

133 Robert W. Wells, "Women Establishing Business Advised by New York Department of Commerce," *Milwaukee Journal*, February 27, 1951, 2.

134 "Homemade and Hopeful," *Life*, October 5, 1953, 73–76.

135 Jhan Robbins and June Robbins, "15 Ways to Make an Extra $1,000 in the Next 12 Months," *McCall's*, March 1959, 32, 94–96.

136 "Could the Lady Be a 'Wildcatter'?," *National Business Woman*, September 1959, 19.

200 • Notes to Pages 67–71

137 "Expanding Occupational Opportunities," 3.

138 New York State Department of Commerce, *Woman's Program*, 13–15.

139 "Thelma R. Davenport," *National Business Woman*, November 1956, 17.

140 Edith Gordon, *Establishing and Operating a Beauty Shop* (Washington, D.C.: Bureau of Foreign and Domestic Commerce and U.S. Department of Commerce, 1953); *Employment Opportunities for Women in Beauty Service* (Washington, D.C.: U.S. Department of Labor, Women's Bureau, 1956).

141 "Ladies! Make Money at Home," *Changing Times*, April 1953, 13.

142 "Ladies! Earn Cash by Typing at Home," *Changing Times*, February 1954, 27–28; Robbins and Robbins, "15 Ways to Make," 32, 94–96; "How to Become a One-Woman Catering Service," *Good Housekeeping*, January 1957, 40; "Earn Extra Money for Extra Work for Extra Women," *Good Housekeeping*, November 1956, 49–50.

143 "May We Present . . . Home Is Her Lab," *Good Housekeeping*, June 1958, 13.

144 Holly G. Miller, "The First Lady of Home Interiors; Mary C. Crowley," *Saturday Evening Post*, April 1983, 58.

145 Direct sales was an important and growing segment of the business and labor market, one that women embraced. For more on this, see Katina Manko, *Ding Dong! Avon Calling! The Women and Men of Avon Products, Incorporated* (New York: Oxford University Press, 2021); Jessica Kay Burch, "'Soap and Hope': Direct Sales and the Culture of Work and Capitalism in Postwar America" (PhD diss., Vanderbilt University, 2015).

146 Miller, "First Lady of Home," 58. See also Anne Bagamery, "Please Make Me Feel Special," *Forbes*, March 28, 1983, 88; "Crowley Named SMU Entrepreneur of the Year," *Southwest Newswire Inc.*, May 16, 1986, Lexis-Nexis Academic Universe.

147 Mary C. Crowley, *Women Who Win: The Proverbs Way to Successful Living* (Fleming H. Revell Company, 1971); Mary C. Crowley, *You Can Too* (Home Interiors and Gifts, Inc., 1973); Mary C. Crowley, *Think Mink* (Fleming H. Revell Company, 1972); Mary C. Crowley, *A Pocketful of Hope: A Book of Devotions for the Family* (Fleming H. Revell Company, 1981).

148 Mary C. Crowley, "Mary C. Crowley, President, Home Interiors and Gifts, Dallas, Texas," in *America's New Women Entrepreneurs: Tips, Tactics, and Techniques of Women Achievers in Business*, ed. Patricia Harrison (Washington, D.C.: Acropolis Books, 1986), 77.

149 Lansing M. Paine and Polly Webster, *Start Your Own Business on Less Than $1000* (New York: McGraw Hill, 1950), 123; Polly Webster, *How to Make Money at Home* (McGraw Hill, 1949).

150 Webster, *How to Make Money*, 19, 51; Other books offered similar advice, among them the popular Helen Stone Hovey, *Making Money in Your Kitchen: Over 1600 Products Women Can Make* (Wilfred Funk, 1953).

151 "May We Present."

152 Taylor, *Exceptional Entrepreneurial Women*, 101; "Rose Totino, 79, Frozen-Pizza Maker," *New York Times*, June 23, 1994, 8B.

153 Bishop was a rather talented woman, going on to develop a leather cleaning product and other cosmetics in the mid-1950s. By 1962, she changed careers, becoming a stockbroker for Bache and Company on Wall Street and later a financial analyst for another firm. Mary Tannen, "Hazel Bishop, 92, an Innovator Who Made Lipstick Kissproof," *New York Times*, December 10, 1998, 48.

154 Berta Crone Horrock, "Perhaps There's a Paying Job for You," *Woman's Home Companion*, January 1953, 46.

155 Hovey, *Making Money*, ix.

156 Jane Whitbread, "Mother Sells Real Estate," *McCall's*, July 1958, 89.

Notes to Pages 72–79 • 201

157 Whitbread, 34, 35, 37, 89.
158 Simmons, interview with the author.
159 Konheim, interview with the author.
160 Not her real name; it is changed here for family privacy. Interview with the author, July 1997.
161 Lois Fenton, "Pauline Trigere—Designing Woman," in *Westchester Wag* (March 2000), www.westchesterwag.com/trigere.htm.
162 Vernon, *Eye for Winners*, 96.

Chapter 3 "Doin' It for Themselves"

1 Chapter title from the feminist anthem, "Sisters Are Doin' It for Themselves," recorded by Aretha Franklin and the Eurythmics in 1985.
2 Mary Smith, "Big Boost for Small Business," *Ebony*, September 1968, 78–79.
3 Smith, 78. Scholars have extensively written about the intrusive nature of the welfare system in the lives (and private lives) of women recipients. For more on this, see the work of Premilla Nadasen, specifically *Rethinking the Welfare Rights Movement* (New York: Routledge, 2012), 19, 75. Nadasen quotes welfare rights activist Johnnie Tillman about caseworkers taking inventory of the contents of her refrigerator, asking about her dating life, and "peeping and peering, telling me what I could do and couldn't do." See also Annelise Orleck, *Storming Caesar's Palace: How Black Mothers Fought Their Own War on Poverty* (Boston: Beacon Press, 2005); and Felicia Kornbluh, *The Battle for Welfare Rights: Politics and Poverty in Modern America* (Philadelphia: University of Pennsylvania Press, 2007).
4 Smith, "Big Boost," 78.
5 Daniel Patrick Moynihan. "The Negro Family: The Case for National Action" (Washington, D.C.: Office of Policy Planning and Research, U.S. Department of Labor, 1965), https://www.dol.gov/general/aboutdol/history/webid-moynihan.
6 Nancy Giesecke, "Soul Food Is Part of Negro History," *Chicago Tribune*, September 16, 1968, 448; Nancy Giesecke, "Soul Food Becomes Big Business," *Chicago Tribune*, September 22, 1968, 18; Dave Hoekstra, *The People's Place: Soul Food Restaurants and Reminiscences from the Civil Rights Era to Today* (Chicago: Chicago Review Press, 2015).
7 Mary Wells Lawrence, *A Big Life (in Advertising)* (New York: Alfred A. Knopf, 2002), 44–45.
8 Author's conversation with Linda Whittenbarger, daughter of Bernice Ratcliff, July 26, 2022. See also Skye K. Moody (Kathy Kahn), *Hillbilly Women: Struggle for Survival in Southern Appalachia* (Anchor, 2014). This book was first published in 1973 and brought attention to the McCaysville story. It was rereleased in 2014. "The Women of McCaysville," *Woman Alive!*, series 1, show 5, November 18, 1975, Vt-30.6, Schlesinger Library, Radcliffe Institute for Advanced Study.
9 Mitra Toosi, "A Century of Change: The US Labor Force, 1950–2050," *Bureau of Labor Statistics Monthly Labor Review*, May 2002.
10 Esther Peterson, with Winifred Conkling, *Restless: The Memoirs of Labor and Consumer Activist Esther Peterson* (Washington, D.C.: Caring Publishing, 1995), 102–103.
11 Katherine Pollack Ellickson "Events Leading to the Formation on the Status of the PCSW," in *The President's Commission on the Status of Women: Its Formation, Functioning and Contribution January 1976*, found in Marguerite Rawalt Papers, box 83-M34, Schlesinger Library, Radcliffe Institute for Advanced Study. Ellickson was the executive secretary of the PCSW from 1961–1963.

202 • Notes to Pages 79-84

12 *American Women: Report of the President's Commission on the Status of Women 1963* (Washington, D.C.: U.S. Government Printing Office, 1963), 85. See also John Thomas McGuire, "From Economic Security to Equality: Frieda Miller, Esther Peterson, and the Revival of the Alternative View of Public Administration, 1945–1964," *American Review of Public Administration* 48, no. 8 (2018): 801.

13 Cynthia Harrison, *On Account of Sex: The Politics of Women's Issues, 1945–1968* (Berkeley: University of California Press, 1988), 1–88, especially 83–88.

14 *American Women*, 14.

15 *American Women*, 28–29. Comparable worth was a revolutionary concept in efforts to secure the Equal Pay Act in the early 1960s when women and men did not often hold the same jobs. Comparable worth advocates argued that women and men should be paid the same for jobs that were comparable, even if not identical. The Equal Pay Act that was passed by Congress and signed by President John F. Kennedy in 1963 did not include comparable worth, however, and only referred to equal pay for equal work.

16 *American Women*, 30–31, 37.

17 *American Women*, 16.

18 *American Women*, 5.

19 *American Women*, 10.

20 *American Women*, 47.

21 Susan M. Hartmann, *From Margin to Mainstream: American Women and Politics since 1960* (New York: Alfred A. Knopf, 1989); William Chafe, "Looking Backward in Order to Look Forward: Women, Work and Social Values in America," in *Women and the American Economy: A Look to the 1980s*, ed. Julia Krebs (Englewood Cliffs, N.J.: Prentice Hall, 1976), 6–30; Sheila Tobias, *Faces of Feminism: An Activist's Reflections on the Women's Movement* (Boulder: Westview Press, 1997), 71–92. See also Harrison, *On Account of Sex*.

22 "Report of Conference: Woman's Destiny—Choice or Chance?," November 21–22, 1963 (Washington, D.C.: U.S. Government Printing Office, 1963), 1.

23 McGuire, 802.

24 The pay act also required all claims of unequal pay be filed within 180 days of beginning employment, making it difficult for women who found out about pay inequities later in their tenure to file a claim.

25 Betty Friedan, "NOW Statement of Purpose," October 29, 1966, https://now.org/about/history/statement-of-purpose/.

26 Friedan, "NOW Statement of Purpose."

27 Jo Freeman, "Political Organization in the Feminist Movement," *Acta Sociologica*, 18, nos. 2–3 (1975): 229.

28 "Biography of Felice Schwartz," Catalyst, Inc., company files, provided by Catalyst, January 3, 2001.

29 Joyce M. Rosenberg, "Catalyst Founder Sees Organization Change with the Times," *Associated Press*, June 19, 1987, Lexis-Nexis Academic Universe.

30 Robert L. Aronson, *Self-Employment: A Labor Market Perspective* (Ithaca: Cornell University Press, 1991), 7.

31 "A Tribute to Catalyst's Founder," *Perspective* (Catalyst Inc. newsletter), February 1996.

32 "A Tribute to Catalyst's Founder." I am especially grateful to Susan Yohn, who shared with me her extensive collection of Catalyst materials (clips, newsletters, research reports) prior to the completed cataloging and availability of these materials at the Hagley Museum and Library.

33 Diane E. Lewis, "End of Line, No Regrets; 'Mommy Track' Essayist to Retire," *Boston Globe*, March 23, 1992, 17.
34 Marilyn Elias, "A Feminist Lightning Rod Retires," *USA Today*, June 3, 1993, 1D.
35 Rosenberg, "Catalyst Founder Sees Organization."
36 Lisa Anderson, "A Pioneer in Workplace Issues Looks beyond the 'Mommy Track,'" *Chicago Tribune*, May 3, 1992, section: Womanews, 3; "Biography of Felice N. Schwartz."
37 Meredith Chen, "Viewpoints: Women at Work: A New Debate Is Born: The 'Mommy Track' Has Authorities Arguing about Women's Roles at Work," *Los Angeles Times*, March 19, 1989, business section, part IV, 3, Lexis-Nexis Academic Universe; Joani Nelson-Horchler, "Felice Schwartz Reflects; Says Her 'Mommy Track' Article Was Misunderstood," *Industry Week*, August 6, 1990, 25, Lexis-Nexis Academic Universe; Anderson, "Pioneer in Workplace Issues," 3; Jillian Mincer, "Schwartz's Legacy Must Not Fade Away; Women's Rights Leader Helped Shatter Barriers in the Workplace," *Kansas City Star*, February 20, 1996, D17; Enid Nemy, "Felice N. Schwartz, 71, Dies; Working Women's Champion," *New York Times*, February 20, 1996, 52.
38 Joan Scobey, "The Best of Both Worlds: For a Career-Minded Wife, Home Can Be an Office, Too," *Mademoiselle*, May 1963, 171–173, 215–218.
39 Among the many women who started employment agencies was Ella Widger Benjamin. See "Biography of Ella Widger Benjamin," in Ella Widger Benjamin Papers, Schlesinger Library, Radcliffe Institute for Advanced Study. The folder containing miscellaneous written works includes a 1982 obituary from the *Boston Globe* for Benjamin.
40 Joseph D. Cooper, *A Woman's Guide to Part-Time Jobs* (New York: Doubleday, 1963).
41 "Forum for Breadwinners and Homemakers," John Hancock Mutual Life Insurance Co., Chicago, March 23–24, 1962, 9, 17, in Margaret Divver Papers, Schlesinger Library, Radcliffe Institute for Advanced Study.
42 Scobey, "Best of Both Worlds," 172.
43 Kahn, *Hillbilly Women*, 3–23, 147–160; *Woman Alive!*, 30 mins., produced by *Ms.*/PBS, 1972, at Schlesinger Library, Radcliffe Institute for Advanced Study.
44 Author's conversation with Linda Whittenbarger; Walter C. Jones, "A Factory the Women Won't Let Die," *Atlanta Journal-Constitution*, October 12, 1980, 227–231.
45 Joseph J. Fucini and Suzy Fucini, *Entrepreneurs: The Men and Women behind Famous Brand Names and How They Made It* (Boston: G. K. Hall, 1985), 96–99.
46 Mary Kay Ash, *Mary Kay*, 3rd ed., *Miracles Happen* (New York: Harper Perennial, 1994), 5–6.
47 Amy Levin-Epstein, "Is Mary Kay a 'Pink Pyramid' Scheme?," *Moneywatch CBS News*, August 12, 2012, accessed January 20, 2023, http://cbsnews.com/news/is-mary-kay-a-pink-pyramid-scheme/. See also Katina Manko, *Ding Dong! Avon Calling! The Women and Men of Avon Products, Incorporated* (New York: Oxford University Press, 2021), 8–9, 211–212, 239.
48 "Pretty Powerful: Mary Kay Inc. Crowned #1 Direct Selling Brand of Skincare and Color Cosmetics in the World," September 5, 2023, accessed September 20, 2023, http://businesswire.com/news/home/20230905783588/en/.
49 Ash, *Mary Kay*, 9.
50 Ash, 10.
51 Stephanie Coontz, *The Way We Never Were: American Families and the Nostalgia Trap* (New York: Basic Books, 1992), 3.
52 Spencer Rich, "Single Parent Families Rise Dramatically," *Washington Post*, May 3, 1982, https://www.washingtonpost.com/archive/politics/1982/05/03/single-parent-families-rise-dramatically/cc4afac4-2764-419e-8bda-66f14bad3dd0/.

204 • Notes to Pages 88–92

53 Ron Ruggless, "Ruth Fertel," *Nation's Restaurant News*, January 1, 1995, 69, Lexis-Nexis Academic Universe.

54 Elaine Dundy, "Can a Welsh Lass of Thirty Six Find Happiness with a Macedonian Rock-and-Roll Star of Twenty-Four? Yes, Says Sybil Burton Christopher. Hear, Hear, Says the Author. (Yeah, Yeah!)," *Esquire*, December 1965, 164–165, 314–315; Albert Goldman, *Disco* (New York: Hawthorne Books, 1978), 46–48.

55 "Ambition for Stage Career," *Ebony*, March 1968, 108.

56 Dundy, "Can a Welsh Lass." See also Goldman, *Disco*, 46–48.

57 Terri P. Tepper and Nona Dawe Tepper, *The New Entrepreneurs: Women Working from Home* (New York: Universe Books, 1980), 57–60.

58 Vernon, *Eye for Winners*, 98–99.

59 Linda Easterlin, "Women & Co.," *New Orleans City Business*, January 2, 1989, section I, 19, Lexis-Nexis Academic Universe; "There's the Beef: New Orleans Restaurateur Ruth Fertel Steaked Her Future on a Business That's a Sizzling Success," *People*, October 20, 1997, 157; John Rebchook, "Ruth's Chris Owner Builds Sizzling Steak House Chain," *Denver Rocky Mountain News*, June 26, 1994, 100A; Richard L. Papiernik, "Ruth's Founder to Pull up Stakes, Sell Majority Holdings," *Nation's Restaurant News*, August 2, 1999, 1, Lexis-Nexis Academic Universe.

60 Tepper and Tepper, *New Entrepreneurs*, 205–206.

61 Cheryl Rene Rodriguez, *Women, Microenterprise, and the Politics of Self-Help* (New York: Garland, 1995), 29. See also Chafe, *Unfinished Journey*; and James H. Binns, "Citizenship with a Shrug," *Vital Speeches of the Day*, January 15, 1969, 207–210.

62 Howard J. Samuels, "Project Own: Compensatory Capitalism," *Vital Speeches of the Day*, vol. 35, February 1, 1969, 250–253; Manning Marable, *How Capitalism Underdeveloped Black America: Problems in Race, Political Economy, and Society* (Chicago: Haymarket Books, 2015), 120, 125–130, 134–141.

63 "Helping the Poor to Be Boss," *Time*, December 16, 1966, 90.

64 Howard J. Samuels, "How to Even the Odds," *The Saturday Review*, August 23, 1969, 24.

65 Mansel G. Blackford, *A History of Small Business in America* (New York: Twayne, 1991).

66 "Banks: Black Capitalism," *Newsweek*, August 26, 1968, 71.

67 References to articles quoting Samuels are mentioned throughout this section. See also Samuels, "Project Own," 250–253.

68 Samuels, "How to Even the Odds," 23; "Aiding Black Capitalism," *BusinessWeek*, August 17, 1968, 32; "The Birth Pangs of Black Capitalism," *Time*, October 18, 1968, 98–99.

69 Whitney M. Young Jr., "The Split-Level Challenge," *Saturday Review*, August 23, 1969, 18. This article was part of a forum on "Black Capitalism" in the magazine.

70 The Editors, "Black Capitalism: Prospects and Problems," *Saturday Review*, August 23, 1969, 15.

71 Charlayne Hunter, "The New Black Businessman," *Saturday Review*, August 23, 1969, 27.

72 "The Seeds for Black Capitalism," *BusinessWeek*, November 15, 1969, 40–43.

73 Wilford L. White, "The Mind Your Own Business," *American Education*, March 1968, 8–11.

74 "Pittsburgh Woman Builds Thriving Business with Unique Party Snacks," *Ebony*, March 1968, 120–121.

75 "Mrs. Roberta Lewis Cited by Businessmen," *Indiana Gazette (Indiana, Pa.)*, May 13, 1968, 19; "Former Fayette Countian Top Businessman," *Evening Standard (Pa.)*, May 13, 1968, 24.

Notes to Pages 92–97 • 205

76 Al Donalson, "Black Women Find Profit Margin Narrow," *Pittsburgh Press*, October 27, 1971, 21.

77 Donalson, 21.

78 Smith, "Big Boost," 79.

79 Smith, 79–80.

80 Samuels, "How to Even the Odds," 24.

81 Smith, "Big Boost," 79.

82 "Soul Food: Where to Find Some of Chicago's Best," *Chicago Tribune*, February 15, 1972, 33.

83 "Birth Pangs," 98–99.

84 John T. Woolley and Gerhard Peters, "Richard Nixon: Statement about a National Program for Minority Business Enterprise," American Presidency Project, University of California–Santa Barbara, March 4, 1969, quoted in Steven J. Gold, *The Store in the Hood: A Century of Ethnic Business and Conflict* (Plymouth, UK: Rowman & Littlefield, 2010), 112–113.

85 Rodriguez, 28–29.

86 Harmon Tupper, "SCORE Spells Help for the Small Businessman," *Reader's Digest*, March 1967, 19–26; Lester Velie, "Big Business Can Help You Be Your Own Boss," *Reader's Digest*, May 1966, 141–144.

87 "Own It Yourself with Assists from the Small Business Administration," *National Business Woman*, November–December 1964, 10–11, 26.

88 These figures are suspect, especially in light of the fact that the agency continues to have a sharp gender imbalance in its loans to women.

89 Muriel Siebert, with Aimee Lee Ball, *Changing the Rules: Adventures of a Wall Street Maverick* (New York: The Free Press, 2002), 43.

90 Julia Montgomery Walsh, with Anne Conover Carson, *Risks and Rewards: A Memoir* (McLean, Va.: EPM Publications, 1996), 116; Sheri J. Caplan, *Petticoats and Pinstripes: Portraits of Women in Wall Street's History* (Santa Barbara: Praeger, 2013), 123–133.

91 Joy Miller, "How Two Mothers Rose to the Pinnacle of Business Life," *Des Moines Tribune*, November 25, 1965, 39; "Place on Exchange Started by Chance," *The Province (Vancouver, British Columbia)*, November 26, 1965, 34; Joy Miller, "All Male Stronghold Invaded by Two Women," *Corpus Christi Caller*, November 21, 1965, 85; Joy Miller, "Two Women Crash Executive 'Party,'" *Miami News*, November 21, 1965, 24.

92 Walsh, *Risks and Rewards*, 80.

93 Walsh, 87, 144, 147.

94 David Clark Scott, "A Pioneer Broker Reorganizes and Expands," *Christian Science Monitor*, July 8, 1985, 17.

95 Siebert, *Changing the Rules*, 29; Caplan, 135–140

96 Siebert, 32.

97 Siebert, 37.

98 "Muriel Siebert: First Woman of Finance," accessed November 5, 2024, https://worthadvisors.com/muriel-siebert-the-first-woman-of-finance/. Muriel Siebert's papers can be found at the Baker Library Special Collections at Harvard University, https://hollisarchives.lib.harvard.edu/repositories/11/archival_objects/3788713.

99 Jocelyn Riley, "'Particular Passions': Women Who've Made a Mark Doing Work They Love," *Christian Science Monitor*, February 10, 1982, 19.

100 Siebert, *Changing the Rules*, 41.

101 This figure was calculated using the tools at Saving.org, https://www.saving.org/inflation/inflation.php?amount=60,000&year=1966.

102 AdAge Encyclopedia. "Wells, Mary (1928–)," September 15, 2003, https://adage
.com/article/adage-encyclopedia/lawrence-mary-wells-1928/98743.

103 Wells, *Big Life*, 42–43.

104 Philip Siekman, "On Lovable Madison Avenue with Mary, Dick and Stew," *Fortune*,
August 1966, 142–146, 167.

105 There were countless articles in business and news publications from 1966 through
the 1970s focusing on Mary Wells, and virtually all of them described her as glamor-
ous. See "Madison Avenue: See Mary Run," *Newsweek*, October 3, 1966, 82–83; "The
Girl Who Painted the Planes," *BusinessWeek*, January 21, 1967, 106; "Girl Wonder,"
Newsweek, April 18, 1966, 80; "Taking Off with Talk," *Time*, June 2, 1967, 61; "The
'Show-Me' Brass Get the Pitch," *Life*, October 27, 1967, 102–104; and Carol J. Loomis,
"As the World Turns—on Madison Avenue or, What Happened in the Ad Biz When
Mary Wells Got Married," *Fortune*, December 1968, 114–117, 187–194.

106 Siekman, "On Lovable Madison Avenue," 146.

107 Maureen O'Donnell, "Barbara Proctor, Pioneering Ad Woman Whose Success Drew
White House Praise, Dies," *Chicago Sun-Times*, January 13, 2019, accessed October 11, 2023, https://chicago.suntimes.com/2019/1/13/18396801/barbara-proctor
-pioneering-ad-woman-whose-success-drew-white-house-praise-dies.

108 Skip Wollenberg, "Wells Rich Greene Agrees to Join French-Led Ad Network,"
Associated Press, April 13, 1990, Lexis-Nexis Academic Universe; Walecia Konrad,
"Can Wells Rich Shine If Its Leading Lady Bows Out?," *BusinessWeek*, October 3,
1988, 79.

109 Loomis, "As the World Turns," 114–117, 187–194. Wells retired in 1996, and within
two years the business she founded and built to $1 billion was in ruins. Dottie Enrico,
"A Star Falls on Madison Avenue; Leadership Problems, Bad Decisions Devastate
Agency," *USA Today*, March 6, 1998, 1B.

110 Walsh, *Risks and Rewards*, 131.

111 Caplan, *Petticoats and Pinstripes*, 130.

112 Cover of *BusinessWeek*, April 17, 1954. See also Kat Eschner, "The Story of Brownie
Wise, the Ingenious Marketer behind the Tupperware Party," *Smithsonian Magazine*,
April 10, 2018, https://www.smithsonianmag.com/smithsonian-institution/story
-brownie-wise-ingenious-marketer-behind-tupperware-party-180968658/.

113 Scobey, "Best of Both Worlds," 172; Adam Ritchie, "Open for Business," *Mademoiselle*, September 1966, 142–143, 206–211.

114 Ritchie, "Open for Business," 142.

115 "Women at the Top," *Newsweek*, June 27, 1966, 76–79. See also Lois Rich-McCoy,
Millionairess: Self-Made Women of America (New York: Harper & Row, 1978),
73–95.

116 Jean Nidetch's weight at her heaviest was frequently noted in the first paragraph of
articles, whereas her firm's rise to a business generating millions in sales would not
appear further down. See "Fortune from Fat," *Time*, February 21, 1972, 71–72; "The
Very First Weight Watcher," *Newsweek*, September 10, 1973, 77; and "Too Much? Is
Pillsbury Getting Trimmed in Buying Weight Watchers?," *Forbes*, May 1, 1975, 16–17.
See also Marisa Meltzer, *This Is Big: How the Founder of Weight Watchers Changed the
World (and Me)* (New York: Little Brown, 2020), 160–161, 164.

117 Thomas B. Congdon Jr., "Ann Lowe: Society's Best-Kept Secret," *Saturday Evening
Post*, December 12, 1964, 74–76.

118 Gerri Major, "Dean of American Designers," *Ebony*, September 1966, 137–142.

119 Smith, "Big Boost," 78.

Notes to Pages 103–107 • 207

Chapter 4   Sisterhood Is (Economically) Powerful

1 "The Woman's Building History: Kirsten Grimstad & Susan Rennie," interview by Jerri Allyn, March 13, 2010, Otis College Archive, published December 7, 2016, https://vimeo.com/194736948.

2 "Woman's Building History"; Kirsten Grimstad, interview with the author, March 17, 2021; "The Sexes Social Survival Kit," *Time*, January 21, 1974, http://content.time .com/time/subscriber/article/0,33009,911028,00.html.

3 Kirsten Grimstad and Susan Rennie, eds., *The New Woman's Survival Catalog: A Woman-Made Book* (New York: Coward, McCann & Geoghegan, 1973).

4 Articles exploring the phenomena of feminist businesses and of the increasing number of women-owned businesses overall were initially interested in them as a novelty but as the 1970s continued, national media treated them more seriously. One of the earliest to address the question of feminism and capitalism ran in the *Wall Street Journal*: Bill Hieronymus, "For Some Feminists, Owning a Business Is Real Liberation," *Wall Street Journal*, April 15, 1974, 1. See also Lois Gould, "Creating a Women's World," *New York Times*, January 2, 1977, 141.

5 Kirsten Grimstad and Susan Rennie, eds., *The New Woman's Survival Sourcebook* (New York: Alfred A. Knopf, 1979), vii.

6 Erica L. Ball, *Madam C. J. Walker: The Making of an American Icon* (New York: Rowman & Littlefield, 2021), 63, 108; A'Lelia Bundles, *On Her Own Ground: The Life and Times of Madam C. J. Walker* (New York: Scribner, 2001).

7 Gertrude Woodruff Marlowe, *A Right Worthy Grand Mission: Maggie Lena Walker and the Quest for Black Economic Empowerment* (Washington, D.C.: Howard University Press, 2003); Shomari Wills, *Black Fortunes: The Story of the First Six African Americans Who Survived Slavery and Became Millionaires* (New York: Amistad, 2018), 203–218; Elsa Barkley Brown, "Womanist Consciousness: Maggie Lena Walker and the Independent Order of Saint Luke," *Signs* 14, no. 3 (1989): 610–633.

8 As quoted in Shennette Garrett-Scott, *Banking on Freedom: Black Women in U.S. Finance before the New Deal* (New York: Columbia University Press, 2019), 74.

9 Robert D. Hirsch, "Women Entrepreneurs: Problems and Prescriptions for Success in the Future," in *Women-Owned Businesses*, ed. Oliver Hagan, Carol Rivchun, and Donald Sexton (New York: Praeger, 1989), 5. The study uses Census Bureau and Labor Department data.

10 Robin Morgan, *Saturday's Child: A Memoir* (New York: W.W. Norton & Co., 2001), 258–259.

11 National Organization for Women, "Statement of Purpose," 1966, https://now.org/ about/history/statement-of-purpose/. For a thorough look at the women's movement as it relates to work and family, see Kirsten Swinth, *Feminism's Forgotten Fight: The Unfinished Struggle for Work and Family* (Cambridge, Mass.: Harvard University Press, 2018).

12 Deborah Babcox and Madeline Belkin, eds., *Liberation Now! Writings from the Women's Liberation Movement* (New York: Dell Publishing, 1971), 2–9.

13 Karen Sacks, "Social Bases for Sexual Equality: A Comparative View," in *Sisterhood Is Powerful: An Anthology of Writings from the Women's Liberation Movement*, ed. Robin Morgan (New York: Random House, 1970), 462.

14 Shulamith Firestone, *The Dialectic of Sex: The Case for Feminist Revolution* (New York: Morrow, 1970), 207.

15 Jill Diane Zahniser, "Feminist Collectives: The Transformation of Women's Businesses in the Counterculture of the 1970s and 1980s" (PhD diss., University of Iowa, 1985), 36.

208 • Notes to Pages 107–111

16 Charles Reich, *The Greening of America* (New York: Random House, 1970), 19; Zahniser, "Feminist Collectives," 36.

17 Gretchen Lemke-Santangelo, *Daughters of Aquarius: Women of the Sixties Counter-culture* (University Press of Kansas, 2009), 90–91.

18 Daniel Zwerdling, *Workplace Democracy: A Guide to Workplace Ownership, Participation, and Self-Management Experiments in the United States and Europe* (New York: Harper Colophon Books, 1978), 9–17, 82–83.

19 Zwerdling, vii, xi.

20 "The Thrust toward Economic Equality," *Ebony*, August 1966, 38.

21 Tiffany M. Gill has written extensively on the subject of Black beauticians and civil rights. Tiffany M. Gill, "Civic Beauty: Beauty Culturists and the Politics of African American Female Entrepreneurship, 1900–1965," *Enterprise & Society* 5, no. 4 (2004): 583–593, http://www.jstor.org/stable/23700183. See also Tiffany M. Gill, *Beauty Shop Politics: African American Women's Activism in the Beauty Industry* (Chicago: University of Illinois Press, 2000).

22 Tiffany M. Gill, "I Had My Own Business . . . So I Didn't Have to Worry: Beauty Salons, Beauty Culturists, and the Politics of African-American Female Entrepreneurship," in *Beauty and Business: Commerce, Gender, and Culture in Modern America*, ed. Philip Scranton (New York: Routledge, 2001), 186.

23 Bernice Calvin, telephone interview with the author, April 28, 1993.

24 Edward Cayton, *The Negro Politician: His Success and Failure* (Chicago: Johnson Publishing, 1964), 76.

25 "Tennessee Beauticians Aid Evicted Voters," *Beauty Trade*, March 1961, 40; "Beauticians Join Poverty War," *New York Amsterdam News*, June 19, 1965, 20.

26 Vernice Marks, *First Edition to the History of the National Beauty Culturists League: 1919–1976* (Ann Arbor: National Beauty Culturists League, 1977), 15.

27 As cited in Gill, *Beauty Shop Politics*, 187.

28 Martin L. Deppe, *Operation Breadbasket: An Untold Story of Civil Rights in Chicago, 1966–1971* (Athens: University of Georgia Press, 2017), 26.

29 "Beauty Culturists Convene," *Jet*, August 28, 1969.

30 Reggie Nadelson, "At Sylvia's, Food Is a Family Affair," *New York Times*, November 16, 2022, https://www.nytimes.com/2022/11/16/t-magazine/sylvias-harlem-soul-food.html; Laura Ruane, "Black-Owned Restaurants Nourished the Activist Soul," *USA Today*, February 18, 2014, https://www.usatoday.com/story/news/nation/2014/02/18/black-history-month-restaurants/5591989/; Margalit Fox, "Sylvia Woods, Soul-Food Restauranteur, 86," *New York Times*, July 19, 2012, https://www.nytimes.com/2012/07/20/dining/sylvia-woods-soul-food-restaurateur-is-dead-at-86.html; "Sylvia Woods, Queen of Soul Food," *Amsterdam News*, June 30, 2016 https://amsterdamnews.com/news/2016/06/30/sylvia-woods-queen-soul-food/.

31 Dave Hoekstra, *The People's Place: Soul Food Restaurants and Reminiscences from the Civil Rights Era to Today* (Chicago: Chicago Review Press, 2015), 163.

32 Hoekstra, 172.

33 Joseph Cripple and Mindy Garret, "Dooky Chase's Restaurant," New Orleans Historical, accessed January 2, 2023, https://neworleanshistorical.org/items/show/1354.

34 Joshua Clark Davis, "Una Mulzac, Black Women Booksellers, and Pan Africanism," *Black Perspectives*, last updated September 19, 2016, https://www.aaihs.org/una-mulzac-black-women-booksellers-and-pan-africanism/; Joshua Clark Davis, *From Head Shops to Whole Foods: The Rise and Fall of Activist Entrepreneurs* (New York: Columbia University Press, 2017), 55–66.

35 Clark Davis, "Una Mulzac, Black Women."

Notes to Pages 111–115 • 209

36 Douglas Martin, "Una Mulzac, 88, Activist Owned Harlem Bookstore," *Boston Globe*, February 17, 2012, B12.

37 *Since: The Drum & Spear Bookstore*, 2018, video, https://www.loc.gov/item/webcast -8548/.

38 "Pacemakers in the World of Fashion," *Ebony*, September 1966, 131–136.

39 Florence De Santis, "Tanzania Joins Fashion World," *Times Colonist (Victoria, British Columbia)*, December 27, 1969, 25.

40 Tanisha C. Ford, *Liberated Threads: Black Women, Style, and the Global Politics of Soul* (Chapel Hill: University of North Carolina Press, 2015), 98, 102, 110.

41 Joan Rattner, "African Queens," *Buffalo Evening News*, November 26, 1966, 89; Florence De Santis, "Hazel Blackman Pioneered with African Fabrics," *Wichita Eagle*, October 12, 1967, 32; Dolores Alexander, "A Midsummer Daydream in Harlem," *Newsday*, August 26, 1968, 65; "Safari in the City," *San Francisco Examiner*, March 16, 1970, 20.

42 Catharine Brewster, "Some Go Abroad to Gain Recognition," *Standard-Star (New Rochelle, New York)* December 2, 1970, 53; Catharine Brewster, "Black Designers Achieve International Success," *Rockland County Journal-News*, December 2, 1970, 16.

43 Laura L. Lovett, *With Her Fist Raised: Dorothy Pitman Hughes and the Transformative Power of Black Community Activism* (Boston: Beacon Press, 2021), 46.

44 Edie Fraser, ed., *Risks to Riches: Women and Entrepreneurship in America: A Special Report* (Institute for Enterprise Advancement, 1986), 65–66; Neil Genzlinger, "Barbara Garner Proctor, Barrier-Breaking Ad Exec, Dies at 86," *New York Times*, January 17, 2019, https://www.nytimes.com/2019/01/17/obituaries/barbara-gardner -proctor-trailblazing-ad-executive-dies-at-86.html; Judy Foster Davis, *Pioneering African-American Women in Advertising: Biographies of MAD Black WOMEN* (New York: Routledge, 2016), 5–6, 27, 79–85.

45 Davis, *Pioneering African-American Women*, 79–80.

46 Davis, 82.

47 "Barbara Proctor: I Made It Because I'm Black and a Woman," *Ebony*, August 1982, 143.

48 Emily Langer, "Barbara Proctor, First African American Woman to Own an Advertising Agency, Dies at 86," *Washington Post*, January 16, 2019, https://www .washingtonpost.com/local/obituaries/barbara-proctor-first-african-american -woman-to-own-an-advertising-agency-dies-at-86/2019/01/16/e338a846-1932-11e9 -88fe-f9f77a3bcb6c_story.html; Davis, *Pioneering African-American Women*, 83–93.

49 Neal Shoemaker, "Cora T. Walker—Harlem Attorney for the People of Harlem—Love Harlem Heritage Tours," May 5, 2010, YouTube video, 4:54, https:// www.youtube.com/watch?v=2BXMDXPmm40; Margalit Fox, "Cora Walker, 84, Lawyer Who Broke Racial Ground, Dies," *New York Times*, July 20, 2006, https:// www.nytimes.com/2006/07/20/nyregion/20walker.html.

50 For more on Black Republicans and the civil rights movement, see Joshua D. Farrington, *Black Republicans and the Transformation of the GOP* (Philadelphia: University of Pennsylvania Press, 2016).

51 Shoemaker, "Cora T. Walker"; "Supermarket Coop Opens in Harlem, June 4," *Morning Call* (Paterson, N.J.), March 25, 1968, 22; Edith Evans Asbury, "Coop Store for Harlem," *New York Times*, December 21, 1967, 1, 42.

52 Bert Shanas, "Food Prices Give Customers a Fair Deal," *New York Daily News*, December 1, 1968, 193.

53 Shoemaker, "Cora T. Walker."

54 Marianna W. Davis, "Black Women in Business," in *Contributions of Black Women to America*, ed. Marianna W. Davis (Columbia, S.C.: Kenday Press, 1981), iii.

210 • Notes to Pages 115–119

55 Kay Mills, *This Little Light of Mine: The Life of Fannie Lou Hamer* (New York: Plume Books, 1993), 192–215, 254–272.

56 Chana Kai Lee, *For Freedom's Sake: The Life of Fannie Lou Hamer* (Urbana: University of Illinois Press, 1999), 147–162.

57 Mills, *This Little Light*, 258–259; Monica M. White, "'A Pig and a Garden': Fannie Lou Hamer and the Freedom Farms Cooperative," *Food and Foodways* 25, no. 1 (2007): 20–39.

58 Quoted in Mills, *This Little Light*, 258; Lee, *For Freedom's Sake*, 147–162.

59 Maegan Parker Brooks, *Fannie Lou Hamer: America's Freedom Fighting Woman* (New York: Rowman & Littlefield, 2020), 146–148, 173; Kate Clifford Larson, *Walk with Me: A Biography of Fannie Lou Hamer* (New York: Oxford University Press, 2021).

60 Lee, *For Freedom's Sake*, 150.

61 Mills, *This Little Light*, 268–271.

62 Frank W. Corrigan, "Women's Lib Takes the Plunge—into Business," *Newsday (Nassau Edition)*, October 9, 1971, 191.

63 "Remembering Sue Sojourner" (obituary), last updated December 12, 2022, https://www.suesojourner.com/fundraising.html.

64 Terri P. Tepper and Nona Dawe Tepper, *The New Entrepreneurs: Women Working from Home* (New York: Universe Books), 113–117.

65 Grimstad and Rennie, *New Woman's Survival Catalog*, 182.

66 Marlene Dixon, "Why Women's Liberation," in *Liberation Now! Writings from the Women's Liberation Movement*, ed. Deborah Babcox and Madeline Belkin (New York: Dell Publishing, 1971), 9–25; Margaret Bentson, "The Political Economy of Women's Liberation," in *Liberation Now!*, 139–144. See also Rachel DuPlessis and Ann Snitow, eds., *The Feminist Memoir Project: Voices from Women's Liberation* (New York: Three Rivers Press, 1998); Alice Echols, *Daring to Be Bad: Radical Feminism in America, 1967–1975* (Minneapolis: University of Minnesota Press, 1990); Ruth Rosen, *The World Split Open: How the Modern Women's Movement Changed America*, revised ed. (New York: Penguin Books, 2006); and Susan Brownmiller, *In Our Time: Memoir of a Revolution* (New York: Dial Press, 1999).

67 Feminists compiled instructions on holding CR groups as early as 1968, insisting that groups be no larger than twelve so that everyone would have a chance to talk. Other rules stressed a nonjudgmental and nondirective approach. William Chafe, *Women and Equality: Changing Patterns in American Culture* (New York: Oxford, 1977), 97–98, 103; "Protective Rules for Consciousness Raising," *Redstockings*, November 27, 1968, 45; Kathie Sarachild, "A Program for Consciousness Raising," in *Feminist Revolution: An Abridged Edition with Additional Writings*, Redstockings of the Women's Liberation Movement (New York: Random House, 1975), 202–203.

68 Boulder (Colorado) Chapter of NOW, "Position Paper to Accompany Resolution #16: Implications of Feminism for the American Economic System," 1973, in NOW Papers, carton #72-25-79-M262; 81M106, folder "Implications of Feminism for the American Economic System," Schlesinger Library, Radcliffe Institute for Advanced Study (hereafter NOW Papers). See also Dawn Chalker, "The Economics of Oppression," *her-self*, March 1975, in *her-self* records, Tamiment Institute Library, New York University.

69 Debra Michals, "From 'Consciousness Expansion' to 'Consciousness Raising:' Feminism and the Countercultural Politics of the Self," in *Imagine Nation: The American Counterculture of the 1960s and '70s*, ed. Peter Braunstein and Michael William Doyle (New York: Routledge, 2002), 41–68.

Notes to Pages 120-121 • 211

70 Anita Shreve, *Women Together, Women Alone: The Legacy of the Consciousness-Raising Movement* (New York: Viking Press, 1989), 199. All the women in this retrospective on CR did not use their real names.

71 New York Radical Women, ed., *Notes from the First Year*, June 1968. There were three editions of *Notes*, including *Notes from the Second Year* and *Notes from the Third Year*, published in subsequent years.

72 Charlotte Bunch and Nancy Myron, eds., *Class and Feminism: A Collection of Essays from THE FURIES* (Baltimore: Diana Press, 1974); Casey Hayden and Mary King, "Sex and Caste" (1965), in *Dear Sisters: Dispatches from the Women's Liberation Movement*, ed. Rosalyn Baxandall and Linda Gordon (New York: Basic Books, 2000), 21; Chicago Women's Liberation Union, "Socialist Feminism" (1972), in Baxandall and Gordon, *Dear Sisters*, 96; Zillah R. Eisenstein, ed., *Capitalist Patriarchy and the Case for Socialist Feminism* (New York: Monthly Review Press, 1979); Evelyn Reed, "Women: Caste, Class or Oppressed Sex" (1970); https://www.marxists.org/archive/reed-evelyn/1970/caste-class-sex.htm. Linda Gordon, "Socialist Feminism: The Legacy of the 'Second Wave,'" *New Labor Forum: A Journal of Ideas, Analysis and Debate* (September 2013), https://newlaborforum.cuny.edu/2013/09/30/socialistfeminism-the-legacy-of-the-second-wave/#_edn11 (no longer extant)

73 Hyde Park Chapter, Chicago Women's Liberation Union, "Socialist Feminism: A Strategy for the Women's Liberation Movement," 1972, https://www.historyisaweapon.com/defcon1/chisocfem.html. See also Barbara Ehrenreich, "What Is Socialist Feminism?," Chicago Women's Liberatio Herstory, 1976, https://www.cwluherstory.org/classic-feminist-writings-articles/what-is-socialist-feminism.

74 Helaine Harris and Lee Schwing, "Building Feminist Institutions," *The Furies: The Final Issue* 2, no. 3 (1973): 3.

75 Bonnie Morris, "Olivia Records: The Production of a Movement," *Journal of Lesbian Studies* 19, no. 3, (July 2015): 290–304; Ginny Z. Berson, *Olivia on the Record: A Radical Experiment in Women's Music* (Aunt Lute Books, 2020).

76 Echols, *Daring to Be Bad*; Brownmiller, *In Our Time*; Marcia Cohen, *The Sisterhood: The True Story of the Women Who Changed the World* (New York: Simon & Schuster, 1988).

77 Carol Seajay, "Our Words in Our Hands: A Brief History of Women's Presses and Bookstore," in *The Woman-Centered Economy: Ideals, Reality and the Space in Between*, ed. Loraine Edwards and Midge Stocker (Chicago: Third Side Press, 1995), 79.

78 Anne Mather, "A History of Feminist Periodicals, Part One," *Journalism History* 3, no. 3 (1974): 82–85, as cited in Mary Thom, *Inside Ms.: 25 Years of the Movement and the Magazine* (New York: Henry Holt, 1997), 4; Martha Shelley, "Voices of Feminism Oral History Project," Sophia Smith Collection, Smith College, interview with Kelly Anderson, October 12, 2003, San Francisco, Calif.

79 Agatha Beins, *Liberation in Print: Feminist Periodicals and Social Movement Identity* (Atlanta: University of Georgia Press, 2017).

80 "The Women's Movement Today," in *A Practical Guide to the Women's Movement*, ed. Deena Peterson (New York: Faculty Press, 1975), 4, 10.

81 Seajay, "Our Words," 79. Seajay describes several incidents where male publishers refused to print women's materials, notably one where printers decided that photos and illustrations for *Ain't I a Woman*'s articles on how to do vaginal self-exams as part of the self-help health movement. They also rejected parodies of feminine hygiene products that spoofed that industry through fictional male-hygiene prototypes. To get an issue of *off our backs* into print, the magazine had to employ a pornography publisher.

212 • Notes to Pages 121-123

82 Hillel Italie, "Pioneer in Women's Publishing Almost Didn't Get off the Ground," *Lakeland Ledger*, August 9, 1995, 7C, Lexis-Nexis Academic Universe.

83 "About the Feminist Press," Feminist Press, November 11, 2024, https://www.feministpress.org/mission#history.

84 "It's a lot Like Falling in Love," *Legacies of Naiad Press and the Tallahassee Lesbian Community, North Florida LGBTQ Oral Histories*, updated May 30, 2024, https://lgbtoralhistory.create.fsu.edu/naiadpress/. See also Barbara Grier—Naiad Press Collection, 1956–1999 (Collection GLC 30), "Biography and Corporate History," The James C. Hormel Gay and Lesbian Center, San Francisco Public Library (2003).

85 Zahniser, "Feminist Collectives," 66; Wendy Kline, "The Making of Our Bodies, Ourselves: Rethinking Women's Health and Second Wave Feminism," in *Feminist Coalitions: Historical Perspectives on Second Wave Feminism in the United States*, ed. Stephanie Gilmore (Urbana: University of Illinois Press, 2008), 63–80.

86 Lois Gould, "Creating a Women's World," *New York Times Magazine*, January 2, 1977, 36.

87 Martha Leslie Allen, "Women's Media: The Way to Revolution," *off our backs* 20, no. 2 (February 1990): 14, 19.

88 Gould, "Creating a Women's World," 36.

89 Judy Hogan, "I Manage Quite a Bit of Mischief," Veteran Feminists of America, Inc., Pioneer Histories Project, interviewed by Virginia Ewing Hudson, March 2019, https://veteranfeministsofamerica.org/vfa-pioneer-histories-project-judy-hogan/interview-judy-hogan/; Judy Hogan, "My Small Press and the Public Library," in Judy Hogan Papers, Special Collections Department, William R. Perkins Library, Duke University; "Women and the Small Press Movement," in Judy Hogan Papers, unpublished speeches, Special Collections Department, William R. Perkins Library, Duke University.

90 Ann Butler, "A Look at Three Distinct Feminists Who Made a Difference," *Pittsburgh Press*, December 19, 1980, B7; David Guo, "'Personal Journey' of Women's Agency Head," *Pittsburgh Post-Gazette*, January 22, 1985; "Anne Pride, Advocate for Women's Rights," *Pittsburgh Post-Gazette*, April 27, 1990, 10.

91 Grimstad and Rennie, *New Woman's Survival Catalog*, 113–114. See also Suzanne Kilpatrick, "Trouble Brewing for Children's Books," *The Spectator*, March 26, 1971, found in the Records of the Carolina Wren Press and Lollipop Power Press, Special Collections Department, William R. Perkins Library, Duke University.

92 Barbara Smith, interview by Loretta Ross, transcript of video recording, May 7, 2003, Voices of Feminism Oral History Project, Sophia Smith Collection, 70–74.

93 Alethia Jones and Virginia Eubanks, eds. (with Barbara Smith), *Ain't Gonna Let Nobody Turn Me Around: Forty Years of Movement Building with Barbara Smith* (Albany: State University of New York Press, 2014), 154–156, 160; Barbara Smith, "A Press of Our Own: Kitchen Table Women of Color Press," *Frontiers: A Journal of Women Studies* 10, no. 3, Women and Words (1989): 11–13; Julie R. Enszer, "'The Black and White of It': Barbara Grier Editing and Publishing Women of Color," *Journal of Lesbian Studies* 18, no. 4 (2014): 362–363.

94 Michele Kort, "Sisterhood Is Profitable," *Mother Jones*, July 1983, 39–43.

95 Judy Dlugacz, "Lesbian Entrepreneur and Activist, Judy Dlugacz, Founder of Olivia Records, Olivia Cruises Interview," August 4, 2015, YouTube video, 13:42, https://www.youtube.com/watch?v=3fsjXsw4NJY.

96 Blair Sabol, "The Roles Some Women Play," *New York Times*, March 12, 1972, 267, 270.

97 "First Women's Liberation LP," Zero to 180—Three Minute Magic, November 12, 2016, https://www.zeroto180.org/?p=16792; Joan Cook, "She's Putting Women's Lib into Ballads," *New York Times*, November 12, 1971, 86.

Notes to Pages 123–127 • 213

98 Jonathan Pont, "The Jett Set," *Working Woman*, December/January 2000, 15–16.

99 Zahniser, "Feminist Collectives," 66; Grimstad and Rennie, *New Woman's Survival Catalog*, 16–20.

100 Dixon, "Why Women's Liberation," 17. See also Anne M. Valk, *Radical Sisters: Second-Wave Feminism and Black Liberation in Washington, D.C.* (Urbana: University of Illinois Press, 2008), 135.

101 Alex D. Ketchum, *Ingredients for Revolution: A History of American Feminist Restaurants, Cafes, and Coffeehouses* (Montreal: Concordia University Press, 2022), 4, 25, 87–107.

102 Anne Enke, *Finding the Movement: Sexuality, Contested Space, and Feminist Activism* (Durham, N.C.: Duke University Press, 2007), 38.

103 Paris Poirier and Karen Kiss, "One Last Call as Maud's Turns 50," *San Francisco Bay Times* (undated, c. 1989), accessed January 11, 2021, www.sfbaytimes.com/one-last-call -as-mauds-turns-50/; Lillian Faderman, *Odd Girls and Twilight Lovers: A History of Lesbian Life in Twentieth-Century America* (New York: Penguin, 1991).

104 Susan Stryker, "Francine Logandise Interview Transcript," *Digital Transgender Archive 1997*, https://www.digitaltransgenderarchive.net/files/5x21tf59w.

105 Nina Siegal, "Overlooked No More: Dorothy Alexander, Feminist Journalist and Activist," *New York Times*, June 25, 2023, https://www.nytimes.com/2023/06/25/ obituaries/dolores-alexander-overlooked.html.

106 Corrigan, "Women's Liberation," 191.

107 As cited in Maria McGrath, "Living Feminist: The Liberation and Limits of Countercultural Business and Radical Lesbian Ethics at Bloodroot Restaurant," *The Sixties* 9, no. 2 (2017): 189–217.

108 The Bloodroot Collective, *The Political Palate: A Feminist Vegetarian Cookbook* (Bridgeport, Conn.: Sanguinaria Publishing, 1980), 175, 193, 249.

109 "Bloodroot: A Feminist Restaurant and Bookstore with a Seasonal Vegetarian Menu," November 5, 2024, https://www.bloodroot.com/.

110 Kristen Hogan, *The Feminist Bookstore Movement: Lesbian Antiracism and Feminist Accountability* (Durham, N.C.: Duke University Press, 2016), xv; Enke, *Finding the Movement*, 14–15.

111 Seajay, "Our Words," 83–84.

112 Seajay, 80–81. See also Susan Loubet, "What's Happening to Feminist Bookstores? Will the Mainstream Destroy a Carefully Nurtured Market?," *Albuquerque Woman*, December 31, 1996, 8, Lexis-Nexis Academic Universe. Karen Kawaguchi, "Feminist Feast and Famine: After Three Decades Feminist Bookstores Are Going through Transition to Stay Viable," *Publishers Weekly*, July 24, 2000, 24, Lexis-Nexis Academic Universe.

113 Kathleen B. Casey, "The Renaissance of Feminist Bookstores," *Ms.*, January 21, 2023, https://msmagazine.com/2023/01/21/feminist-bookstores/.

114 Grimstad and Rennie, *New Woman's Survival Catalog*, 50.

115 Davis, *Head Shops*, 129–130.

116 Enke, *Finding the Movement*, 247–248; John Adkins, "Old Lady, New Life: A Club for Today's Women," *Detroit Free Press*, April 9, 1976, B1, B4; Fran Moira, "FEN: Do the Facts Speak for Themselves?," *off our backs* 6, no. 6 (1976): 5, 15; Kathie Barry, "F.E.N.," *off our backs* 6, no. 10 (1977): 16–17.

117 Coletta Reid, "Taking Care of Business," *Quest*, 1 no. 2 (1974): 8, 16.

118 Gould, "Creating a Woman's World," 11.

119 Bunch, *Passionate Politics*, 224.

120 "Olivia Records Talks about Collectivity—Part II," in the records of the Lollipop Power Press, Special Collections Department, William R. Perkins Library, Duke University.

214 • Notes to Pages 128–131

121 "Sisters," *off our backs* 1, no. 2 (March 19, 1970): 1, as quoted in Zahniser, "Feminist Collectives," 177–178.

122 Bill Hieronymus, "For Some Feminists, Owning a Business Is Real Liberation: Women's Movement Spurs Female Entrepreneurship; Politics and Profits Mix," *Wall Street Journal*, April 15, 1974, 1.

123 Reid, "Taking Care of Business," 19.

124 Zahniser, "Feminist Collectives," 84.

125 Thom, *Inside Ms.*, 21.

126 Hieronymus, "For Some Feminists," 1.

127 Thom, *Inside Ms.*, 52, 52, 188.

128 Reid, "Taking Care of Business," 19.

129 As quoted in Zahniser, "Feminist Collectives," 178.

130 Zahniser, 178.

131 Bunch, *Passionate Politics*, 237.

132 Zahniser, "Feminist Collectives," 185.

133 Kort, "Sisterhood Is Profitable," 44.

134 Jackie Robinson, *I Never Had It Made: An Autobiography* (HarperCollins, 2013), 64.

135 Gainer, "Overlooked No More"; Rose Morgan, The HistoryMakers A2002.009, interviewed by Julieanna L. Richardson, January 28, 2002, HistoryMakers Digital Archive, session 1, tape 5, story 5, Rose Morgan talks about starting Freedom National Bank in 1965, https://da-thehistorymakers-org.ezproxy.bpl.org/story/71434;q=Rose %20Morgan.

136 Lila Ammons, "The Evolution of Black-Owned Banks in the United States between the 1880s and 1990s," *Journal of Black Studies*, 26, no. 4 (March 1996): 477. See also Mehrsa Baradaran, *The Color of Money: Black Banks and the Racial Wealth Gap* (Cambridge, Mass.: Belknap Press of Harvard University Press, 2017), 171–172, 196–199, 241.

137 Edward Cowan, "Freedom National Bank Ready to Open in Harlem on Monday," *New York Times*, December 19, 1964, 37, 42.

138 Suzanne M. Snell, "Harlem's Freedom National Bank—Exploiters or Soul Brothers?," *Harvard Crimson*, July 5, 1966, accessed August 12, 2021, https://www.thecrimson .com/article/1966/7/5/harlems-freedom-national-bank-exploiters-or-soul/.

139 Stephanie Strom, "Failed Dreams—the Collapse of a Harlem Bank; Freedom Bank's Demise: A Trail of Risky Loans and Fast Growth," *New York Times*, December 3, 1990, section A, 1.

140 Corrigan, "Women's Lib Takes," 191.

141 Various pamphlets from the Feminist Federal Credit Unions exist among the papers of the Feminist Economic Alliance at the Special Collections Department, William R. Perkins Library, Duke University. See also NOW Papers, 72-25-79-M262, m106, carton 21, folder "General—Old Credit Stuff"; and Cynthia Harrison Papers, carton 2, 83-M238, folders 7, 13, 25, Schlesinger Library, Radcliffe Institute for Advanced Study (hereafter Cynthia Harrison Papers). I have also written about feminist credit unions and women's banks; Debra Michals, "The Buck Stops Where? 1970s Feminist Credit Unions, Women's Banks, and the Gendering of Money," *Business and Economic History On-Line* 16 (2018), https://thebhc.org/ index.php/beh-online/2018/buck-stops-where-1970s-feminist-credit-unions -womens-banks-and-gendering-money.

142 Debra Law, Feminist Federal Credit Union, letter to Susan Onaitas, Credit Task Force Chair, January 16, 1976, in NOW Papers, 72-25-79-M262, 81-m106, carton 21, folder "Misc."; "Socially Responsible Investing Resources," in the papers of the Feminist

Economic Alliance, Special Collections Department, William R. Perkins Library, Duke University.

143 "Feminist Theory and Economic Practice," *Sistershares: The Newsletter of the Massachusetts Feminist Federal Credit Union* 2, no. 3 (June 1976): 3. Only three feminist credit unions remained in 2001—two in Texas and one in California. But in the 1980s and 1990s, these credit unions began accepting male members, who comprised up to 10 percent of depositors at California Feminist Credit Union. See also Liz Harman, "To Their Credit, These Feminists Bank on Success; California Feminist Credit Union," *San Diego Business Journal*, August 23, 1993, 1; and Melinda Rice, "To Her Credit: Local Credit Union Is Devoted to Empowering Women Financially," *Dallas Morning News*, April 28, 1999, 5C.

144 "Feminist Theory and Economic Practice," 3.

145 Cynthia Harrison Papers, carton 2, 83-M238, folders 13, 23, 28, and also carton 1, folders 3, 4, 7; NOW Papers, 72-25-79-M262, 81-M106, carton 21, folder "Credit under Cohen, '76–'77"; NOW Papers, 72-25-79-M62, M106, folder "Credit Task Force."

146 "Where Credit Is Due: An Update," *WEAL Washington Report*, June 1978, 1, found in Cynthia Harrison Papers, 83-m238, carton 1, folder 3.

147 Hoel, Erik, "The Joy and Privilege of Growing Up in an Indie Bookstore," *LitHub*, April 6, 2021, https://lithub.com/the-joy-and-privilege-of-growing-up-in-an-indie-bookstore/.

148 NOW Papers, folder "Letters."

149 Betty Rae Worthington, Sundance Wyoming, Letter to NOW, February 22, 1973, found in NOW Papers, 72-25-79-M262, 81-M106, box "Credit," folder "Sharyn Campbell." In fall 1972, NOW received one letter in particular from a twenty-four-year-old woman who was turned down for a small business loan, even though she had just reached the break-even point with an aquarium store she opened two months earlier. See NOW Papers, 72-25-79-M262, 81-m106, carton 21, folder "Connecticut"; Letters to *Ms.* (unpublished), carton 1, folder Credit 72–73. One woman wrote that she was recently turned down for a credit card by a major company because "it was not their policy to issue cards to separated women."

150 Andrea Bennett, "Women's Banks Rethink Market," *American Banker*, September 19, 1983, 1.

151 N. R. Kleinfield, "A Bank of His Own: Martin Simon; Running First Women's Bank," *New York Times*, February 8, 1987, III, 6; Lynn Langway, "A Woman's Touch," *Newsweek*, October 20, 1975, 79.

152 Wendy Gristmacher, "Women's Banks Learn to Assume Expanded Roles in Their Communities," *Christian Science Monitor*, November 20, 1980, Financial, 9, Lexis-Nexis Academic Universe.

153 Susan Harrington and Laura L. Castro, "When a Woman's Bank Isn't," *New York Newsday*, May 16, 1988, City Business section, 1; Patricia Bergeron, "Women's Bank Remains Anomaly and Enigma," *Denver Business Journal*, September 21, 1987, 12, Lexis-Nexis Academic Universe.

154 "Women's Bank Plans BHC," *American Banker*, May 13, 1980, 14, Lexis-Nexis Academic Universe; Jane Seaberry, "New Women's National Bank Now Part of Establishment," *Washington Post*, March 29, 1979, C1; "Feminism Takes a Backseat at Women's Banks," *BusinessWeek*, October 9, 1978, 125.

155 Gristmacher, "Women's Banks Learn," 9.

156 "Feminism Takes a Backseat," C1.

157 Andrea Bennett, "Women's Banks Rethink Market," *American Banker*, September 19, 1983, 1.

216 • Notes to Pages 134–142

158 Don Munro, "Erasing 'Woman' from Names of Banks: Has Gender Outlived Its Usefulness in Identifying Institutions?," *American Banker*, September 16, 1986, 24; Bennett, "Women's Banks Rethink"; "Five Women's Banks Endure to Do Battle with 'Attitude' Problem," *Chicago Tribune*, October 19, 1986, Jobs 1, Lexis-Nexis Academic Universe.

159 Rudolph A Pyatt Jr., "Women's Banks Losing Special-Interest Role," *Washington Post*, May 7, 1982, E1.

160 Anne M. Valk, "Living a Feminist Lifestyle: The Intersection of Theory and Action in a Lesbian Feminist Collective," *Feminist Studies* 28, no. 2 (Summer 2002): 317, 319.

161 Joanne Parrent, conversation with the author, July 9, 2021; Fran Moira, "FEN: Do the Facts Speak for Themselves?," *off our backs* 6, no. 6 (1976): 5, 15; Kathie Barry, "F.E.N.," *off our backs* 6, no. 10 (1977): 16–17. See also Davis, *Head Shops*, 129–130; and C. Corday, Kana Trueblood, and Sonny Tufts, "Feminist City Club: FEN Fatale," *Fifth Estate*, no. 272 (May 1975), accessed March 18, 2018, https://www.fifthestate.org/archive/272-may-1976/feminist-city-club/.

162 Susan Sojourner, "Profit—That Nasty, Ugly Word," in *Dealing with the Real World: 13 Papers by Feminist Entrepreneurs* (New York: Feminist Business Association, 1973), 1, 4.

163 Marthey Abernathy, "Transphobic Radical Hate Didn't Start with Brennan: The Sandy Stone-Olivia Records Controversy," *TransAdvocate*, August 24, 2011, https://www.transadvocate.com/transphobic-radical-hate-didnt-start-with-brennan-the-sandy-stone-olivia-records-controversy_n_4112.htm; "An Open Letter to Olivia Records," *Lesbian Connection* 3, no. 5 (November 1977): 3–4, https://www.digitaltransgenderarchive.net/files/ft848q88b and https://www.jstor.org/stable/community.28039177; Ginny Berson, "Olivia on the Record, Letters," *off our backs* 8, no. 4 (April 1978): 16.

164 Cristan Williams, "TERF Hate and Sandy Stone," TransAdvocate, August 16, 2014, accessed November 12, 2018, http://www.transadvocate.com/terf-violence-and-sandy-stone_n_14360.htm.

165 Toni Carabillo and Judith Meuli, "Another View: Toward a Feminist Business Ethic," *Ms.*, April 1976, 69–70; Heidi Fiske and Karen Zehring, "How to Start Your Own Business," *Ms.*, April 1976, 55–70.

166 Anne Pride, "Underpricing Our Own Work—Devaluing Women's Work," in *Dealing with the Real World*, 9.

167 Claudia Jessup and Genie Chipps, *Supergirls: The Autobiography of an Outrageous Business* (New York: Harper & Row, 1972), 1, 10.

168 Jessup and Chipps, *Supergirls*, 21–37.

169 Jessup and Chipps, 68–70.

170 Jessup and Chipps, 140–141.

171 Claudia Jessup and Genie Chipps, *The Woman's Guide to Starting a Business*, 3rd ed. (New York: Henry Holt, 1991).

172 Berson, "Olivia on the Record," 249.

Chapter 5   Becoming "Entrepreneurs"

1 "On the Record: Reagan on Women's Issues," *New York Times*, April 6, 1984, 24.

2 Francis X. Clines, "Reagan Defends His Record on Women," *New York Times*, April 6, 1984, 24.

3 As discussed throughout this book, I maintain here that the numbers of women entrepreneurs in the 1940s, 1950s, and 1960s were grossly undercounted due to the

Notes to Pages 142–145 • 217

lack of uniform data collection. Even with the understanding that there were more women business owners in the earlier decades than noted by the government, the 1970s and especially 1980s still stand apart for the dramatic upward spike in women's entrepreneurship.

4 Robert D. Hirsch, "Women Entrepreneurs: Problems and Prescriptions for Success in the Future," in *Women-Owned Businesses*, ed. Oliver Hagan, Carol Rivchun, and Donald Sexton (New York: Praeger, 1989), 5. The study uses Census Bureau and Labor Department data.

5 Hirsch, 5, 8.

6 Mansel G. Blackford, *A History of Small Business in America* (New York: Twayne, 1991), 117–118; Lois Therrien, "What Do Women Want? A Company They Can Call Their Own," *BusinessWeek*, December 22, 1986, 60, Lexis-Nexis Academic Universe.

7 George Gendron, "The Big Business of Women-Owned Companies: Some Surprising Statistics about Women-Owned Businesses," *Inc.*, May 1, 1992, https://www.inc.com/magazine/19920501/4055.html.

8 Gendron.

9 U.S. Small Business Administration, Office of Advocacy, "Business Ownership by Gender in 1982, Small Business in the American Economy" (Washington, D.C.: U.S. Government Printing Office, 1988), 130, as cited in Blackford, *History of Small Business*, 118.

10 Blackford, *History of Small Business*, 119–120.

11 U.S. Department of Labor, Bureau of Labor Statistics, *Handbook of Labor Statistics, 1978*, as cited in Bettina Berch, *The Endless Day: The Political Economy of Women and Work* (New York: Harcourt College Publishers, 1982), 133; U.S. Department of Labor, Bureau of Labor Statistics, Employment *and Earnings 1979 and 1980*, as cited in Berch, 133.

12 U.S. Department of Labor Statistics, *Employment and Earnings*, January 1976 and 1980, as cited in Berch, 134–135.

13 Angel Kwolek-Folland, *Incorporating Women: A History of Women and Business in the United States* (New York: Twayne, 1998), 199.

14 Kwolek-Folland, 205.

15 Kwolek-Folland, 177.

16 Erin Hatton, *The Temp Economy: From Kelly Girls to Permatemps in Postwar America* (Philadelphia: Temple University Press, 2011), 85; See also Louis Hyman, *Temp: How American Work, American Business, and the American Dream Became Temporary* (New York: Viking, 2018).

17 Erin Hatton, "The Rise of the Permanent Temp Economy," *New York Times*, January 26, 2013, https://archive.nytimes.com/opinionator.blogs.nytimes.com/2013/01/26/the-rise-of-the-permanent-temp-economy/; Louis Hyman, *Temp: How American Work, American Business, and the American Dream Became Temporary* (New York: Viking, 2018), 50–66.

18 Carol Grever, interview with the author, telephone tape recording, August 2001.

19 Figures from Congressional Hearings, *Legal Remedies beyond Title VII to Combat Sex Discrimination in Employment*, as cited in Berch, 127. For a comprehensive study on Title VII, see Katherine Turk, *Equality on Trial: Gender and Rights in the Modern American Workplace* (Philadelphia: University of Pennsylvania Press, 2016).

20 Kwolek-Folland, *Incorporating Women*, 180.

21 "Women Rise as Entrepreneurs," *BusinessWeek*, February 25, 1980, 85, Lexis-Nexis Academic Universe.

218 • Notes to Pages 146–152

22 Mary Jo Lass Woodfin, "Found Women: Catron County, New Mexico," *Ms.*, February 1976, 58–59.

23 Grever, interview with the author.

24 Marsha Serlin, conversation with the author, December 29, 2023.

25 Diane Jennings, *Self-Made Women: Twelve of America's Leading Entrepreneurs Talk about Success, Self-Image and the Superwoman* (Dallas: Taylor Publishing, 1987), 92.

26 Diane von Furstenberg, *Diane: A Signature Life* (New York: Simon & Schuster, 1998), 21.

27 von Furstenberg, 81.

28 von Furstenberg, 89.

29 von Furstenberg, 93.

30 von Furstenberg, 123.

31 Debbi Fields and Alan Furst, *One Smart Cookie: Mrs. Fields* (New York: Simon & Schuster, 1987), 141.

32 Fields has told this story repeatedly. Along with her memoir, see "How to Build a Multi-Million Dollar Company: The Story of Mrs. Fields Cookies," *Forbes*, November 20, 2012, https://www.forbes.com/sites/learnvest/2012/11/20/how-to-build-a -multimillion-dollar-company-the-story-of-mrs-fields-cookies/?sh=66e9ed22467e; and Bettina Makalintal, "If You Give a Woman a Cookie," eater.com, February 22, 2023, https://www.eater.com/23599456/mrs-fields-cookies-business-profile-history -feminism.

33 Tom Richman, "A Tale of Two Companies," *Inc.*, July 1984, 38, Lexis-Nexis Academic Universe; Bob Webster, "Homemade Success: The Real Life Mrs. Fields Bakes up an International Cookie Empire," *Bergen Record*, October 1, 1986, B03, Lexis-Nexis Academic Universe.

34 Rosenberg International Franchise Center, University of New Hampshire Peter T. Paul College of Business and Economics, "Debbi Fields," accessed December 18, 2023, https://paulcollege.unh.edu/rosenberg/pioneers/debbi-fields.

35 Jennings, *Self-Made Women*, 81.

36 "Starting a Business: Women Show It's Not Just a Man's World," *US News & World Report*, August 29, 1977, 55, Lexis-Nexis Academic Universe.

37 Myra MacPherson, "Commentary: GOP Women in the Age of Ferraro; Money, Motherhood and Fighting off the ERA," *Washington Post*, August 22, 1984, B1, Lexis-Nexis Academic Universe.

38 "Enterprises Run by Women Widen Customer Base," *New York Times*, May 30, 1983, 37, Lexis-Nexis Academic Universe.

39 "Starting a Business," 55.

40 National Association of Women Business Owners, *NAWBO: The Many Faces of NAWBO, 25 Years of Powerful Connections, 1975–2000* (Washington, D.C.: National Association of Women Business Owners, 2000).

41 "Women Rise as Entrepreneurs," 85.

42 Marilyn Hoffman, "Corporation Helps Women in Running Small Businesses," *Christian Science Monitor* January 26, 1983, July 28, 2019, https://www.csmonitor.com/ 1983/0126/012612.html.

43 Deborah Rankin, "A Business Course for Entrepreneurial Women," *New York Times*, July 17, 1978, D-9. Extensive news clippings from regional and national publications are included in Administration and Management Research Association of New York City, Inc., and American Woman's Economic Development Corporation, "Establishment of the American Woman's Economic Development Corporation: Including a Model Entrepreneurial Assistance Program—Final Report January 1,

1979–December 31, 1979" (Submitted to the U.S. Department of Commerce, Economic Development Administration).

44 Michele Willens, "Women at Work: Her Business Is Business," *USA Today*, February 24, 1989, https://www.proquest.com/newspapers/women-at-work-her-business -is/docview/306161869/se-2.

45 Jennifer Szalai, "The Complicated Origins of 'Having It All," *New York Times*, January 2, 2015, https://www.nytimes.com/2015/01/04/magazine/the-complicated -origins-of-having-it-all.html.

46 Szalai, "Complicated Origins." The article mentions a 1980 book by Joyce Gabriel and Betty Baldwin entitled, *Having It All: A Practical Guide to Managing a Home and Career.*

47 Arlie Hochschild, with Anne Machung, *The Second Shift: Working Parents and the Revolution at Home* (New York: Viking Penguin, 1989).

48 Alex Taylor III, "Why Women Managers Are Bailing Out," *Fortune*, August 18, 1986, 16–20.

49 *Baby Boom*, directed by Charles Shyer (United Artists, 1987; Sandpiper Video, 2021), DVD.

50 Claudia Jessup and Genie Chipps, *The Woman's Guide to Starting a Business*, 3rd ed. (New York: Henry Holt, 1991).

51 Charlotte Taylor, *Women and the Business Game: Strategies for Successful Ownership* (Washington, D.C.: Venture Concepts Press, 1980), 10, 14, 19–22.

52 Terri P. Tepper and Nona Dawe Tepper, *The New Entrepreneurs: Women Working from Home* (New York: Universe Books, 1980), 34–38.

53 Phyllis Gillis, *Entrepreneurial Mothers: The Best Way in the World for Mothers to Earn Money without Being Tied to a 9-to-5 Job* (New York: Rawson, 1984), 16.

54 Rachel Treisman, "Remembering Marilyn Loden, Who Gave a Name to the Glass Ceiling," *NPR*, September 5, 2022, https://www.npr.org/2022/09/05/1121132384/ marilyn-loden-glass-ceiling.

55 Melissa Lockert, "Understanding What the Glass Ceiling Is and How It Affects Women in the Workplace," *Business Insider*, March 10, 2022, https://www.businessinsider.com/ personal-finance/glass-ceiling; Diana Furchtgott-Roth and Christine Stolba, *Women's Figures: The Economic Progress of Women in America* (Arlington, Va.: Independent Women's Forum, 1996), 12. See also Allison Elias, *The Rise of Corporate Feminism: Women in the American Office, 1960–1990* (New York: Columbia University Press, 2022).

56 Carol Smith, "Glass Ceiling Is More like a Rubber Roof," *Seattle Post-Intelligencer*, August 14, 1992.

57 Special thanks to historian Pamela Walker Laird for pointing me toward "the rubber roof." Pamela Walker Laird, "Parallel Ladders to the Glass Ceiling: Presidential and Corporate Appointments," in *The President and American Capitalism since 1945*, ed. Mark H. Rose and Roger Bile (Gainesville: University Press of Florida, 2017), 155, 159; Steven P. Galante, "Venturing Out on Their Own," *Wall Street Journal*, March 24, 1986, 4D; Robin Pogrebin, "Ways to Rise above the 'Glass Ceiling,'" *New York Times*, August 14, 1988, section 3, 11.

58 Laurie Wilson, "Getting a Leg Up: Pioneering Businesswoman Is Sold on Helping Sister Entrepreneurs," *Dallas Morning News*, March 19, 1995, 5C, Lexis-Nexis Academic Universe.

59 Curt Schleier, "Snugli Creators Ann and Michael Moore," *Investor's Business Daily*, March 5, 1999, A6, Lexis-Nexis Academic Universe; Mirka Knaster, "Mrs. Gooch: The First Lady of Natural Food Stores," *East West*, August 1990, 43, Lexis-Nexis Academic Universe.

220 • Notes to Pages 155–156

60 Nola Sarkisian, "Gooch," *Los Angeles Business Journal*, July 18, 1999, https://labusinessjournal.com/news/gooch/.

61 Kwolek-Folland, *Incorporating Women*, 192.

62 Micki Siegel, "We Salute Six Women Who Changed Their Lives," *Good Housekeeping*, July 1990, 80, Lexis-Nexis Academic Universe.

63 Jenna Goudreau, "Building a Business on Scrap," *Forbes*, May 1, 2009, https://www.forbes.com/2009/05/01/small-business-recycling-forbes-woman-entrepreneurs-careers.html?sh=61dc6bb1ec84.

64 Alison Gutterman, "A Conversation with Marsha Serlin of United Scrap Metal," *CLR Leadership Blog*, September 15, 2017, https://clrbrands.com/News/Blog/A-Conversation-with-Marsha-Serlin-of-United-Scrap. "Women in Metals and Mining: Marsha Serlin, Founder and CEO, United Scrap," *S & P Global Commodity Insights* (blog), https://www.spglobal.com/commodityinsights/en/market-insights/special-reports/metals/marsha-serlin-united-scrap.

65 Marsha Serlin, conversation with the author, December 29, 2023.

66 "Scrap Makes Family Success," *CNN Money*, May 12, 1998, https://money.cnn.com/1998/05/12/smbusiness/scrap_pkg/; William Hageman, "Remarkable Woman: Marsha Serlin," *Chicago Tribune*, August 5, 2012, https://www.chicagotribune.com/lifestyles/ct-xpm-2012-08-05-ct-tribu-remarkable-serlin-20120805-story.html; "Diverse Business Spotlight: United Scrap Metals," *Facebook*, April 1, 2022, https://www.facebook.com/watch/?v=979632692915858; Michelle Mariola, "Making a Positive Impact: The Empowered Women of United Scrap," *Mariola Unlimited*, July 19, 2021, https://mariolaunlimited.com/2021/07/29/making-a-positive-impact-the-empowered-women-of-united-scrap-metal/.

67 United Scrap Metal, "United Scrap Metal Celebrates 40 Years: Gives Each Team Member Founder's Seed Money," October 15, 2018.

68 Therrien, "What Do Women Want?," 60; Barbara Sullivan, "Gold Miners' Prospect for Recyclable Metal; Successful Subcontractor Started from Scrap," *Chicago Tribune*, April 29, 1996, 1C, Lexis-Nexis Academic Universe.

69 Kathy Rebello, "High-tech Wizard Seeks ASK's Old Magic: Start-Up Mode Returns at 18-Year Old Firm; about Kurtzig," *USA Today*, August 15, 1990, Lexis-Nexis Academic Universe; Jonathan Glater, "ASK's Kurtzig Returning to Retirement," *San Francisco Chronicle*, July 18, 1992, B1, Lexis-Nexis Academic Universe; Ronald Rosenberg, "Silicon Valley's Software Queen; Sandra Kurtzig Found the Right Formula—and Made It Work," *Boston Globe*, June 16, 1991, 77, Lexis-Nexis Academic Universe; Lois Rich-McCoy, *Millionairess: Self-Made Women of America* (New York: Harper & Row, 1978), 127.

70 "Women Rise as Entrepreneurs," 85.

71 Christopher Grove, "Money Matters: Org Keeps Tabs on $100 Million Club," *Daily Variety*, March 20, 1998, Lexis-Nexis Academic Universe.

72 James Bates, "Market Research Firm to Buy Entertainment Data," *Los Angeles Times*, December 19, 1997, https://www.latimes.com/archives/la-xpm-1997-dec-19-fi-109-story.html.

73 Lillian Faderman and Stuart Timmons, *Gay: A History of Sexual Outlaws, Power Politics, and Lipstick Lesbians* (New York: Basic Books, 2006), 245–246.

74 Julia Carmel, "How Are There Only Three Lesbian Bars in New York City?," *New York Times*, April 15, 2021, https://www.nytimes.com/2021/04/15/nyregion/lesbian-bars-new-york-city.html. See also "The Vanishing Lesbian Space," *curve magazine*, June 9, 2014, https://www.curvemag.com/blog/history/the-vanishing-lesbian-space/; and The Lesbian Bar Project, https://www.lesbianbarproject.com/.

75 Carmel, "How Are There Only"; Jen Jack Gieseking, "On the Closing of the Last Lesbian Bar in San Francisco: What the Demise of the Lex Tells Us about Gentrification," *HuffPost*, October 28, 2014, https://www.huffpost.com/entry/on-the-closing-of-the-las_b_6057122.

76 Blackford, 119.

77 Kwolek-Folland, *Incorporating Women*, 197.

78 Martha Shirk and Anna S. Wadia, *Kitchen Table Entrepreneurs: How Eleven Women Escaped Poverty and Became Their Own Bosses* (Cambridge, Mass.: Westview Press, 2002), xxv, 1–8, 73–80, 114–115.

79 Jo Ann Zuniga, "Ninfa's Restaurant Possible Here: South Texas Native Planning Expansion," *Corpus Christi Times*, May 10, 1984, 3.

80 "And How? Ninfa Laurenzo Finds Success!," *Taylor (Tex.) Daily Press*, April 12, 1978, 7.

81 Greg Bowan, "Restauranteur Shares Stories of Struggles," *Victoria (Tex.) Advocate*, May 3, 1989, 1, 10.

82 Greg Morago, "Remembering Ninfa: The Mother Houston Called 'Mama,'" *Houston Chronicle*, May 12, 2014, https://www.houstonchronicle.com/entertainment/restaurants-bars/article/remembering-ninfa-the-mother-houston-called-5466650.php.

83 "Ninfa's Restaurant Chain Files for Bankruptcy Protection," *Longview (Tex.) News-Journal*, November 3, 1996, 64. In 1984, Sonia Melara founded a business that created the Hispanic Yellow Pages to forge networking potential between ethnic entrepreneurs. See Joline Godfrey, *Our Wildest Dreams: Women Entrepreneurs Making Money, Having Fun, Doing Good* (New York: Harper Business, 1992), 180–181.

84 Laura L. Lovett, *With Her Fist Raised: Dorothy Pitman Hughes and the Transformative Power of Black Community Activism* (Boston: Beacon Press, 2021), 103.

85 Dorothy Pitman Hughes, *Wake up and Smell the Dollars! Whose Inner City Is This Anyway!* (Phoenix: Amber Books, 2000).

86 Sam Staley, "Women and the Market," in *Free to Try* (Irvington-on-Hudson, N.Y.: Foundation for Economic Research, 1995), 25.

87 Ruth S. Finney, *Self-Employed Women in Hawaii: Their Work and Family Lives, 1977*, data and report found at the Henry A. Murray Research Center: A Center for the Study of Lives, Radcliffe, Cambridge, Mass.

88 Ruth S. Finney, Papers from "The Business and Family Life of Self-Employed Women," box 1, folders for Subjects 001–030, 032–075, Henry A. Murray Research Center, Radcliffe Institute for Advanced Study.

89 Alexandra Wohl, "Biography: Martha Stewart," *Biography*, May 1998, 14–16; Robin Pogrebin, "Master of Her Own Destiny," *New York Times*, February 8, 1998, III, 1, 14.

90 Eileen Daspin, "French Quarters: Designer Josie Natori on Lingerie, Luxury, and Life in Paris," *In Style*, July 1997, 146; Anne-Marie Schiro, "Natori Planning to Cast a Wider Net," *New York Times*, April 25, 1992, 35.

91 Daniel Slotnik, "Mitzi Shore, Whose Comedy Store Fostered Rising Stars, Dies at 87," *New York Times*, April 12, 2018, https://www.nytimes.com/2018/04/12/obituaries/mitzi-shore-whose-comedy-store-fostered-rising-stars-dies-at-87.html.

92 A. David Silver, *Enterprising Women: Lessons from 100 of the Greatest Entrepreneurs of Our Day* (New York: American Management Association, 1994), 141.

93 Pat Colander, "Oprah Winfrey's Odyssey: Talk-Show Host to Mogul," *New York Times*, March 12, 1989, section 2, 31.

94 Ruth Umoh and Brianne Garrett, "Black in Business: Celebrating the Legacy of Black Entrepreneurship," *Forbes*, February 3, 2020, accessed September 20, 2021, https://www.forbes.com/sites/ruthumoh/2020/02/03/celebrating-black-history-month-2020/?sh=5af5fe132b45.

222 • Notes to Pages 163–167

95 Bill Hieronymus, "For Some Feminists, Owning a Business Is Real Liberation," *Wall Street Journal*, April 15, 1974, 22; "Women Learn How to Start a Business," *New York Times*, June 25, 1977; Denise Davidoff, "Pre-Feminist Entrepreneurs," *New York Times*, June 25, 1977.

96 Caroline Bird, *Enterprising Women: A Bicentennial Project of the Business and Professional Women's Foundation* (New York: W. W. Norton, 1976), 13–14.

97 Martha Stuart, "Are You Listening: Women Business Owners," transcript of PBS documentary, 1972, in Martha Stuart Papers, carton 4 and carton 10.

98 "Magazines That Mirror Women's Success," *BusinessWeek*, January 11, 1982, 39, Lexis-Nexis Academic Universe; Paul Richter, "'New Woman' Theme Selling Many Magazines," *Bergen Record*, June 22, 1986, B1, Lexis-Nexis Academic Universe. Sadly, many of the urban women's and entrepreneurial magazines would fold within a few years. *Savvy* lasted longer, enduring until 1991, and *Working Woman* ran the longest, closing up shop in 2001.

99 Nancy Flexman, "Women of Enterprise: A Study of Success and Failure Rates from Self-Employed Women" (PhD diss., University of Illinois at Urbana-Champaign, 1976), 57, data and study found at the Henry A. Murray Research Center, Radcliffe Institute for Advanced Study.

100 Janice Lyski Demarest, "Women Minding Their Own Businesses: A Pilot Study of Independent Business and Professional Women and Their Enterprises" (PhD diss., University of Colorado at Boulder, 1977).

101 James DeCarlo and Paul Lyons, "A Comparison of Selected Personal Characteristics of Minority and Non-Minority Female Entrepreneurs," *Journal of Small Business Management*, October 17, 1979, 22–29, cited in U.S. Department of Commerce, *Women and Business Ownership: An Annotated Bibliography* (Washington, D.C.: U.S. Government Printing Office, July 1986), 12. Other studies include James Schreier, *The Female Entrepreneur: A Pilot Study* (Milwaukee: Center for Venture Management, 1975).

102 Henry E. Bender, *American Management Association's Survey of Women Business Owners, 1978, 1979*, data and study at the Henry A. Murray Research Center, Radcliffe Institute for Advanced Study.

103 Bender, 214.

104 Harold Welsch and Earl Young, "Comparative Analysis of Male and Female Entrepreneurs with Respect to Personality Characteristics, Small Business Problems, and Information Source Preferences" (Chicago: DePaul University, 1982, mimeographed), cited in U.S. Department of Commerce, *Women and Business Ownership*.

105 Ellen WoJahn, "Why There Aren't More Women in This Magazine," *Inc.*, July 1, 1986, https://www.inc.com/magazine/19860701/4433.html.

106 A. David Silver, *Enterprising Women: Lessons from 100 of the Greatest Entrepreneurs of Our Day* (New York: American Management Association, 1994).

107 Martha Shirk and Anna S. Wadia, *Kitchen Table Entrepreneurs: How Eleven Women Escaped Poverty and Became Their Own Bosses* (Boulder: Westview Press, 2002), xxv.

108 Shirk and Wadia, xxv.

109 U.S. Department of Commerce, *Women and Business Ownership*, 6.

110 U.S. Department of Commerce, 7.

111 Report of the President's Interagency Task Force on Women Business Owners, *The Bottom Line: Unequal Enterprise in America* (Washington, D.C.: U.S. Government Printing Office, June 1978), 4, 60–62.

112 Fiske, 63.

113 "Starting a Business," 55.

114 "Women and Business Ownership," 22.

115 Committee on Small Business, House of Representatives, *Selected Documents Pertaining to the Women's Business Ownership Act (Public Law 100–533)* (Washington, D.C.: U.S. Government Printing Office, December 1988), 1.

116 Committee on Small Business, House of Representatives, 100th Congress, 2nd sess., *New Economic Realities: The Rise of Women Entrepreneurs* (Washington, D.C.: U.S. Government Printing Office, 1988).

117 Committee on Small Business, House of Representatives, *Selected Documents Pertaining*, 13, 48.

118 Committee on Small Business, House of Representatives, 52.

119 Committee on Small Business, House of Representatives, 37, 53.

120 National Women's Business Council, "History," November 11, 2024, https://www.nwbc.gov/about-us/.

121 Committee on Small Business, House of Representatives, *Selected Documents Pertaining*, 53.

122 Committee on Small Business, House of Representatives, 43.

123 Philip Shenon, "Transition in Washington," *New York Times*, January 19, 1989, https://www.nytimes.com/1989/01/19/us/transition-in-washington-bush-names-choice-for-information-agency.html?searchResultPosition=5; George Bush, "Statement on the Resignation of Susan S. Engeleiter as Administrator of the Small Business Administration," January 22, 1991, *American Presidency Project* https://www.presidency.ucsb.edu/documents/statement-the-resignation-susan-s-engeleiter-administrator-the-small-business.

124 The Entrepreneurship Institute, "How to Create and Manage Your Own Business" (flier), in Martha Stuart Papers, folder "Entrepreneurship Institute"; William McCrea, letter to Martha Stuart, July 10, 1978, in Martha Stuart Papers, folder "Entrepreneurship Institute."

125 Harold C. Livesay, "Entrepreneurial History," in *Encyclopedia of Entrepreneurship*, ed. Richard C. Scott (Englewood Cliffs, N.J.: Prentice Hall, 1982), 7–11; Robert H. Brockhaus Sr., "The Psychology of the Entrepreneur," in Scott, *Encyclopedia of Entrepreneurship*, 39–41.

126 Jeannette M. Oppedisano, *Historical Encyclopedia of Women Entrepreneurs: 1776 to Present* (Westport, Conn.: Greenwood Press, 2000), xi.

127 Flexman, "Women of Enterprise," 82.

128 Therrien, "What Do Women Want?," 60.

129 I authored this article for *Ms.* based on my work as a business journalist with an expertise on women. The title of that article inspired the title of this book. Debra Michals, "She's the Boss: What Happens When the Tables Are Turned and Women Entrepreneurs Hire Their Husbands to Work for Them?," *Ms.*, November 1989, 58–61.

Epilogue

1 Emily Canal. "Kevin O'Leary: Why I Prefer to Invest in Women-Led Businesses," *Inc.*, September 26, 2017, https://www.inc.com/emily-canal/kevin-oleary-women-led-companies-shark-tank-inc-womens-summit.html.

2 Jack Otter, "Shark Tank's Kevin O'Leary Prefers Investing with Women. Here's Why," Barrons.com, June 21, 2019, https://www.barrons.com/articles/shark-tanks-kevin-oleary-invests-only-with-women-heres-why-51561159764.

3 Ali Montag, "'Shark Tank' Star Kevin O'Leary: Women-Run Businesses Make Me the Most Money—Here's Why," CNBC.com, March 22, 2018, https://www.cnbc.com/2018/03/22/shark-tanks-kevin-oleary-women-make-me-the-most-money.html.

224 • Notes to Pages 172–174

4 David Horowitz, *Entertaining Entrepreneurs: Reality TV's Shark Tank, and the American Dream in Uncertain Times* (Chapel Hill: University of North Carolina Press, 2020).

5 Leigh Buchanan, "American Entrepreneurship Is Actually Vanishing. Here's Why," *Inc.*, May 2015, https://www.inc.com/magazine/201505/leigh-buchanan/the-vanishing-startups-in-decline.html; Joint Economic Committee Republicans, "Entrepreneurship and the Decline of American Growth," December 2022, https://www.jec.senate.gov/public/index.cfm/republicans/2022/12/entrepreneurship-and-the-decline-of-american-growth; Congressional Budget Office, "Federal Policies in Response to Declining Entrepreneurship," December 2020, https://www.cbo.gov/publication/56945.

6 U.S. Senate Committee on Small Business and Entrepreneurship, "Women's Small Business Ownership and Entrepreneurship Report" (Washington, D.C.: U.S. Government Printing Office, July 2023); NAWBO Expert Reviews, "What Percentage of Businesses Are Small Businesses?," NAWBO.org, February 9, 2024, https://nawbo.org/expert-reviews/small-business-statistics/; National Women's Business Council, *A Compendium of Statistics on Women-Owned Businesses in the US* (Washington, D.C.: U.S. Government Printing Office, September 1994).

7 Gabrielle Carpenter, "Small Business Statistics in 2024," NAWBO Expert Reviews, March 6, 2024, https://nawbo.org/expert-reviews/blog/small-business-statistics/.

8 Lydia Dishman, "Women of Color Are Starting New Businesses Faster Than Anyone Else," *Fast Company*, September 23, 2019, https://www.fastcompany.com/90408156/women-of-color-are-starting-businesses-faster-than-anyone; Andre M. Perry, Manann Donoghoe, and Hannah Stephens, "Who Is Driving Black Business Growth? Insights from the Latest Data on Black-Owned Businesses," *Brookings Institute*, May 24, 2023, https://www.brookings.edu/articles/who-is-driving-black-business-growth-insights-from-the-latest-data-on-black-owned-businesses/.

9 Farah Z. Ahmad, "How Women of Color Are Driving Entrepreneurship," Center for American Progress, June 10, 2014, https://www.americanprogress.org/issues/race/reports/2014/06/10/91241/how-women-of-color-are-driving-entrepreneurship/; National Foundation for Women Business Owners, *The Spirit of Enterprise: Latina Entrepreneurs in the United States* (Washington, D.C.: NFWBO, 2000).

10 U.S. Senate Committee, "Women's Small Business Ownership," 6.

11 Gabrielle Carpenter, "What Percentage of Businesses Are Small Businesses?," *NAWBO Expert Reviews*, May 9, 2024, https://nawbo.org/expert-reviews/blog/percentage-of-small-businesses/.

12 Sammi Caramela, "Startup Costs: How Much Cash Will You Need?," *Business News Daily*, November 20, 2023, Accessed December 1, 2023, https://www.businessnewsdaily.com/5-small-business-start-up-costs-options.html.

13 U.S. Senate Committee, "Women's Small Business Ownership," 6; Isabel Solal and Kaisa Snellman, "For Female Founders, Fundraising Only from Female VCs Comes at a Cost," *Harvard Business Review*, February 1, 2023, https://hbr.org/2023/02/for-female-founders-only-fundraising-from-female-vcs-comes-at-a-cost.

14 PWC and the Crowdfunding Center, "Crowdfunding: Releasing Women's Entrepreneurial Potential," July 2017, http://womenunbound.org; Lydia Dishman, "Is Crowdfunding Leveling the Playing Field for Female Entrepreneurs," *Fast Company*, June 29, 2015, https://www.fastcompany.com/3047942/is-crowdfunding-leveling-the-playing-field-for-female-entrepreneurs; Melissa Houston, "The Power of Crowdfunding for Women-Owned Businesses," *Forbes*, November 15, 2022, https://www.forbes.com/sites/melissahouston/2022/11/15/the-power-of-crowdfunding-for-women-owned-businesses/?sh=1c90d9662b64.

15 Kate MacArthur, "Angelica Ross, TransTech and Voice and Value for Transgender People," *Chicago Tribune*, June 4, 2015, https://www.chicagotribune.com/business/blue-sky/ct-angelica-ross-transtech-social-enterprise-bsi-20150604-story.html.

16 National Gay and Lesbian Chamber of Commerce, "First Ever 'America's LGBT Economy' Report Suggests LGBT Businesses Add $1.7 Trillion to US Economy," press release, January 18, 2017, https://www.prnewswire.com/news-releases/first-ever-americas-lgbt-economy-report-suggests-lgbt-businesses-add-17-trillion-to-us-economy-300392041.html.

17 Stanford University Center for Comparative Studies in Race and Ethnicity, "Valerie Red-Horse Mohl," accessed April 1, 2022, https://ccsre.stanford.edu/people/valerie-red-horse-mohl.

18 Raul Gouvea and Jaye Francis, *Indigenous Women Entrepreneurs of New Mexico: Surpassing Barriers and Stereotypes* (self-published, 2016).

19 "NWL's Origin Story," Native Women Lead, accessed March 17, 2023, https://www.nativewomenlead.org/.

20 Babita Persaud, "End of a Chapter: Southern Sisters, Durham's Feminist Bookstore, Is Closing, a Victim of Chain Stores," *News & Observer*, May 16, 1999, section E, 1; Karen Kawaguchi, "Feminist Feast and Famine: After Three Decades, Feminist Bookstores Are Going through Transition to Stay Viable," *Publishers Weekly*, July 24, 2000, 24; Marie Kuda, "Feminist Bookstore News Closes," *Outlines: The Voice of Chicago's Gay and Lesbian Community*, July 26, 2000, www.outlineschicago.com/ooutlines/2000726/fembooks.html.

21 During its brief history, sales at Nasty Girl topped $100 million. Revenue began declining in 2015; in 2016, the company sold for $20 million. As of 2024, she has become involved with venture capital. For more, see Jessica Bennett, "Sofia Amoruso Is Ready to Retire Girlboss for Good," *Elle*, February 29, 2024, https://www.elle.com/culture/a46716954/sophia-amoruso-interview-2024/.

22 Petra C. Kassun Mutch, "Are You a Feminist Entrepreneur?," *Medium*, March 23, 2018, https://pkmutch.medium.com/are-you-a-feminist-entrepreneur-d79f003dd53a.

23 Tim Worstall, "Capitalism Has Shown Itself to Be the Most Feminist System," *Foundation for Economic Education*, March 11, 2018, https://fee.org/articles/capitalism-has-shown-itself-to-be-the-most-feminist-system/; Dawn Foster, "Capitalism Is Co-Opting and Ruining the Feminist Movement," *huck*, January 16, 2019, https://www.huckmag.com/article/capitalism-is-co-opting-and-ruining-the-feminist-movement; Jennifer Stefano, "Feminists Should Thank God for Capitalism," *The Hill*, April 25, 2019, https://thehill.com/opinion/civil-rights/440477-feminists-should-thank-god-for-capitalism/.

24 Jennifer Sey, "I'm Glad to See the 'Girl Boss' Moniker Phased Out," *Sey Everything*, October 11, 2023, https://jennifersey.substack.com/p/im-glad-to-see-the-girl-boss-moniker. See also Orianna Rosa Royle, "Genz Is over the 'Girl Boss' Era, Now It's All about 'Snail Girl' and Experts Approve," *Fortune*, October 4, 2023, https://fortune.com/2023/10/04/snail-girl-workplace-trend-girlboss/; and Daisy Jones, "Yes, the Girlboss Is Dead—but Her Replacement Isn't So Great Either," *Vogue*, August 10, 2023, https://www.vogue.com/article/girlboss-is-dead-but-her-replacement-isnt-so-great-either.

25 Barbara Orser and Catherine Elliot, "The Feminist Entrepreneur," *Stanford University Press Blog*, April 28, 2015, https://stanfordpress.typepad.com/blog/2015/04/the-feminist-entrepreneur.html. See also Barbara Orser and Catherine Elliott, *Feminine Capital: Unlocking the Power of Women Entrepreneurs* (Stanford: Stanford University Press, 2015).

26 Carpenter, "Small Business Statistics."

Index

Page numbers in *italics* refer to figures.

activism and entrepreneurship, 106–107,
110–113, 115, 118–119, 122–128, 131, 159
American Women's Economic Development
Corporation (AWED), 152
anticommunism, 3–4
Arden, Elizabeth, 7, 11, 22, 37
Ash, Mary Kay, 64, 86–87, 89
Asian American entrepreneurs. *See* entrepreneurs, ethnic

Baby Boom, 153
Ball, Debra, 1
banks, women's, 7, 132–134
beauty business, 11, 20, 22, 27, 35–37, 38,
53–54, 109–110, 132
bias: age, 38, 50–51, 83, 173; gender, 38, 46, 75,
96, 98, 100, 111, 136–137, 144, 153–154, 155,
163–164, 167, 175, 177; racial, 35–39, 46, 54,
75, 92–94, 101, 111, 143, 155
Black capitalism, 75, 77, 78, 90–96, 101,
118
Black Enterprise, 78
Black Power, 106, 110–111
Black women's businesses, 53–55, *55, 56*, 56,
74–75, *76, 92–93, 93*, 104–105, 108–109,
110–118, 123, 159, 173
Black women's cooperatives, 114–118
books on starting a business, 20, 25, 30–31, 32,
33, 69, 85, 136–139, 151, 153–154, 163
bookstores, 110–111, 118, 125, 132

BPW, 14–15, 18, 24–25, 30, 39, 42, 58–59
Brown, Helen Gurley, 152–153

capitalism: and feminism, 106, 118–123,
127–129, 135–136, 137, 139, 145–146, 176–177;
language of, 3–4; and patriarchy, 106–107;
practice of, 14, 60–62
Carter, Jimmy, 95, 142, 166–167
celebrity entrepreneurs, 88, 160–162
Census Bureau (1972), 5, 106, 166
Chamber of Commerce, 21, 46, 60–61
Chen, Joyce, 44, *49*, 49–50
civil rights, 2, 47, 53–57, 74–102, 103–139,
108–114, 130
Cold War, 43–46, 51–52, 57–58, 61, 63, 65, 67
Coleman, Charlotte, 52
consciousness raising (CR), 119–120
consumerism, 57–58, 64–66
cooperatives, 108, 114–118
COVID-19, 1, 173–174
Crowley, Mary, 63, 69, 150–151

Daughters of Bilitis, 52
Detroit Feminist Federal Credit Union
(DFFCU), 131
Dewey, Thomas, 15, 28–29, 45
divorce, 87–90, 165, 167
domesticity, 3–4, 43–73; language of,
47–50, 73
"Double V" campaign, 14

228 • Index

Eagle Forum, 151
economic rights, 2–3
employment agencies, 84, 144, 154–155
entrepreneurs, ethnic, 52, 157–158, 160,
    173; Asian American, 33, 49–50, 160;
    Hispanic/Latina, 46, 146, 158–159,
    173–174; Jewish, 52–53, 146; Native Ameri-
    can, 49–50, 158, 175–176
entrepreneurship, 19, 63–64, 73, 74–102, 140,
    169–170
Equal Credit Opportunity Act (1974),
    132–133, 167, 168
Equal Employment Opportunity Commis-
    sion (EEOC), 144
Equal Pay Act, 81, 96, 106, 144
ethnic entrepreneurs. *See* entrepreneurs,
    ethnic

femininity, 40–41, 146–147
feminism, 19, 25–26, 28–30, 99, 103–139,
    119–120, 145–146
feminist business models, 119, 127–130
feminist credit unions, 105, 131
Feminist Economic Network (FEN),
    126–127, 135–136
feminist publishing, 52, 104, 120–123, 128
feminist spaces, 124–127
Fertel, Ruth, 88–89
Fields, Debbi, 147–149
financing, 30–31, 32, 33–35, 63, 69–71, 114,
    125, 141, 165, 166–168; alternative options,
    130–131, 133–134; biases in, 90–93,
    95–96, 132–133, 158; SBA and, 90–93, *93*,
    168–169, 174
Fitzpatrick, Bea, 152
Freedom Bank, 130–131
Freedom Farm Cooperative, 115–118

Gilman, Charlotte Perkins, 7
glass ceiling, 84, 100, 154
Good Housekeeping, 66, 68–69
government initiatives, 13, 20
Graham, Bette Nesmith, 48, 64, 163
Great Depression, 8–9, 16–17
Great Society, 77
Grimstad, Kirsten, 103–104, 118, 120, 128

Hamer, Fannie Lou, 82, 115–118
Harlem Food Co-op, 105, 114–115
Harrison, June, 89
Hawes, Elizabeth, 15

Hispanic entrepreneurs. *See* entrepreneurs,
    ethnic
Hochberg, Lillian, 43–44, 45, 52–53, 64, 72.
    See also Vernon, Lillian
home businesses, 3, 19–20, 32–35, 39, 47, 50,
    67, 89, 153–154. *See also* small businesses
Hughes, Dorothy Pitman, 85, 113, 159

internet, 173–174

Jewish entrepreneurs. *See* entrepreneurs,
    ethnic

Keckly, Elizabeth Hobbs, 7
Kitchen Table: Women of Color Press, 123
Korean War, 62, 64

Ladies Home Journal, 17, 56
Latina entrepreneurs. *See* entrepreneurs,
    ethnic
Laurenzo, Ninfa, 158–160
lavender scare, 52
Leopold, Alice, 57
lesbian entrepreneurs, 46, 51–52, 120–121, 123,
    124–125, 136–137, 156–157
Lewis, Roberta, 91–92
LGBTQ+ businesses, 2, 4, 105, 136–137,
    156–157, 174–175
Liquid Paper, 48
Lowe, Ann, 55, 55–57, 101
Lukens, Rebecca, 6–7

Martin, Marion, 29–30
McCaysville Industries, 76, 85–86, *87*, 163
Mildred Pierce, 31
Minority Business Enterprise (MBE), 3, 95,
    158
"Mommy Track," 84
Morgan, Rose, 35–37, 53–54, 130–131
motherhood, 43–73, 96, 153
Ms. magazine, 121, 122–123, 128, 135, 137, 163

National Association of Manufacturers
    (NAM), 21, 60, 65
National Association of Women Business
    Owners (NAWBO), 142, 151–152, 155
National Federation of Business and Profes-
    sional Women's Clubs (BPW), 14–15, 18,
    24–25, 30, 39, 42, 58–59
National Organization for Women (NOW),
    81–82, 107, 119, 132, 135, 145

Index • 229

Native American entrepreneurs. *See* entrepreneurs, ethnic
"New Forgotten Man," 60
New Woman's Survival Catalog (NWSC), 103–104, 118, 120
New York Woman's Program, 21, 23–24, 25, 33, 34, 39–40

Olivia, 120, 123–124, 127, 129–130, 131, 136, 139

"pin money," 6, 23–24, 39, 47, 59, 68
President's Commission on the Status of Women (PCSW), 77, 79–80, 82, 83, 88–89
Proctor, Barbara, 113–114
Project Own, 75, 77, 90, 101

race, 74–102
Reader's Digest, 25, 30–31, 34
Reagan, Ronald, 140–142, 167–168
recession, 140–142, 143–144
reconversion, postwar, 18, 19–20
Red-Horse Mohl, Valerie, 175
Redmond, Mary Lou, 74–77, 78, 93–94, 102
Rennie, Susan, 103–104, 128
restaurants, 74–77, 78, 93–94, 102, 110, 124–125
Riley, Mary Velasquez, 49–50
Ross, Angelica, 175
rubber roof, 154–155
Rubenstein, Helena, 7, 37
Rudkin, Margaret, 32

Schwartz, Felice, 83–84
self-publishing, 120–121
Serlin, Marsha, 146, 155–156, *157*
Shark Tank, 171–172
Shore, Mitzi, 161–162
Siebert, Muriel, 96–97, 99
silent generation, 60

Small Business Administration, 20–21, 46, 62–64, 90, 92–96, 108, 167–169
small business clinics, 11–12, 22–25, *26*, 39–40, 58–59, 68
small businesses, 18–20, 32–39. *See also* home businesses
soul food businesses, 74–77, 78, 93–94, 102, 110
Stewart, Martha, 160–161
suffrage, 28, 29
Supergirls, 137–139, 153

Title VII, 77, 81, 96, 106, 144
Todd, Jane, 1–2, 11, 12, 13–14, 22, 24, *26*, 27–30, 41–42, 58–59
Totino, Rose, 52, *70*, 70–71
Trigere, Pauline, 52–53, 72, 133
Truman, Harry, 28

Vernon, Lillian, 4, 43–44, 45, 64, 89
von Furstenberg, Diane, 146–147, 160–161

Walker, Cora, 114–115
Walker, Madam C. J., 7, 104
Walker, Maggie Lena, 7, 105
Wall Street, 96–97, 106, 160
Walsh, Julia Montgomery, 96–97, 99
Webster, Polly, 32, 69
Wells, Mary, 76, 97–99
Winfrey, Oprah, 152, 161
Wise, Brownie, 100
woman entrepreneur, 165–170
Women's Business Enterprise (WBE), 3, 95
Women's Business Ownership Act (1988), 3, 5, 167–169
Women's Equity Action League (WEAL), 82, 132
Women's International Terrorist Conspiracy from Hell (WITCH), 106
Working Woman, 163–165
World War II, 2, 4, 15–20

About the Author

DEBRA MICHALS is an associate professor of women's and gender studies and chair of the Department of Humanities at Merrimack College, North Andover, Massachusetts. A twentieth-century women's historian, her research and teaching center on how "out groups"—those on the margins of mainstream U.S. society—survive, thrive, and bring about social change. She earned her PhD in American History from New York University. Her published work includes the essays "Selling Out or Staying True? Fear, Anxiety, and Debates about Feminist Entrepreneurship in the 1970s Women's Movement," in *The Business of Emotions in Modern History*; "Dads Can Cuddle Too: Feminism, 1960s Sitcoms, and the Making of Modern Fatherhood," in *Feminist Fathers/Fathering Feminists* (2020); "The Buck Stops Where? 1970s Feminist Credit Unions, Women's Banks, and the Gendering of Money," in *Business and Economic History On-Line* (2019); "The Stealth Feminist Generation" (a term she coined), in *Sisterhood Is Forever* (2003); and "From 'Consciousness Expansion' to 'Consciousness Raising:' Feminism and the Countercultural Politics of the Self," in *Imagine Nation: The American Counterculture of the 1960s and '70s*. Before becoming a historian, she worked as a journalist, publishing articles in *BusinessWeek*, *Women's Wear Daily*, *Ms.*, *Working Woman*, the *Smith Alumnae Quarterly*, and the *New York Daily News*. Additionally, she has served as a consultant to the online National Women's History Museum (womenshistory.org) where she coauthored an exhibit on 100 years of women's entrepreneurial history. In 2016 she was invited to serve as a consultant/member of the scholar working group assisting the Congressional Commission for the proposed American Museum of Women's History in Washington, D.C.